Economic Behaviour
As If
Others Too Had Interests

Raymond Chegedua Tangonyire, SJ
&
Lawrence Kyaligonza Achal, SJ

Langaa Research & Publishing CIG
Mankon, Bamenda

Publisher
Langaa RPCIG
Langaa Research & Publishing Common Initiative Group
P.O. Box 902 Mankon
Bamenda
North West Region
Cameroon
Langaagrp@gmail.com
www.langaa-rpcig.net

Distributed in and outside N. America by African Books Collective
orders@africanbookscollective.com
www.africanbookcollective.com

ISBN: 9956-727-43-1

DISCLAIMER
All views expressed in this publication are those of the author and do not necessarily
reflect the views of Langaa RPCIG.

Table of Contents

Acknowledgements

We are greatly indebted to many people whose moral, editorial, and material support led to the composition and logical completion of this book. In gratitude, we remember Rev. Professor Laurenti Magesa of Hekima College whose unrelenting encouragement and guidance led to the composition and completion of this book. He is our highly revered lecturer, mentor, and friend who is always available to show us the way to academic heights. In a special way, we would like to thank professor Emeritus Dominic Kofi Agyeman, fellow Ghana Academy of Arts and Sciences, and formerly of University of Cape Coast, Ghana. We are grateful to you for your insightful contribution toward the enrichment of the manuscript and the final title of the book. Our gratitude will be incomplete without mention of Dr. Charles A. Abugre, Director, United Nations Millennium Development Campaign, Africa region, for providing us with the conducive space and all the necessary material needs that enabled us to put together the first draft of the manuscript.

To our Jesuit family, we are also grateful but more particularly to Rev. Dr. Gabriel Mmassi, SJ rector of Hekima College, Rev. Dr. Agbonkhianmeghe E. Orobator, SJ, the Provincial superior of the Eastern Africa Province of the Society of Jesus, and Rev. Dr. Odumaro Mubangizi, SJ for their invaluable editorial support and encouragement. Their insights helped to deeply enrich our manuscript.

Finally, we would like to express our sincerest gratitude to Rev. Fr. Kevin O. Odey, SJ, a true friend whose unwavering and unfailing love, inspiration, and moral support were useful to the realization of this book.

Introduction

The twenty-first century has witnessed the dilemma of seven billion people having to share only one Planet Earth. Each of the seven billion people needs to survive and so the competition for resources has become stiffer than it used to be in those days when world population was still a few millions. Moreover, the world is not only crowded by human beings but also by visible and invisible non-human entities. Thus, twenty-first century humans and nonhumans need sober and moderate ways of meeting their interests.

In this book, we wish to discuss two levels of competition in which human beings participate. The first level is among human beings themselves while the second level is between human beings on one hand and non-human entities on the other hand.

At the first level, human beings compete among themselves basically to meet their interests in order to survive. Usually some individuals or groups of individuals dominate the rest. Those who belong to the domineering group go about their activities as if the rest of humanity did not have interests. This is what we shall be referring to as human egoism. However, human egoism manifests itself in different degrees: solipsism, selfishness, and self-interest.

There is no such thing as pure altruism; nobody ever acts *only* in the interests of other people. People usually act in their own interests. The most 'altruistic' people you can get are those who act in their own interests and at the same time in the interests of others. Such a mixture of egoism and altruism is what we shall be referring to as altruistic egoism. Instances of altruistic egoism include deferred gratification, symbiotic reciprocation, scrupulous benefactors, composite beneficiaries, emotively egoistic people, advertisers, consanguineous altruism, deontological altruism, and philanthropic altruism.

The sphere of economics is usually the most fertile ground for selfishness. People who have strong economic muscles pursue their goals as if they are the only ones who have interests or as if other human beings do not matter at all. Resources are said to be scarce while human needs are assumed to be unlimited. Private property is locked up for private use only.

Economic systems are nothing but institutions of selfishness. Selfishness becomes more prevalent as a people move from primitive economic systems such as subsistence economics, communitarian economics, feudalism, and mercantilism to modern economic systems such as liberal capitalism, socialism, mixed economics and geocentric economics. Indeed, the major reason why economic systems collapse is selfishness.

Despite all the efforts and the advancement in science and technology, the world has not yet achieved true economic development mainly because development models and processes are driven by human selfishness. Income disparities continue to widen as a few individuals continue to get richer at the expense of the poor who are usually the majority, the gap between rich and poor countries is not getting narrower, and corruption has become an economic virtue.

Multinational Corporations disguise themselves into agents of development but they are largely motivated by selfish interests. In today's world, they are the most official and efficient channel through which the rich and strong continue to exploit the poor and weak. Given their technological and monetary power, Multinational corporations find it easy to operate as if it is only their interests which matter. They are able to manipulate the decision makers of poor countries in order to buy raw materials at throw-a-way prices and to sell their finished products at exorbitant prices.

Needless to say, the economic challenges which we are experiencing today are a warning against human selfishness. Consequently, the solution to today's economic challenges does not lie in coming up with more abstract economic theories but in taming the evil of human selfishness. Moderating our selfishness is especially imperative for a crowded planet like ours. The seven billion people have no better choice than to cooperate with one another. In other words, if I need to survive in this crowded world I must not act against other people's interests. The twenty-first century requires an economic system in which every human being matters and his interests are taken seriously by everyone. It is no longer sustainable to take care of my interests at the expense of or without putting into consideration other people's interests.

The second level of competition exists between human beings and non-human entities. As a species, human beings compete with all non-human entities to meet their interests. Most a time, human interests are met at the expense of the interests of non-human entities. Indeed, especially in their economic activities, human beings behave as if they are the only beings that have interests; the interests of non-human entities are either assumed to be non-existent or they are deliberately ignored or suppressed. We are still caught up in what the experts have referred to as a dangerous anthropological error. Rich countries have achieved high economic growth rates but at the expense of the environment. Poor countries want to pursue the same route since high economic growth figures are adored by everyone. The environment is still regarded as a pool of resources which can be exploited unscrupulously for human interests.

However, the contemporary environmental crisis is the response from the non-human entities against human selfishness. Their message can be paraphrased thus, 'we too matter; we too have interests'. Humans can no longer continue to exploit the environment without experiencing hazards such as global warming, floods, or tsunamis. It is no longer tenable for human beings to continue behaving as if non-human entities do not matter or do not have interests. More so, the solution to the crisis should not be expected from the rhetoric of environmental experts and politicians which is largely motivated by selfishness. The solution to the contemporary environmental crisis lies in taming human selfishness. Human beings, irrespective of whether they belong to rich or poor countries, must begin to moderate their selfishness as they relate with non-human entities. Indeed, it is in their own interests for human beings to take care of the interests of non-human entities.

So far we have only mentioned that human beings need to moderate their selfishness in order for them to alleviate the contemporary economic and environmental challenges but we have not mentioned any concrete tool which might enable them to become less selfish. As an important tool, education is certainly inevitable for moulding people into better humans. This is the tool which we are suggesting and describing at the end of this book. The kind of education which we are referring to here has nothing to do with what seems to be the goal of most of our schools today, namely, cramming abstract concepts for passing examinations and acquiring degree certificates at the end of the course. It is an education process based on people's daily experiences and we shall be referring to it as education for altruistic egoism. Education for altruistic egoism can be conducted within homes, in institutions of learning, within civil society organizations, and in religious institutions. It is a type of education to which even young children can be introduced. People who have gone through this education process should be able to work for their interests without preventing other people from meeting their own interests and they should be able to respect the interests of non-human entities. Education for altruistic egoism is an indispensable tool for achieving what every sensible contemporary man or woman is dreaming about, namely, sustainable development. Sustainable development cannot be achieved until we begin to carry out our economic activities with the conviction that others too have interests and by 'others' we do not only mean fellow human beings but non-human entities as well.

Chapter 1

The Hegemony of Human Egoism

Humans as Egoistic Beings

It is not uncommon to see people assisting one another, for example, by giving directions to strangers, contributing to charities, volunteering to work in refugee camps or in hospitals, sending aid to victims of natural calamities, visiting prisoners, feeding the hungry, paying school fees for orphans, and binding the wounds of survivors of accidents. Such interventions are usually described as altruistic acts in comparison to the pursuit of self-interest.[1] However, at least in real life, all human acts are pursued for certain self-interests irrespective of whether we refer to the actors as altruistic or egoistic people. Acting out of self-interest is characteristic of each one of us whether we are male or female, white or black, tall or short, rich or poor, religious or atheist. We normally act in our own interest. In other words, we are largely egoistic.[2] Obviously, other people do benefit from our activities but this does not necessarily mean that their welfare is what initially motivates us to carry out those activities. What initially and primarily motivates us is self-interest. Other people's interests are secondary or even unintended or they are sometimes unavoidable.

Certain egoistic acts are sometimes mistaken for purely altruistic acts. This is due to a narrow understanding of what pure altruism would mean and what acting out of self-interest means. Many people erroneously think that any assistance rendered by one person to another is an act of pure altruism. Yet, charitable people are never motivated by altruism *alone*. The people we mistakenly refer to as *altruistic*[3] are those who spare some of their time and effort to work for other people's welfare. But even for such people, the welfare of other people is only a secondary motivation. They intend to meet their own interests and only as a second intention the interests of other

---

[1] David Kelly, "Generosity and Self-Interest," *The Atlas Society* (January 2005) http://www.atlassociety.org/generosity_self-interest (25th February 2012)

[2] Alasdair MacIntyre, *After Virtue: A Study in Moral Theory*. 2nd ed (Notre Dame: University of Notre Dame Press, 1984), 228-34.

[3] We shall later on argue that pure or absolute altruism does not exist.

1

people. Purely altruistic acts do not exist. At best we have acts that are motivated by a mixture of self-interest and some degree of altruism. Of course, there are some moral geniuses, such as Mother Teresa of Calcutta, Mahatma Gandhi and Nelson Mandela of South Africa. But, they are extremely rare; moral geniuses are individuals who, at least occasionally, put the interests of other people prior to their own personal interests. Nevertheless, even for moral geniuses, the self-interest motivation cannot be ruled out – purely altruistic acts do not exist!

In real life most people are instinctively egoistic and altruistic only cognitively. Our first, immediate, primary, and usual instinct is to act out of self-interest. Most, if not all the so-called altruistic people are indeed motivated by their own interests, at least partially. Their egoism is piously sugar-coated with altruistic spices.

The Human Instinct for Survival: the Origin of Egoism and Altruism

The human person can hardly survive without the assistance of other people.[4] Unlike other animals, human beings leave their mother's womb when they are still too feeble to fend for themselves. They spend a long time before they are weaned from their mother's breast and even after they have been weaned, the inevitability of some kind of support from other people continues until death. The support of others is indeed needed until the person has been buried. In other words, dependence on other people characterizes the person's whole journey here on earth; it begins from the womb and ends until the person rests in his tomb.

Given its fragility, a baby can only depend on the mercy of other people. Soon after it is born, the baby instinctively realises that the only way for it to survive is to depend on the mother for everything. In fact the baby gradually develops the illusion that everything the mother does is for its own survival; whatever the mother does is in the interest of the baby. Psychologists tell us that between 8 and 12 months, infants develop a fear for strangers, stranger anxiety, and instead they develop an intense bond with those who care for them. "No social behaviour is more striking than this intense and mutual infant-parent bond, called attachment – a powerful survival impulse that

---

[4] Adam Smith, *An Inquiry into the Nature and Causes of The Wealth of Nations*, ed. Bruce Mazlish (Indianapolis: Bobbs-Merrill Educational Publishing, 1961), 14.

keeps the infant close to its caregivers."[5] Thus, in order for it to survive, the infant needs to attach itself to those who provide it with its needs: warmth, security, food, and so on.

Since values and social attitudes are not innate but emerge through the interactions we have with others,[6] a baby is neither egoistic nor altruistic at its birth; it is tabula rasa. It is however born with the instinct to survive. This instinct to survive compels the baby to begin to behave egoistically. It begins by depending on its mother for everything and then it gradually develops the belief that the mother is there wholly for its interests. The baby's interests must be met if it is to survive. Whenever the baby feels uncomfortable, all it does is to ring the bell by simply crying so that the mother can fulfil her duties more attentively.

We need to emphasize that this learning process is largely instinctual. According to Sigmund Freud's psychoanalysis theory, the development of social identity is influenced by strong instinctual impulses. In other words, the mind unconsciously shapes human behaviour.[7] Basing on this theory, despite the criticisms which have been levelled against it, we can assert that a child's egoistic behaviour results from its strong instinctual impulse to survive.

With time, however, the child begins to learn that in order for some of its interests to be met, it has to cooperate with its playmates and caretakers. The child learns to behave somewhat altruistically. This altruism is basically for egoistic purposes. The child behaves altruistically in order for its interests to be met. Thus, it is still the instinct for survival which compels the child to behave a little bit altruistically.

A more important reason why the child begins to behave altruistically is the way other people take care of its interests. The child learns to take care of other people's interests from the way its mother takes care of its interests. Most importantly, by meeting other people's interests, it meets some of its own interests. For example, when a child does something altruistic and it receives a reward from the parents, it feels good and this motivates it to keep

---

[5] David G. Myers, *Psychology*, 5th ed. (Michigan: Worth Publishers, Inc, 1998), 95.

[6] Margaret L. Andersen and Howard F. Taylor, *Sociology: Understanding a Diverse Society* (Belmont: Thomson Learning/Wadsworth, 2000), 92.

[7] Andersen and Howard F. Taylor, *Sociology: Understanding a Diverse Society,* 94.

behaving altruistically. Learning to behave altruistically is an unconscious process, at least basing on Sigmund Freud's psychoanalysis theory. According to this theory, identity is developed from dynamic tensions between strong instinctual impulses and social standards of society. Thus, a child's altruistic behaviour unconsciously results from a dynamic tension between the strong instinct for it to survive and the way other people take care of its interests. Similarly, Object Relations Theorists such as Nancy Chodorow argue that the social relationships experienced by a child unconsciously determine adult personality.[8] From these theories we can conclude that children who grow up in highly egoistic societies are more likely to become more egoistic than those who grow up in largely altruistic societies.

Note that the instinct to survive is the origin of both egoism and altruism. The baby learns to behave egoistically before it learns to behave altruistically. Whether the baby behaves egoistically or altruistically it does so in order for it to survive. But, most a time, the child behaves egoistically because egoism is closer to the instinct to survive than altruism is.

Society as a School of Both Egoism and Altruism

We do not only learn by instinct but also through socialization. Learning by instinct is when we acquire certain skills and beliefs on our own without any instructions from other people. Through socialisation, however, we acquire knowledge about the beliefs and behaviours of our society by being instructed by other people and by interacting with other people. We are introduced to the way things are and ought to be done in a given society. The process of socialization is carried out through formal and informal settings. We are socialized in schools (formal education), by going through different stages of initiation in our cultures (informal education), religion, by our peers and the media.

Socialisation creates the inclination for someone to act in socially acceptable ways; it is the process through which people learn to behave according to the expectations of society and the normative values associated with social situations. According to Social Learning Theorists such as Jean Piaget, the formation of identity is a learned response to the expectations of society and Symbolic Interaction Theorists such as Charles Horton Cooley and George Herbert Mead argue that through the socialization process,

---

[8] Andersen and Howard F. Taylor, *Sociology: Understanding a Diverse Society*, 95.

humans learn, internalize, and appropriate the social meaning that different behaviours imply.[9] From these two theories, we can argue that through the process of socialisation, a person acquires traits of egoism and/or altruism.

Egoism is passed on from one generation to the next. As Piet Schoonenberg insightfully points out, human beings are born and immersed into networks of relationships in which sin (selfishness) has already taken place.[10] We are born and bred in societies in which selfishness has already had a strong grip on the people's way of living. Such a poisonous situation influences us in one way or another and in turn we too influence others to become selfish when we begin to act selfishly. The influence goes unnoticed because selfishness is seen as a normal way of doing things about which nobody is supposed to feel guilty. For example, when corruption becomes a normal practice in a given country, corrupt people are the most respected because they are fabulously wealthy and so they do not feel guilty at all. Paying bribes, cheating, jumping the queue, or embezzling public funds become normal ways of earning a living. Corrupt parliamentarians pass laws that shield their selfishness, the state is run by kleptomaniacs, accountants re-write the accounting rules to hide names of criminals behind dirty monies, lawyers defend criminals in the courts of law and instead the innocent are convicted, media men and women are bribed to do selective dissemination of information against the norm of telling the truth, the police are the cheapest people to be bribed by law-breakers, and the custom and immigration officers flourish on tips. Everybody participates in selfish acts, knowingly or unknowingly. The web of selfishness becomes so strong that it can hardly be broken by a single individual.

The virus of selfishness is transmitted from one generation to the next through bad processes of socialization and the examples of bad people in society. Especially in rich urban areas where individualism is more prevalent due to modernism and the neglect of traditional value systems, parents teach their children to become selfish by not allowing them to interact with others. They basically play computer games and so computers become their best friends. The children are not taught how to share with others what their

[9] Andersen and Howard F. Taylor, *Sociology: Understanding a Diverse Society,* 94 and 97-99.

[10] Xavier Thevenot, *Sin: A Christian view for today* (Missouri: Liguori Publications, 1984), 43-45.

parents give them. A child moves from its family's apartment into the car[11] to be taken to school and back to the apartment. There is minimal interaction with other children, except in unavoidable situations like at school. The child grows up thinking only about itself and its interests. Unfortunately, since children who come from rich urban areas are most likely going to become leaders in the future, their selfishness will contaminate the whole society.

Egoism is intensified when children go to school. School is the place where children are first exposed to a hierarchical and bureaucratic environment[12] and are officially introduced to the world of professional competitors. Students generally compete more than they cooperate in academics and in sports. Each student is consciously or unconsciously aspiring for the first position in class. It is a capitalist ethic according to which being better than the rest is the best thing that can happen to someone. Most a time the competition is so stiff that students work against one another's progress, for instance by hiding the best textbooks from their classmates, stealing classmates' notebooks, refusing to share insights with others, or even cheating in examinations. Parents and teachers worsen matters by giving desserts to the best students and or remaining silent about the selfishness that exists among the students. The media announces the results of the best and the worst students. Students are therefore forced to compete with one another in order to make their parents and teachers proud. This unnecessary fuss is what forced Sylvia Wanjiku and Mercy Chebet to hang themselves on 29th December, 2011 just a day after the Kenya Certificate of Primary Education (KCPE) results were released and announced by the ministry of Education.[13] Sylvia had scored an aggregate mark of 303 out of 500. This score was good enough for her to join a secondary school but she was not satisfied by her performance because she had not emerged as the best student in the school and so she was not going to become famous in society. At the tender age of 14, Sylvia and Mercy terminated their lives because they had lost the race of competitive selfishness – they had done their best but their best was not good enough for the lucrative first position. Their death, moreover during the joyful season of

---

[11] Some of those flamboyant cars are bought using embezzled public funds and the children are proud to be driven in such expensive cars.

[12] Andersen and Howard F. Taylor, *Sociology: Understanding a Diverse Society,* 108.

[13] Benedict Tirop and Jackline Moraa. "Two Girls commit suicide over KCPE results." (Saturday Nation, 31st Dec, 2011).

Christmas, is a clear protest against the competitive spirit that exists in our schools. At their tender age, children are made to believe that life means being number one. This belief, accompanied with the spirit of deadly competition, is found even in universities. Like Sylvia and Mercy, some university students do commit suicide simply because they did not get the best mark. For example, on 22nd March, 2012, Hemed Athuman, a journalism student at Morogoro School of Journalism in Tanzania, hanged himself for scoring badly in his first semester examinations.[14]

Teachers do not penalise the students' competitive selfishness because they themselves have gone through the same system and they are beneficiaries of that system. As students graduate, they go to the world with the same competitive and selfish spirit. They want to get the best job in order to make more money than others. This is the reason why most of the corrupt people in our societies are actually highly learned people. Some even hold doctorates but they are not ashamed of embezzling public funds. They become models and a source of inspiration for students who are still in school.

Of course, through the socialisation process, we also learn to act altruistically. For example, when our parents, especially in rural areas, teach us how to share what we have with others or when teachers encourage us to form discussion groups instead of always competing with one another, we learn to act altruistically. However, we are trained more in egoism than in altruism because our societies are more saturated with egoism than with altruism. Moreover, at least in the short run, being egoistic is more beneficial than being altruistic. A corrupt politician, for instance, prefers embezzling public funds in order to get rich quickly than being trustworthy but remain poor or take long to get rich. Selfishness prevails and it is attractive because it contains an apparent good. On the other hand, the good that is contained in altruism takes long to be realized. Thus, more people are inclined to egoism than to altruism. The fact that we are more attuned to egoism than to altruism is the major reason why we have laws in our societies. Laws are basically meant to regulate human egoism; they protect us against one another's selfishness. Obviously, there are many laws that would be irrelevant if human beings became less egoistic but more altruistic.

---

[14] Erick Mchome. "Suicide: Why Students are Killing Themselves." (The Citizen: 5th June, 2012).

Degrees of Egoism

So far we have been using the terms egoism and selfishness interchangeably. But, it is important to make a distinction between these two terms even though that distinction is not an easy one to make. Egoism means "Concern for one's own interests and welfare."[15] When people act in their own interests we usually say that they are egoistic. However, some people are more egoistic than others. Different people are concerned about their interests in different ways and with different intensities. The different intensities with which different people are concerned with their interests and welfare are what we are referring to as degrees of egoism. In this book, the word egoism is used as an umbrella term to include solipsism, selfishness, and self-interest.

Being concerned with one's interests is certainly good and necessary for human existence. We can hardly survive without meeting or at least being concerned about our interests. However, the different ways by which we meet our interests are sometimes unethical and bad. It is also unethical if by meeting our interests we prevent *others*[16] from meeting their own interests. Thus, as we shall see in a moment, certain degrees of egoism are ethical while others are unethical.

Solipsism

Solipsism is acting in your interest based on the belief that you are the only existing human being. It is "the theory that only the self exists, or can be proved to exist." It is the "extreme preoccupation with and indulgence of one's feelings, desires, etc."[17] The consequence of this belief is self-centredness. The solipsist is concerned with the interests of the only human being that is believed to exist, his own interests. Everything else that exists is believed to have no interests and it is important if and only if it can be used as a means to achieve the solipsist's interests. The solipsist acts as if fellow human beings were less human or even as if they were non-existent. Their interests do not matter. Solipsism is the most unethical form of egoism because other human beings are treated as if they were mere things, a means

---

[15]Collins English Dictionary Online: http://www.collinsdictionary.com/dictionary/english/egoism (Accessed: Nov.30th 2011).

[16] By *others* here we mean fellow human beings and the environment.

[17] http://dictionary.reference.com/browse/solipsism (accessed: July 24th 2011).

8

to somebody else' end. This attitude extends even to the use of non-human resources. For example, solipsists tend to use resources in an extravagant way because they believe that everything is abundantly available for their interests.

It can be a psychological disease for a person to behave in a solipsistic way. Most solipsists live with other human beings and yet they sustain the belief that they are the only human beings that exist. This contradiction can only be an illusion if not a mental disease that might require psychological therapy. Solipsists, however, do not know that they are disillusioned or that they need help because in the first place they do not believe in the existence of any other person who could offer such help. It is a kind of insanity that might lead to the extermination of other human beings. A solipsist kills other people in the same way as he would for example kill a goat or an insect. Whatever else that exists is simply a thing and it must be used for his own interests. This creates a lot of disharmony in society.

Traces of solipsism are detectable in some leaders, be they religious, political or cultural leaders. The most common symptom of leaders who suffer from the disease of solipsism is the strong belief that they are the only ones who can lead. Solipsistic leaders are fond of making statements such as "I am the *only* one who knows where we are coming from and where we are going as a community or country". They consider themselves to be indispensable vision-bearers and so they do not imagine that one day somebody else will replace them. This has been the case with African political leaders such as Mobutu Sese Seko of Zaire, Robert Mugabe of Zimbabwe, Muammar Gaddafi of Libya, Hosni Mubarak of Egypt, Paul Biya of Cameroon, and Yoweri Kaguta Museveni of Uganda. All these men did everything possible to remain in power because of the illusion that they were the only sane people capable of leading their countries. Such self-acclaimed visionary leaders tend to be dictators. They think of their subjects as weak, incapable of leadership, less intelligent, or even less human. Due to these misconceptions, African presidents with solipsistic tendencies have been accused of using national resources for their own interests. The interests of their subjects are at best thought of as secondary concerns. A solipsistic president goes to bed and sleeps soundly well whether or not the citizens have the basic needs of life. The president's luxurious needs are considered to be more urgent and necessary than the basic needs of the citizens. Surely, there is nothing as unethical as this! It is indeed a stupid thing for a person to disregard others and or to place one's security in material possessions. "Watch, and be on your guard against avarice/greed of any kind, for a man's life is not made secure by what he owns, even when he has more than he needs" (Lk 12:15). Both Gaddafi and Mobutu were not saved by their monies – they died like dogs!

The concept of solipsism can also be used to refer to the belief systems of the so-called superior groups of people. Pathological ideologies such as racism, colonialism, and slavery are all instances of what we might describe as group or collective solipsism. One group believes that it is superior to the other(s). The colonizers believe that they are the only human beings who exist while the colonized are believed to be mere things or at best potential but not yet real human beings. With this kind of mental conviction, if not misconception or actually a pathological mind-set, all the things of this planet earth are believed to be meant for the interests and welfare of the superior group. This is the philosophy which pertains during a colonial era and which justifies racism and slave trade. The colonizer takes away all the resources for his own interests because the colonized is believed to be less human or an animal or simply any other thing except a human being. For instance, at a banquet of commemorating the abolition of slavery, Victor Hugo encouraged his fellow Europeans saying, "Go forward, the nations! Grasp this land! Take it! From whom? From no one. Take this land from God! God gives the earth to men. God offers Africa to Europe. Take it"![18] Africa was generally seen as free land because those who were occupying it before were not really human. God was offering Africa to men (true human beings), to Europeans. Slavery had ended but now it was time for colonialism; a time to conquer lands that were initially occupied by semi-humans or non-humans.

In a solipsistic colonial situation, the colonized cannot claim any human rights since such rights belong only to true human beings whose existence is not indubitable. Likewise, the slave owner can do anything to the slave since the latter is said to be less human – is irrational or has no soul. All resources are therefore used for the interests of the *only existing* human group, namely, of the colonizers or superior race or slave masters/mistresses. It is believed that the only interests that actually matter are those of the superior group; the inferior group does not exist as a group of human beings and therefore its interests can be ignored or at best postponed.

The environment is currently in a crisis because of group solipsism. One group of the world's inhabitants, the human species, has for a long time been

---

[18] Gilbert Rist, *The History of Development: From Western Origins to Global Faith* (London: Zed Books, 1997), 51.

behaving in a solipsistic manner. Humans have been relating with the environment as something that has no interests and feelings. The existence of non-human entities is affirmed only when humans think of them as resources to meet their interests. In retaliation against this mistreatment, the environment has begun to make its existence felt. We now have no choice but to respect the interests of other creatures lest we perish since our existence depends on their existence.

Selfishness

When Dolan, Adela and Dinah[19] were still very little children, they used to fight for toys. Whenever their mothers left them to play together, the three little cousin sisters would each try to grab all the toys from the pool. Each of the three little children tried to take all the toys and by so doing deny the other two sisters the privilege of playing with the toys. Because of their limited worldviews and the inability to foresee long-term costs and benefits, Dolan, Adela and Dinah, like all little children, were under the spell of selfishness. When a child sees its counterparts, it acknowledges their existence but each of them knows that in order to meet its personal needs, it must compete with the others and also try to prevent them from meeting their individual needs.

Sibling jealousy is a more common concept that is used by psychologists to describe symptoms of selfishness. What sibling jealousy boils down to is one child becoming envious of the other when the parents' attention is shifted to the other child.[20] For example, when a child sees its mother with a new baby, it takes the new baby for a rival as far as meeting personal interests is concerned. The child soon realizes that some of the mother's care and love is being shifted to the new baby. Gradually, almost all the mother's attention shifts to the new baby. The child competes with the baby for the parents' attention but usually in vain.

Selfishness means "acting in your benefit without regard, and often harming, other individuals."[21] For the selfish person, it is not enough to meet

---

[19] Dolan, Adela, and Dinah are Kyaligonza Lawrence's nieces.

[20] http://ezinearticles.com/?What-Causes-Sibling-Jealousy---What-Can-You-Do-About-It?&id=321373 (Accessed June 10th 2012)

[21] Ethan Lee Vita, "On Selfishness and Self-Interest": (Date of Publication Friday Dec 21, 2007), http://ethanleevita.blogspot.com/2007/12/on-selfishness-and-self-interest.html (Accessed May 15th 2011)

personal interests; in addition to meeting personal interests, he harms the interests of other people. Ethically speaking, selfishness is a little better than solipsism because the selfish person at least recognizes the existence of other people. However, selfishness is not very far from solipsism; in both cases the interests of other people do not matter. The selfish person tries as much as possible to work against the interests of other people. It seems as if preventing other people from meeting their interests is part of the selfish person's interests. Selfishness is unethical not because it involves acting in one's interest but because it also involves harming other people's interests. Certainly, if everybody would act selfishly, the world would be very chaotic and life would be impossible for those who cannot defend their interests against the greed of those who are powerful. The young, the lame and all those who are physically weak would simply die since nobody would take care of their needs but instead everybody would be trying to harm their interests.

Selfishness, as Reinhold Niebuhr maintains, means "life taking advantage of life."[22] Those who have the power to do so undermine the interests, rights, privileges, and advantages of those without such power. This eventually generates social unrest as those whose interests have been undermined begin to revolt against the despots. An example of this is what we saw in 2011 when the Arab world experienced a wave of mass uprising against selfish governments. Selfishness is indeed the source of all human evils.

When some African kings and chiefs exchanged huge parcels of land with the colonialists for a piece of mirror or a kilogram of sugar or just a candy they acted selfishly. Of course, they were a bit ignorant of what they were doing but it is also true that they were concerned about their immediate interests only. They did not mind about their people's long term interests let alone the interests of future generations. They harmed the interests of many contemporary Africans who do not have sufficient land. This spirit of selfishness cum ignorance did not die with the pre-colonial chiefs and kings. Africa still has leaders who sell huge pieces of land to foreign investors at a throw away price while the citizens do not have sufficient land. As long as the leader is given some money to meet his own interests, the citizens can languish in poverty.

---

[22]Wiley Tatha, *Original Sin* (New York: Paulist Press, 2002), 138.

For instance, between 2006 and 2008, President Yoweri Kaguta Museveni of Uganda was willing to sell away Mabira forest to foreign investors; the investors must have promised to give him his own fill and so he did not care about the interests of the whole country in that forest. If the people had not taken to the streets, this forest might have gone just like that. Corruption is the most obvious symptom of selfishness in today's world. Public and civil servants embezzle public funds for selfish reasons. "Greedy, corrupt and unethical politicians in positions of power and influence use their influence to make laws work for them, to loot the state in consort with crooked rent-seeking business people (mostly men) in local and multinational companies who often have close business relationships with the most important politicians to launder their loot."[23]Corruption prevents the rest of the citizens from meeting their interests. It is a vice that has infected many institutions, including religious ones, and it has a long history. For instance, the renaissance popes lived in great splendour. They selfishly acquired a lot of wealth through the sale of indulgences and generally flourished on people's ignorance. Overwhelmed by the extravagance of the time, Pope Leo X (1513-1521) is said to have exclaimed, "God has given us the papacy let us enjoy it!"[24] By 'us', he was not referring to the whole Church but to himself and probably a few relatives and friends in crime. The same selfishness and extravaganza was characteristic of the emperors and princes of the time.

Many people join politics for selfish reasons. Some politicians care about becoming rich and powerful, even when the people they are supposed to be serving languish in poverty and suffering. As with Papi Silvio who, when confronted with a bribery case proclaimed that 'If I, in taking care of everyone's interests, also take care of my own, you can't talk about a conflict of interest;' many politicians pretend to be motivated by the people's interests. The fact, however, is that a person joins politics mainly to serve his own interests but not those of everyone. Most of our contemporary politicians would not agree with Aristotle's position that seeking the common good is a more complete and divine good than seeking individual interests. Most seek their individual interests.[25] Just before joining politics, for instance,

---

23 From a discussion with Dr. Charles Abugre, Director of the Millennium Development Goals, Africa Region (Nairobi, 18th February 2012).

24 http://www.mgr.org/TruthAboutSomePopes.html

25 Aristotle, *Nicomachean Ethics*, trans.Terence Irwan (Indianapolis: Hacket Publishing company, 1985), 1094 b 5-10.

Papi Silvio himself once said "I am forced to enter politics, otherwise they will put me in prison."[26] This impunity is one of the factors that motivate people to join politics; politics enables people to conceal their past and present records of corruption. Also, the political office carries honour, status, wealth, comfort, prerogatives, and the freedom from doing humbling tasks.[27] Selfish office bearers insist on honour more than they regard performance. The motivation to seek power over others leads to a blindness to people's interests and the security gained by acquiring power entails insecurity for those who do not have power.[28]

Selfishness exists even among religious institutions. Some religious sects preach negatively against others in order to get more members. One sect steals members from another sect by claiming that it is the most authentic religious sect. This is the case with newly established protestant churches within Christianity which have very few followers. The pastor aggressively hunts for more members partly because the more the members the higher the offertories.

The selfishness that exists in institutions is what we might refer to as group selfishness. One group prevents other groups from meeting their interests. This is the case with sectarianism. Tribalism, for example, is a situation where one tribe meets its interests at the expense of another tribe's interests. Some work places in Africa are dominated by people from a single tribe; for example, in Nigeria most army men/women are from the Tiv tribe and in Ghana, the civil sector is dominated by the Ewes. In some countries, commerce is dominated by certain tribes – the Igbo and Hausa in Nigeria, the Kikuyu in Kenya, the Baganda in Uganda, the Chaga and Haya in Tanzania, and the Akan in Ghana. Unfortunately, tribalism is also common in religious institutions; some religious congregations are dominated by certain tribes as if God has become sectarian in calling people for certain vocations. If somebody from any other tribe joins a congregation that is already infected by group selfishness, he will be frustrated by the dominant group; he might end up leaving the congregation believing that he probably has no vocation to religious life. Similarly, one wonders why women cannot be ordained to the priesthood within the Roman Catholic Church. This

---

[26] From a discussion with Abugre

[27] Michael Walzer, *Spheres of Justice: A Defense of Pluralism and Equality* (Oxford: Basil Blackwell, 1983), 155.

[28] Tatha Wiley, *Original Sin* (New York: Paulist Press, 2002), 145.

14

controversial issue is to some extent an example of group selfishness; priesthood has been monopolized by men and indeed the Roman Catholic Church is largely androcentric. The situation is even worse in Islam where women have been suppressed by the selfishness of their male counterparts.

Selfishness is characterized and catalysed by stiff competition. The world of selfish people is like a jungle where survival is for the fittest. In such a world, nothing (even what is in plenty) can ever be enough for everyone. Each member tries to take more than what he needs because the goal is not simply to meet one's interests but to also prevent the other members from meeting their interests. The selfish person works for his greed not needs; indeed, greed is the other name for selfishness. Competition is the only reliable weapon in the world of selfish people. However, sometimes competition can and does work against its adherents. In certain situations, even for selfish people, it is better to cooperate than to compete with one another. The famous example of the prisoners' dilemma illustrates this point very clearly.[29] In this example, we hypothetically imagine two prisoners (A and B) being interrogated separately for a crime they are suspected to have committed together. Each of them is secretly told that if he confesses but his counterpart does not confess, he will serve a sentence of three months only while his counterpart will serve three years. But if both of them do not confess, then each will serve a sentence of nine months; if both of them confess, then each will serve two years in prison. What do you think the prisoners will do? The most rational and selfless thing to do is not to confess because by not confessing, each of the two prisoners saves his counterpart from serving a sentence of three years. However, due to human selfishness, each of the two prisoners feels attracted to the mild punishment of serving three months and ignores the welfare of his counterpart. None of them is willing to sacrifice the three months sentence for the other. Each of them selfishly confesses in order to serve three months with the hope that his counterpart will not confess and so will be sentenced for three years. This is the prisoners' dilemma; they both end up confessing because of their selfishness and so each of them earns two years in prison; both of them lose not only the three months' sentence but also the nine months' sentence.

The prisoners' dilemma is a hypothetical example but it says a lot about the reality of our life as human beings. Most of us think only about what can

---

[29] Philip Hardwick, John Langmead and Bahadur Khan, *An Introduction to Modern Economics*, 5th ed. (London: Pearson Education Limited, 1999), 211-2.

benefit us as individuals; we do not mind about others or we even try to harm their interests. It is only in the aftermath of our choices that we begin to see the light, namely, we later on realise that if we had put our selfishness at bay and instead had cooperated, we might have been better-off. By trying to harm other people's interests, we end up harming our own interests too. Thus, there are only two options set before us: we either learn to care for one another or we all perish as fools. Selfishness is indeed costly not only for the selfish person but also for the entire society. It is responsible for most of the conflicts in the world and human-made disasters. When they run out of patience, those who feel that their interests have been harmed protest against the perpetrators.

One day, John was told by his landlord to ask for a Christmas gift for his good behaviour. The only condition was that whatever John would ask for his neighbour James[30] would be given twice as much. John thought to himself, should I ask for a tax-holiday of one month? But his neighbour would be given two months without paying rent! This troubled John and so instead of asking for a favour, he asked for something harmful. John told his landlord to disconnect one of the two lights in his apartment. The landlord did not understand John's motive until James had lost his two lights and came to him to complain. Selfishness can be as dangerous as that. It transforms people into brutes. Most selfish people make very irrational and dangerous decisions. Sometimes they are more interested in harming other people's interests than in meeting their own interests.

Sometimes, however, people feel guilty for having acted in a seemingly selfish manner and yet the situations in which they acted were such that nobody could have acted otherwise. This is common with acts which we might refer to as mutually exclusive interest acts. These are acts whereby it is not possible to meet the interests of one person without frustrating the interests of another person. What distinguishes mutually exclusive interest acts from pure selfish acts is that the beneficiary of a mutually exclusive interest act regards and cares about the interests of the other beneficiaries but he cannot do anything to have their interests met. Meeting their interests would mean forfeiting his interests because it is impossible to meet the interests of both parties. The pure selfish actor deliberately, maliciously and unnecessarily prevents others from meeting their interests but a mutually exclusive interest actor does so unavoidably, necessarily, and usually

---

[30] John and James are mythical figures.

regrettably. If it were possible for the interests of the two parties to be met, the mutually exclusive interest actor would not act in a seemingly selfish way. Imagine, for example, a woman with a cancerous uterus. Both the mother and the foetus will die if nothing is done. In order to save the life of the mother, the uterus must be removed but then the foetus will have to die.[31] It makes sense to remove the uterus because by doing so one of the two lives is saved while if it is not removed both lives will be lost. The mother might feel guilty afterwards thinking that she acted selfishly. However, what she has done is actually the best possible alternative; the foetus was not going to survive anyway. The mother's life is saved at the expense of the foetus living for a few more days or weeks.

A second and more complicated imaginary example is a situation where a person has limited resources and is supposed to make a choice to use those resources for saving one or the other person but not both. Imagine that a man and his wife are suffering from a disease that can only be treated at a high cost. The resources available can only save one life but not both lives. Should the resources be used to save the life of the man or of his wife? A lot of factors will have to be considered before the decision can be made. The question of who acquired the resources might not be as important as which of the two would be in a better position to look after the children. In this situation, saving one of the lives and letting-go of the other is not a case of selfishness. It is a way of trying to act rationally in an absurd situation. Of course, the one whose life is saved might feel guilty afterwards thinking that he acted selfishly. This requires psychological counselling. The survivor needs to be reminded that it was not possible for him to save the life of the deceased given the limitedness of their resources. What he needs to do is to carry out the responsibilities for which his life was saved, for instance, looking after the orphans. This would be the only way to overcome the unnecessary guilt – a way of appeasing the spirit of the deceased partner.

A third and a more common example is the situation where only one person can be employed but two or more people qualify for that job. After all the interviews have been conducted, meritocracy might not be the only criterion to follow since two or more candidates qualify. The job might be given to the candidate whose application was received first or by considering

---

[31] Richard M. Gula , *Reason Informed by Reason: Foundations of Catholic Morality* (New Jersey, Paulist Press, 1989), 270.

other qualities in the candidates.[32] Sometimes a draw might be done so that the job is given on the basis of meritocracy plus sheer luck. But, if the interviewers favour one of the candidates on the basis of gender, religion, tribe, colour, or race then they will have acted selfishly unless, through affirmative action, they are trying to redress a past inequality which was based on gender, religion, tribe, colour, or race. The candidate who ends up getting such a job is not selfish even though by taking the job he prevents the other candidates from getting it. It is simply impossible to have two or more people employed for a job of one person. However, if he gets the job by bribing the interviewers or the employer then he is selfish.

Self-interest

A common ambiguity is the tendency to equate the pursuit of self-interest with selfishness. Indeed most people, especially those who think of themselves as perfectly good-willed, selfless, charitable, or virtuous, hate to be told that their acts are motivated by some degree of self-interest. This is because for them pursuing self-interest means being selfish and yet selfishness belongs to the litany of vices. Such good people would like their acts to be described as altruistic acts but not as self-interest acts in order to avoid being associated with selfishness. The truth however is that they are neither purely altruistic people nor are they selfish. Their acts are self-interest acts and it is actually good and necessary for people to carry out such acts.

Self-interest refers to acting in one's own benefit, but with some consideration of other people's interests or at least without preventing other people from meeting their interests.[33] The condition of not preventing other people from meeting their interests is what we can refer to as the *negative law of egoism*. We can also describe the possibility of considering other people's interests as the *positive law of egoism*. These two laws are the ones that distinguish self-interest from selfishness. A selfish person is not satisfied by meeting his own interests; he must also prevent other people from meeting their interests. But the self-interest person aims at meeting his interests without aiming at harming other people's interests or, if possible, with some consideration to assist others in meeting their interests. Unlike a selfish

---

[32] Walzer, *Spheres of Justice,* 136.

[33] Ethan Lee Vita, "On Selfishness and Self-Interest".

person, a self-interest person hardly feels bad when other people meet their own interests. Acting out of self-interest is therefore ethically good.

Self-interest is necessary for the survival of individuals, companies, or nations. All normal human beings act out of self-interest. Self-interest is the healthiest and therefore the most acceptable form of egoism. An example of self-interest would be fair trade; John sells mangoes to James. Both John and James are happy with the transaction because each of them meets his interests without harming the interests of the other. Self-interest requires some sacrifice in order to facilitate the other person to meet his personal interests. It is the middle ground between giving everything to the other person (the so-called pure altruism) and taking everything for your interests (solipsism).

Self-interest is intimately connected to the instinct for survival. Human beings have to meet their interests in order for them to survive. Our survival depends on our willingness and ability to meet our interests. The axiom is simple, namely, you either meet your interests or you perish – unless your life depends on some kind of charity. The intimate connection between self-interest and the instinct for survival greatly influences all human activities. Most of the things people do are aimed at meeting certain personal interests and those interests are connected to the instinct for survival. People work hard to meet their interests because they do not want to die. The easiest way of inviting death is to stop working for one's interests.

Self-interest motivates people to work hard and to be innovatively creative. People will do anything to meet their interests and more especially when they realise that their interests are at stake because it is their survival which is at stake. Normal human beings will immediately shun their job or task as soon as they realise that it can no longer help them to meet their interests. People do not feel motivated to do something out of which they will not benefit in some way. Without the self-interest motivation, people have to be forced to do anything and they cannot do it as perfectly and willingly as they would do if that motivation was there. Prisoners, for instance, have to be compelled to do their tasks due to the absence of the self-interest motivation. No prisoner will enthusiastically do his task since most prison tasks do not meet the prisoners' needs and interests.

Another good example is that of taxation policies. Most tax defaulters evade paying taxes especially when they suspect that they will not get anything in return for their money. Surely, why should anybody pay taxes if the tax revenues are not used to meet tax payers' interests through the provision of public goods and services? The same thing can be said about associations. If an association is formed for certain interests, its survival will depend on how it enables the members to meet those interests. As soon as the members realise that the association or community is no longer helping them to meet their interests, they begin to opt out of that association or community. People will for example not pay allegiance to a nation-state which does not help them to meet their personal interests. The same applies to religious institutions. People pay no allegiance to a Church that does not assist them to achieve their spiritual needs. It is therefore important not only to be aware of people's interests but also to promote and protect those interests. Those personal interests are what motivate people to creatively work hard and to pay allegiance to institutions and communities. Thus, self-interest is good. People tend to be more productive when they are motivated by self-interest than when they are forced to do something that will not help them to meet their personal interests. This, as we shall see later, might be the main reason why capitalistic economies tend to progress faster than socialist economies and why perpetual aid prevents people from developing.

Self-interest is a good motivation for a successful education program. School children need to be told by their parents and teachers that the education which they are pursuing will benefit them in one way or another otherwise they might not take their studies seriously. If they are not motivated by some self-interest or if for some reason children develop the illusion that being in school is for their parents' or other people's interests only, they might not take their studies enthusiastically. Without some self-interest motivation, education is a bitter pill to swallow. Nobody goes to school solely for the interests of other people. It is therefore not enough to take your children to school and to provide them with all the school requirements. In addition to all these, children need to be told that that education is, at least to some extent, for their own good. Once children have been convinced that education will benefit them, they will make all possible sacrifices to take their studies seriously. In fact even if they might be from very poor families, they will struggle hard and try everything possible, including begging for school fees, to make sure that they complete their education.

Self-interest is also important for motivating people to unite and to become a little bit generous. People form institutions such as families, villages, nation-states, and supra-national organizations with the aim of meeting some of their personal interests. Self-interest is the main reason why

20

we have institutions, communities and organizations. Institutions are formed for the survival of individual human beings. People form institutions primarily for meeting interests which they cannot meet as individuals but as groups of people. However, the members of the group soon realise that in order to meet some of their personal interests, they have to also work for the interests of the other members. Eventually, the individuals might end up doing things for the other members' interests without any strong concern for their personal interests. The established institution or community teaches its individual members to let-go of some of their personal interests and to sacrifice for the other members' interests. Thus, even though communities are formed mainly for self-interests, the members end up becoming a little bit generous, at least to their fellow community members.

Chapter 2

Altruism

When people do generous things such as voluntary work in refugee camps, guiding strangers, contributing to charities, and giving aid to victims of natural disasters, we quickly conclude that they are altruistic because for us altruism means acting in other people's interests. There is nothing wrong with referring to generous and charitable people as altruistic but what we want to correct in this book is the illusion that such people are not influenced by some degree of self-interest. We want to emphasize the fact that all those so-called altruistic acts have some strings attached to them, the actors' interests.

Absolute Altruism

Absolute or pure altruism means acting in the interest of other people at the expense of one's own interests without expecting *any* benefit for oneself.[34] Acting in the interest of other people is what we referred to as *the positive law of egoism*. Let us refer to 'acting at the expense of one's own interests' as *the first degree of altruism* and 'acting without expecting *any* benefit for oneself' as *the second degree of altruism*. Absolute altruism can only happen in a world of angels but not in a world of ordinary human beings like us. There is no such a thing as pure altruism or selflessness in our world. All human beings are motivated by some degree of self-interest. At best, some are motivated by a mixture of self-interest and altruism. True, some people do act in the interest of others and sometimes even at the expense of their own interests but nobody ever acts in the interest of others without expecting some benefit for himself. The expectation might be implicitly hidden but it is always there. Similarly, the cost of helping others might be higher than the benefit derived by the helper but, however little, that benefit is always there. The benefit can be material, psychological or spiritual. Pure or absolute altruism is simply an illusion. At best people fulfil the positive law of egoism and the first degree of altruism but nobody can ever fulfil the second degree of altruism.

---

[34] http://en.wikipedia.org/wiki/Enlightened_self-interest (accessed: 25th February 2012).

When a mother spends a sleepless night attending to the needs of her sick baby, she acts in the interests of the baby but also in her own interests. Her interests include the fact that that baby is her child; she is fulfilling her parental obligations, and the implicit hope that the baby will be of some help to her when it grows up. More so, it is in the mother's interest to meet the interests of the baby so that when it falls asleep the mother too can sleep. The mother cannot meet her interest of sleeping until those of the child have been met by her. Meeting the interests of the child is for the good both of the child and of the mother. Thus, even in such situations pure or absolute altruism does not exist. There is always some aspect of self-interest on the side of the actor. People can sacrifice their interests for other people's interests but there is always a way they expect to compensate for their foregone interests or to benefit from their sacrifices.

Acquired Altruism

Although we have asserted that there is no such a thing as an absolutely or a purely altruistic act, people try to be generous in numerous ways. Some are more altruistic than others. People become somewhat altruistic because of the experiences of life through which they go and also because of cultural socialisation and religious instruction. When people experience hardships and they are helped by others to go through them, they will most likely become generous after that experience. By experiencing the benevolence of other people, a person becomes benevolent. However, most people become charitable because of cultural socialization and religious instructions. Because of certain experiences, as Reinhold Niebuhr argues, societies come to realize that too much self-centredness is ultimately counterproductive[35] and that a little bit of altruism is very necessary for individual and communal survival. Certain personal and communal interests cannot be met unless individuals form groups to work jointly for those interests. For instance, from the Akan community of Ghana there is a concept called *Innoboa* which literally means communal help. This concept is common among people of rural farming communities. Individual youths come together and work as groups on each of the member's farm. Individual members benefit by having their farms cultivated on time. The whole community benefits by being food secure. Also, as they work together the members share personal stories and this

---

[35] Tatha, *Original Sin*, 144.

unites them and they learn from one another about their culture. The *Innoboa* group becomes a form of social capital for the benefit of the individual members and the whole community even beyond the farming activity.

Societies therefore try to inculcate altruism in their members especially when they are still young in order to create a mechanism by which such interests can be met. For example, mothers teach their children to become generous by giving them something such as a candy and asking them to share it with other children. This is because they know that a certain degree of altruism will enable their children to survive in life and it will also sustain the community. Thus, altruism is something we acquire. Some of our egoistic energies must be transformed into altruism if we are to survive as individuals and as communities. Examples of people who through the process of cultural socialization acquired the charisma of altruism and practised it include moral geniuses such as Nelson Mandela of South Africa, Mahatma Gandhi of India, and Mwalimu Julius Nyerere of Tanzania and many others whose names have not attracted international attention because they did not acquire influential political positions in their societies.

Religion is another important agent of socialisation which makes people a little bit altruistic. Religion is so influential that even those who renounce it are deeply affected and influenced by the attitudes, self-images, and beliefs instilled by early religious training.[36] It influences its members to act in a certain way, whether they like it or not. Most religions emphasize the need to be generous. Altruism is an important ideal in most, if not in all religions. It is one of those virtues that enable religious institutions to continue existing. Actually without generous members, the religious community cannot survive and the religious leaders might not get their bread. One important religious symbol that has influenced the members to become generous is the Christian belief in a Triune God. According to the doctrine of the Trinity, God is not a monad but a perfect community of three distinct but equal persons. The three persons of the Trinity are interconnected by a strong bond of mutual self-giving and love. The Triune God is a community of three persons that are 'addicted' to self-giving love, sharing, self-sacrifice, cooperation, equality, respect of difference, solidarity, peace, etc. It has been pointed out, especially by liberation theologians, that the doctrine of the Trinity is an invitation for Christians to transform the world into a community of mutual love, respect,

---

[36] Andersen and Howard F. Taylor, *Sociology: Understanding a Diverse Society*, 101.

solidarity, justice, peace, etc.[37] Christians are supposed to act not only in their own interests but also in the interests of their neighbours since humans can only live by giving life to one another and receiving it from one another. Examples of Christians who have heeded this teaching are quite numerous but a few deserve mentioning here, Mother Teresa of Calcutta, Archbishop Oscar Romero of El Salvador, and Archbishop Hélder Pessoa Câmara of Brazil.

Altruistic Egoism[38]

We have already alluded to the fact that the human acts which we commonly refer to as altruistic acts are to some extent also influenced by the interests of the actors. However, we need to emphasize that just as it would be wrong to refer to those acts as purely altruistic acts so it would also be wrong to refer to them as purely egoistic acts. They are neither altruistic acts nor egoistic acts but composite acts of altruism and egoism. The actors are influenced by certain self-interests and the interests of the beneficiaries. The acts are partially egoistic and partially altruistic. Both the actor and the beneficiary benefit from an act of altruistic egoism. The actor does not act out of pure benevolence; he is at least convinced that it is for his own advantage for him to do something for the beneficiary. As Adam Smith puts it, "man has almost constant occasion for the help of his brethren [but] it is in vain for him to expect it from their benevolence only. He will be more likely to prevail if he can interest their self-love in his favour, and show them that it is for their own advantage to do for him what he requires of them."[39]

For some acts of altruistic egoism, the actor is influenced more by self-interest than by the interests of the beneficiaries while for others the interests of the beneficiaries are more influential. In any case, it is hard to measure these influences and their extents. However, the actor usually knows which interests influence him more. The following are some examples of situations where the actor is influenced by both self-interest and the interests of the beneficiaries.

---

[37] Leonardo Boff, *Holy Trinity, Perfect Community*, trans. Phillip Berryman (New York: Orbis Books, 1988), xiv; 2; 47.

[38] Concept coined by the authors of this book.

[39] Smith, *An Inquiry Into the Nature and Causes of The Wealth of Nations*, 14.

Deferred Gratification

This refers to situations where someone decides to sacrifice his short-term interests in order to maximize his long-term interests.[40] A shop owner, for example, might decide to offer discounts and after-sell services in order to attract more customers. Most customers will be attracted to his shop thinking that he is a very generous/altruistic person. Indeed, in the short-run, the shop owner will sacrifice his gains for the interests of his customers but in the long-run, he will maximise his profits from increased trade volume and be able to make up for the short-term losses. It is in the interest of the shop owner to reduce prices in the short-term in order to maximise profits in the long-run; it is not just for the benefits of his customers. Both the actor and the beneficiaries benefit from the act. In most cases, the actor benefits more than the beneficiaries, at least in the long run.

Most human acts which we refer to as altruistic acts are cases of deferred gratification. They are forms of investment. Immediate benefits are sacrificed for the sake of enjoying more benefits in the future. For example, Tinkasiimire, a charitable man in Kasungu village – Kasese district – western Uganda, was known by all his neighbours to be an altruistic man because he was paying school fees for several poor children and orphans who were not even related to him. However, later on during his old age, Tinkasiimire started complaining that although some of those children had become important and wealthy people, they were not doing enough to support him. Tinkasiimire's neighbours had canonized him without knowing that he was making an investment for his interests, the interests of the children notwithstanding. He had sponsored the children with the hope that they would reciprocate his support in the future. His sponsorship was like an investment in an insurance company. He sacrificed his immediate interests with the hope that the future would be brighter. A lot of charitable people like Tinkasiimire are usually motivated partly, if not majorly, by self-interest but they disguise their acts as if they were purely altruistic acts. The same might be said about the assistance which we sometimes give to strangers. Most of us forego our present comforts to help strangers but with the hope that they will in future become our friends or that they will in turn help us in one way or another. If they do not remember to reward us, we get annoyed with them or we might even stop assisting strangers.

---

[40] http://en.wikipedia.org/wiki/Enlightened_self-interest (accessed: 25th February 2012).

The concept of deferred gratification can be used to categorize the acts of many religious people. Some religious acts are mainly motivated by the desire to go to heaven or the fear of going to hell. Religious acts are "like an investment in a retirement program where it costs (someone) a little in this life for a huge return in the next life."[41] Since every investment requires some sacrifices to be made in the present in order for some benefits to be earned in the future, many religious people forego present satisfactions in order to be gratified in the next life. Their acts are teleological because the main concern is the end for which the actor acts. The motivation is the future reward but not the act-in-itself. For example, instead of using their resources to meet personal needs, some believers give alms to the poor so that their reward in heaven might be increased. They fast and forego the so-called earthly pleasures for the sake of the promised heavenly glory. The alms-giver is more interested in the reward than in the act of assisting the recipients. However, when they do charitable works, religious people appear to be purely altruistic (and indeed most of them want to be referred to as purely altruistic people) but in actual fact their acts are tainted by a certain degree of self-interest. A certain woman was terminally ill in a hospital and the members of her Christian community kept visiting her to comfort her. One day she asked them whether they had come to see her or to see Jesus in her. They were taken aback by the question because the truth is that they had gone to fulfil the command, namely, they had gone to visit Jesus by visiting 'the least of his sisters' in order to be counted among the sheep that will sit on the right hand of God on judgment day. The visitors had not gone to see their friend just because visiting the sick is a good thing but because they hoped that visiting the sick would earn them a place in heaven. Likewise, some Christians visit prisoners or give food to the hungry or water to the thirsty not for the sake of being generous but in order to fulfil a command so that they might earn some reward in heaven as Jesus Christ promised in Matthew 25: 31-46. Without the solemn expectation for some compensation in heaven or if the fear of going to hell is transcended, not many people would be as generous as they appear to be. Self-interest is at the core of some religious activities. People have made great contributions towards the construction of churches or for the welfare of their pastors simply because the pastor has convinced them that in heaven they will receive a hundredfold of what they are willing and able to offer now.

---

[41] http://www.churchof reality.org/wisdom (accessed: 5th April 2011).

Motivated by deferred gratification, countries assist their counterparts especially during difficult times. When a country is experiencing a natural hazard such as an earthquake, floods, tsunami, or hurricane, other countries provide it with relief aid mainly because they believe that if something like that happens to them in the future, they too will need the assistance of other countries including the one that is being assisted now. A country treats its troubled counterparts as it would like to be treated in similar circumstances. However, sometimes the motive might not necessarily be deferred gratification but to grab certain resources from the country that is being assisted. Countries that are naturally endowed with precious resources always get assistance as soon as they are challenged by any calamities but those without such resources hardly get anybody to come to their rescue. When countries rush to assist Libya, Iraq, or the Democratic Republic of Congo they do so partly in order to loot the resources of those countries. They are motivated mainly by the oil and the gold. Why was Rwanda not assisted during the 1994 genocide? It was mainly because there was nothing much to gain afterwards.

Symbiotic Reciprocation[42]

Most human beings are members of certain communities and they are aware that belonging to a community involves a lot of responsibilities and obligations. In order to remain a good member of a community, the person has to fulfil certain tasks and duties. A member who is simply a parasite will be seen as a burden to the community. Community solidarity is built and sustained by symbiotic relationships where the members uphold the philosophy of give-and-take. Members render certain services to one another. They are involved in a mutual relationship of give and take. Each member receives from the community and gives back to the community. Nevertheless, in the process of paying back, the members might appear to be purely altruistic but in actual fact, they are moved by some sort of self-interest. People do certain things for the community as a way of 'paying back' (reciprocating) what the community has already done for them in the past. "Through socialization, we learn the reciprocity norm, the expectation that we should return help, not harm, to those who have helped us."[43]

---

[42] Concept coined by the authors of this book.

[43] Myers, *Psychology*, 587.

Reciprocation, however, is not the same thing as pure altruism. It is a way of paying back for one's interests that were met in the past by another person or community. For example, it is not pure altruism when a government minister assists people from his village. Such a minister is moved by the impulse to appreciate how the village contributed to his upbringing and education. Of course, the minister is also motivated by the desire to be appreciated by those whom he assists. He is at once concerned about the future interests of the community and his own past interests that were fulfilled by the community. This is a situation of an act that is motivated by both self-interest and altruism.

Many business organisations are also once in a while involved in acts of symbiotic reciprocation. This happens especially after a business entity has made huge profits. The business organization decides to 'give back' to the community, for example, by paying school fees for a number of children in the community, constructing a road or a bridge for the community, or by throwing a party for the community. Such acts are not instances of pure altruism even if they might be portrayed as so. They are acts of symbiotic reciprocation – a mixture of self-interest and altruism. The business enterprise does such 'charitable' acts as a way of appreciating the benefits it has already received from the community. As a matter of fact, no serious business entity can offer services to the community if it has been making losses in the past. It does not make any economic sense to appreciate the community for business losses. Businesses give a token of appreciation if and only when their interests of making profits have been met. They meet community interests if and only after their own interests have been met by the community.

Sometimes the reciprocation takes place in advance. It is a form of pre-payment for the services that will be rendered in future to an individual by the community. Such a pre-payment is not pure altruism but a mixture of self-interest and altruism. In a typical African village, for instance, everyone is expected to be present at funerals. People attend funerals partly because they know that they too will need community support when they lose a family member in the future. They are motivated by the expectation that the community will reciprocate in the future. They assist the grieved family with certain necessities and carry out certain tasks that cannot be done by those who are grieving. By attending community celebrations, the individual meets the current interests of the community and his future interests of being assisted by the community when the time comes. A person who does not participate in community celebrations risks being ostracized by the community. Such a person will not be supported by the community when he faces problems. The community will reciprocate in the same currency when his turn comes. For example, a certain wealthy man in a Ugandan village used to send money to grieved families but he was never present at funeral celebrations. For him money was enough to soothe the community. One day he lost his son. Each member of the community sent him money and continued with their business. This was a lesson not only for him but for all the members of the community.

In democratic countries, politicians are the most common example of people who are usually involved in acts of symbiotic reciprocation. Whenever politicians do anything for their communities, they want to be perceived as purely altruistic people if they are to win another term in office. Yet, all that they do is to pay the community for having voted them into power or supported them financially during the electioneering campaigns. As a way of reciprocating, some politicians give positions of leadership to those who supported them during the campaigns even if they might not be qualified for those positions. If the people were to come to the realisation that what their leaders do for them is not motivated by pure altruism but mainly by self-interest, they would consider other important factors before voting for them again. Because it is the voters' right, symbiotic reciprocation should not be a means for politicians to earn another term in office. After their first term in office, they can be voted for another term if and only if they have fulfilled what they promised to do for the people. If they have not been faithful to their manifestos, they must be replaced by somebody else who can do a better job. This was the conviction of a certain old and illiterate woman at Paga-Buru, a village in northern Ghana. In 2008 she refused to vote for her incumbent member of parliament even though he had given her two bags of rice, three litres of cooking oil, and some money. Her main reason was that the man was claiming to be generous but in actual fact he was paying back for the votes which he got during the first campaigns. These gifts were not supposed to be used as a way of luring the community to vote for him for another term. Politics should not be left to selfish sophists but to those who can maintain a balance between meeting their own interests and the interests of their people. Likewise, leaders should not give positions of leadership to people simply because they supported them financially or materially during the campaigns. Meritocracy is the only authentic means of getting people to occupy positions of leadership that require expertise. As a way of symbiotic reciprocation, leaders are free to use their personal resources to pay back for what they were given during the campaigns but using public resources for such purposes is immoral. It is acceptable only in countries where nepotism and corruption have been legalized.

Symbiotic reciprocation can also mean what Haley Joel Osment uses as title for his inspirational movie – *Pay It Forward*. As an act of symbiotic reciprocation, when a person receives something from another, he does not pay back to that same person but to any stranger. The recipient pays forward what he has received from a stranger or even from a member of his community. His interests were met by someone and so he too meets the interests of another. Sometimes, however, by paying it forward, the recipient might accidently pay it backward, for example, by assisting a stranger without knowing that that stranger is related to the person who assisted him. This situation is conveyed in the following forwarded story:[44]

One day a man saw an old lady, stranded on the side of the road, but even in the dim light of day, he could see she needed help. So he pulled up in front of her Mercedes and got out. His old Pontiac was still sputtering when he approached her. Even with the smile on his face, she was worried. No one had stopped to help for the last hour or so. Was he going to hurt her? He didn't look safe; he looked poor and hungry.

He could see that she was frightened, standing out there in the cold. He knew how she felt. It was that chill which only fear can put in you.

He said, 'I'm here to help you, ma'am. Why don't you wait in the car where it's warm? By the way, my name is Bryan Anderson.'

Well, all she had was a flat tyre, but for an old lady, that was bad enough. Bryan crawled under the car looking for a place to put the jack, skinning his knuckles a time or two. Soon he was able to change the tyre. But he had to get dirty and his hands hurt.

As he was tightening up the lug nuts, she rolled down the window and began to talk to him. She told him that she was from St. Louis and was only just passing through. She couldn't thank him enough for coming to her aid.

Bryan just smiled as he closed her trunk. The lady asked how much she owed him. Any amount would have been all right with her. She already imagined all the awful things that could have happened had he not stopped. Bryan never thought twice about being paid. This was not a job to him. This

---

[44] http://finance.groups.yahoo.com/group/jfcnigeria/message/624 (accessed: 25th December 2011).

was helping someone in need, and God knows there were plenty, who had given him a hand in the past. He had lived his whole life that way, and it never occurred to him to act any other way.

He told her that if she really wanted to pay him back, the next time she saw someone who needed help, she could give that person the assistance they needed, and Bryan added, 'And think of me.' He waited until she started her car and drove off. It had been a cold and depressing day, but he felt good as he headed for home, disappearing into the twilight.

A few miles down the road the lady saw a small cafe. She went in to grab a bite to eat, and take the chill off before she made the last leg of her trip home. It was a dingy looking restaurant. Outside were two old gas pumps. The whole scene was unfamiliar to her. The waitress came over and brought a clean towel to wipe her wet hair. She had a sweet smile, one that even being on her feet for the whole day couldn't erase. The lady noticed that the waitress was nearly eight months pregnant, but she never let the strain and aches change her attitude.

The old lady wondered how someone who had so little could be so giving to a stranger. Then she remembered Bryan.

After the lady finished her meal, she paid with a hundred dollar bill. The waitress quickly went to get change for her hundred dollar bill, but the old lady had slipped right out the door. She was gone by the time the waitress came back. The waitress wondered where the lady could be.

Then she noticed something written on the napkin. There were tears in her eyes when she read what the lady wrote: 'You don't owe me anything. I have been there too. Somebody once helped me out, the way I'm helping you. If you really want to pay me back, here is what you do: Do not let this chain of love end with you.'

Under the napkin were four more $100 bills. Well, there were tables to clear, sugar bowls to fill, and people to serve, but the waitress made it through another day. That night when she got home from work and climbed into bed, she was thinking about the money and what the lady had written. How could the lady have known how much she and her husband needed it? With the baby due next month, it was going to be hard....

She knew how worried her husband was, and as he lay sleeping next to her, she gave him a soft kiss and whispered soft and low, 'Everything's going to be all right. I love you, Bryan Anderson.'

33

Scrupulous Benefactors[45]

Some people acquire a lot of wealth through dubious and unjust means. For example, when a given group of people colonizes another group, the colonizers might acquire a lot of wealth by exploiting the resources of the colonized. Likewise, there are some politicians who enrich themselves by swindling public funds and there are business people who become rich by cheating their customers. With time, however, such rich people might be tormented by their own conscience – they begin to feel scrupulously guilty for having robbed from their fellow human beings. Consequently, they might decide to return to the victims some of what they stole from them but in a seemingly charitable manner, for example, by giving grants to the victims' descendants or by sponsoring certain public works. Such grants might be presented as donations and the donors might claim to be offering assistance but the truth is that the donors are scrupulous benefactors. Scrupulous benefactors are never purely altruistic people. Their acts are motivated by a sense of guilt but not by genuine generosity. They try to pacify their conscience by compensating those from whom they unjustly acquired their wealth. Certainly, scrupulous benefactors meet some of the interests of the beneficiaries but they too benefit by soothing their own conscience. Thus, they are largely motivated by self-interest and only to a small extent by altruism. It is very unfortunate, however, that scrupulous benefactors usually conceal the reason as to why they do their 'charitable' works. They instead want to be appreciated for being purely altruistic. Indeed, the recipients are sometimes misled to the extent that they even go as far as adoring scrupulous benefactors as if what has been returned to them was a privilege but not a right.

Composite Beneficiaries

Certain acts satisfy not only the interests of the actor but also the interests of his group members. The whole group benefits from the individual's act. For example, when a footballer endangers his leg to score a goal, he does not win alone; the whole team wins. Similarly, when a soldier risks his life to fight in a war, his country begins to enjoy security. He does not enjoy that security alone. Also, when someone works hard for the sanitation of his city, he does not benefit alone. The whole city enjoys staying in a clean and safe environment. Thus, the actor benefits at two levels,

---

[45] Concept coined by the authors of this book.

34

namely, at a personal level and at the group level. At the personal level, the actor becomes famous and he might win an award while at the group level, he benefits like any other group member does. What we need to emphasize here is the fact that the actor is motivated more by his own interests than by the interests of his fellow group members. Of course, he knows that the other group members will benefit from his act but their benefit is not the primary motivation. However, a composite beneficiary might claim that his acts are motivated solely by the interests of the group.

Emotively Egoistic[46] People

There are some people who simply feel good for helping somebody else.[47] Because of their appetite to give, emotively egoistic people spend a lot of resources helping other people in order to feel good afterwards. They usually assist flatterers who can praise them afterwards. What motivates such people is not pure altruism but a mixture of altruism and self-interest. Emotively egoistic people feel good for assisting those who are less fortunate. It burdens them, at least psychologically, to see other people suffering. They meet the interests of the beneficiaries but they also benefit by experiencing some joy or some psychological calmness after offering the help. When people offer charity they do so primarily because they secretly expect that they will be appreciated or that they will at least be thought of as good people. Without such solemn expectations, there could hardly be a single charitable person in this world. If a helper suspects that he will not feel good after offering the help, he withholds the assistance. Also, if from experience he realises that the recipients of his assistance do not show any sign of gratitude and so instead of feeling good after offering the assistance he gets frustrated, he will immediately stop assisting. It is however a bit difficult to accept the fact that such helpers, such good people are to some extent motivated by some degree of self-interest. We often think that they are motivated by nothing else but the interests of the recipients. The reason why we think that they are purely altruistic is that emotively egoistic people usually assist people in pathetic situations, such as people who are soaked in abject poverty. Moreover, some donors decide to remain anonymous and so they are not motivated by the beneficiaries' acclaim. Nevertheless, anonymous donors too feel good for having assisted other people;

---

[46] Concept coined by the authors of this book.

[47] Aristotle, *Nicomachean Ethics*, 1121a 30 – 1121b 1

sometimes by remaining anonymous, the donor feels even more fulfilled and convinced that he is more virtuous than people who parade their generosity.

Advertisers

In order to attract people, an advertiser, using the media which is a significant agent of socialization, must use linguistic devices that are altruistic. Potential customers are made to believe that they will benefit a lot from the goods or services being advertised and that the provider is indeed a selfless person. The provider pretends to be altruistic as if he has nothing to gain from the transaction. Advertisers use catch phrases to lure customers, for instance, 'your happiness is our only goal', 'your health is our only concern', and 'we are here just for you'. However, the fact is that all business entities are more concerned with their own interests than with the customers' interests. In fact they only care about the customers' interests because if they do not then the customers will run away from them and go to other providers. It is in the interest of the business to meet the customers' interests. But, we always think that businesses are there to meet our interests. Adverts keep misleading us into buying unnecessary things just because we believe that the advertisers are genuine in promising that our interests are their only motivation. If business enterprises were there to meet our interests only they would be making a lot of losses and therefore there would be very few business people, if any. Business people are motivated by profits but not losses. Adverts are meant to boost the interests of the business even though the customers somehow benefit from them. There is no business enterprise in this world that sells high quality products at low prices unless its manager is experiencing some kind of mental breakdown or wants to close the enterprise altogether. It is too expensive to run adverts in newspapers or on televisions. No sane business manager can spend huge sums of money on adverts unless he is convinced that the benefits will be more than the costs. It is simply unimaginable that a business enterprise can advertise its products for purely altruistic purposes. Even sales promotions are aimed more at boosting business profits than at enabling customers to buy more products at lower prices.

Some advertisements are forms of deferred gratification. A business entity might decide to advertise its products by offering low prices or by announcing that it has improved the quality of its products. Such moves are meant to attract more customers. The business will not benefit in the short-run but the long-term benefits are sufficient to cover not only the costs of the advertisements but also any losses that might have accrued to the enterprise in the short-run when the products were being sold at lower prices. This is possible because once the customers have been misled to the extent that they now think of the business as a purely altruistic enterprise they will continue buying the same products even at higher prices.

Politicians who cannot advertise themselves to the people can hardly win elections. Many politicians win elections by pretending to be purely altruistic. During the campaigns they try to convince the people that they have been motivated by altruism but not by any personal interests. They must conceal their interests from the voters and instead claim in their manifestos, usually in an exaggerated way, that they will work for nothing else but for the interests of the people. The people cast their votes for the candidate who succeeds in convincing them that he is going to be a selfless leader. They vote for someone whom they have been made to believe that he will work for the common good and one who will serve instead of being served. However, at least in the world of human beings, it is unimaginable that anybody can campaign for a position of leadership without expecting some personal benefits. Because of its complexity and demands, leadership is embraced not for altruistic reasons but because of the benefits that are associated with it. Once we see somebody campaigning for a position of leadership we can as well already conclude that that person is not looking forward to serving us but to meeting personal interests. If the opportunities of meeting certain self-interests are removed from a leadership position nobody will campaign for it. True leadership is supposed to be servant leadership but that kind is not lucrative. Leadership for pure service is never anybody's cup of tea; it is a burdensome undertaking. People accept to shoulder the burdens of leadership after carrying out a detailed cost-benefit analysis and convincing themselves that the burdens will be less than the satisfaction they will get as individuals. People have to be forced or persuaded to accept servant leadership positions otherwise nobody can campaign for them because of the lack of possibilities to meet self-interests. All campaigns for leadership are motivated by some degree of self-interest. The best leader we should expect to get is someone who can meet both his own interests and our interests. If a candidate tells us during the campaigns that he has been motivated by his own interests and our interests, he would be the right one to vote for simply because he is genuine and therefore most likely reliable.

Consanguineous benevolence[48]

It is not pure altruism that motivates people to help their relatives. People help their relatives mainly because they are related to them. This might sound tautological but it is true. People do anything to assist their siblings, parents or any other relatives apparently for no other reason but because they share the same blood. The motivation is the blood bond that they share as relatives. Because of the strong blood bond, parents passionately take care of their children, even physically or mentally handicapped ones. People assist their delinquent relatives or terminally ill spouses mainly because they are related to them. "If a man who is passionately in love with his wife spends a fortune to cure her of a dangerous illness, it would be absurd to claim that he does it as a "sacrifice" for her sake, not his own, and that it makes no difference to him, personally and selfishly, whether she lives or dies."[49] The survival of the wife is of great importance to the husband, his happiness requires her survival.

Assistance between relatives and by extension between friends and spouses should never be mistaken for purely altruistic acts; such assistance is hardly, if ever, extended to strangers. The beneficiary's interests are met but the actor also benefits by feeling good that he has assisted his relative or has paid back to the family for what he received from it. Consanguineous benevolence is usually characteristic of emotively egoistic people and symbiotic reciprocators. It can also be a form of deferred gratification where a person helps his relatives partly because he expects that they will assist him or his children in the future. In any case, consanguineous benevolence is influenced not only by altruism but also by self-interest.

If people who are in influential positions offer jobs to their relatives partly because they are related to them, that is a case of consanguineous altruism; the job is offered because of meritocracy and consanguinity. The person benefits from reducing the burden of having to assist the relatives with his own salary while the relatives benefit by earning their own salaries. This practice is common in many societies and it has a long history. For instance, during the medieval period, the so-called renaissance popes did not hesitate to offer ecclesiastical benefices to their sons. What is unethical is

---

[48] Concept coined by the authors of this book.

[49] Ayn Rand and Nathaniel Branden, *The Virtue of Selfishness: A New Concept of Egoism* (New York: Signet, 1964), 51.

pure nepotism, offering the job to someone just because he is related to you irrespective of his ability to do the job.[50]

Deontological Altruism[51]

Sometimes we do certain acts to fulfil specific laws and regulations, for example, when we pay taxes or when we obey traffic rules or when we try to keep our cities clean by putting rubbish in the public rubbish bin. Such acts are not purely altruistic acts; they are acts done to fulfil certain laws and regulations – they are deontological acts. If laws and regulations were not put in place, such acts would hardly be done; some individuals would definitely act differently. Deontological acts are largely motivated by the fear of punishment. It is in the interest of the actor to obey and to fulfil the law. Of course, other people end up benefiting from his obedience but their benefit is secondary.

Philanthropic Altruism

A person who has integrated the virtue of altruism through cultural socialization or religious instruction and who loves humanity is likely to act in the interests of humanity. Such a person is referred to as a philanthropist. Philanthropists think of humanity as one big family. Their altruism is not limited to their families or relatives or countries. They assist any human being because of the conviction that human beings are in one way or another related to one another. Philanthropists extend their altruism even to strangers. Because their altruism is open to the whole of humanity, philanthropists are sometimes referred to as humanitarians. In most cases they form agencies to offer humanitarian assistance especially to people who are in difficulties, for example, the poor, refugees, and people who have been hit by natural disasters such as earthquakes, floods, landslides, droughts, tsunamis, etc.

However, even though philanthropists appear to be purely altruistic, they too are to some extent motivated by their own hidden interests. Some might be emotively egoistic or scrupulous benefactors or symbiotic reciprocators or others might be doing some kind of deferred gratification. In any case, such

---

[50] Walzer, *Spheres of Justice*, 148.

[51] This concept is derived from Immanuel Kant's theory of Deontological Ethical Theory which is described as rule or obligation or duty based ethics – rules/laws bind you to your ethics. Thus, a person does something because he is required by the law to do so.

aspects are usually never explicit when humanitarian assistance is offered. The beneficiaries are falsely made to believe that their Good Samaritan has nothing to gain from the act. The beneficiaries usually receive some tangible assistance but the actor also benefits, at least psychologically or socially. Some philanthropists gain international recognition as charitable people and some even win awards because of their work. Such benefits can motivate people to become humanitarian. Genuine philanthropists are motivated more by the interests of the beneficiaries than by their own interests while counterfeit philanthropists are motivated more by their own interests than by the interests of the beneficiaries. For instance, so many counterfeit Samaritans have used the Masai people of Kenya and Tanzania and the slum-dwellers of Kibera to write attractive project proposals but most of the money is used by these so-called Samaritans to buy flamboyant vehicles for themselves. The beneficiaries are given peanuts. Because of this abuse, the Masai no longer accept to be photographed by the so-called Good Samaritans.

Community Formation

Before we conclude this chapter, it is important to discuss the process of community formation. Humans are largely egoistic and yet they are social animals. How is altruism possible in a community of humans who are largely egoistic? The main reason why communities are formed and sustained is the strong instinct for survival. In actual fact the community is a consequence of the failure to survive on our own. In other words, the community is a means but not an end in itself. Human beings form or join communities in order to survive and more specifically in order to acquire those economic goods and services which can only be produced by joint efforts. Otherwise, most social encounters are mechanical, impersonal and opportunistic. Howland Sanks affirms this maxim by acknowledging that "although we do have face-to-face social exchanges, such as buying groceries, working with others in the office or factory, or visiting a doctor when sick, undergirding these social encounters are vast impersonal social and economic systems of production, distribution, marketing, advertising, banking and credit."[52] To a very large

---

[52] Howland T. Sanks "Reading the Signs of the Times: Purpose and Method" in *Resources for Social and Cultural Analysis: reading the Signs of the Times*. Eds. Howland T. Sanks and John A. Coleman, (New York: Paulist Press, 1993), 5.

extent, we cooperate with other people not necessarily because we love them but especially because we *need* one another. We do not visit the doctor just because we want to 'be' with him but because we need his relieving help. The patient is interested in getting healed while the doctor is above all else lured by his own self-interests, namely, the profit that will accrue from the medical bill and/or the heroic feeling he will experience after healing the patient. In this example we notice that the patient is moved by the instinct to survive while the doctor is to a very great extent motivated by profit.

According to Aristotle, the family is the first necessary human association to be formed[53] and it is formed primarily for procreation purposes. Human beings, just like other animals, have the strong desire to leave their image behind. The belief is that after death, the human person continues to exist through his offspring. Following this understanding, we can assert that the bringing forth of children is the main reason why a man and a woman willingly accept to unite with each other to form a family. Since they cannot procreate without the assistance of each other and since child-upbringing is easier when father and mother are in fellowship, man and woman unite in order to find a solution to their fear of absolute extinction.[54] The family is to a large extent formed as a means of satisfying human self- interest and as a way to overcome human limitations. When a man unites with a woman it is not for the welfare of the woman but mainly because of his own welfare that he does so and likewise when the woman accepts the man's invitation to form a family it is what she will benefit from the union that ultimately persuades her. It is not pure love or altruism that brings the two together.

When a child is born in a family, it remains in that family for its own survival. The child cannot survive on its own because of its defencelessness. As soon as the child becomes an adult and develops some degree of independence, it 'leaves' its parents' family to form its own with a partner. Of course, the family institution is sustained by the strong bond that develops

---

[53] Aristotle, *The Politics*, ed. Steven Everson (Cambridge: Cambridge University Press, 1988), 1252a 25.

[54] With the advancement in technology, the family institution might become less attractive for some people. More and more people are deciding not to marry since they can have children without necessarily having spouses, for example, buying sperms for IVF and surrogate motherhood. People are able to meet the primary goal of the family without necessarily forming a family. The phenomenon of single mothers is becoming common especially in cities such as Nairobi.

among the members. The members remain connected in one way or another. However, that bond too is to some extent an aspect of egoism and the instinct to survive. Each member somehow knows that cooperating with the other family members will facilitate the acquisition of his interests.

The bond among family members gives birth to altruistic gestures and activities. In an ideal family, for example, most parents will do anything to fend for their children. Real parents do sacrifice their own comfort for the sake of their children's welfare. Especially during very difficult times, most parents try to suspend their own interests for the survival of their children. For example, in situations of serious famine, authentic mothers decide to starve themselves in order to give to their children the little food that is still available. This kind of sacrifice can only happen among people who are strongly bonded. Family members share a very strong bond, a bond that is thickened not by water but by blood and so they can easily sacrifice their individual interests for the sake of one another. The family is an ideal institution that teaches people how to turn their egoism into some kind of altruism. A person can easily forget about his own interests for the sake of the interests of his family members. Because of the love that exists in the family, none of the members feels satisfied by simply meeting his interests; the interests of all the members must be met before any of the members can be at peace. No genuine mother will sleep before she is sure that all her children are comfortable. When her child cries at night, the mother forgets all about the comfort of sleeping and instead attends to the needs of the child. This altruistic spirit is gradually passed on to the child. The child learns from its family members, especially from the mother, that life is not about taking care of one's interests only but also the interests of others.

We must however insist that the altruism that exists among family members is itself to some extent motivated by self-interest. When parents take good care of their children, they do so first of all because those children are 'theirs' – the children are an extended self of each of the two parents. Secondly, the parents believe that their children will look after them during old age - deferred gratification. More so, parents simply feel fulfilled by taking care of their children. The parents' egos are satisfied when they see their children happy; most parents are emotively egoistic people. The family members must practice some kind of altruism if each of them is to meet their individual interests.

The family is an association established not only for procreation purposes but also for the supply of basic human needs. Certain needs, usually referred to as basic needs, including food, shelter, clothing and basic knowledge are necessary for the sustenance of human life. Fortunately, nature has made available certain resources (plants and animals) for the satisfaction of most of our needs and therefore for the sustenance of human life.[55] However, even though nature has been generous enough, the human person must appropriate natural resources in order to satisfy his needs since some resources cannot automatically avail themselves to him. Now, the way human beings utilize available resources to satisfy their needs is what is referred to as economics. Usually, individual human beings find it very hard to satisfy their needs without the direct or indirect assistance of other people. Human needs are easily met when people cooperate with one another.

The family is the primary unit of economics. Economics has a lot to do with the Greek term *Oikonomia* which means household management. Economics refers to the ways the members of a household (a family) meet their necessities through the utilization of available resources. However, it is not pure altruism that moves the individual members of the family to participate in the family's economic activities. True, the individual knows that his efforts will benefit other family members but that is not the primary reason why he gets involved in household economic activities; he is first of all moved by self-interest and the interests of other family members serve only as a secondary motivation. Thus, the family as an association for economic welfare is to a larger extent initiated and sustained by egoistic intentions than by altruistic motives.

A village is formed by several individual families coming together mainly to form an economic unit. When individual family units realise that they cannot meet all their needs by themselves, they seek the assistance of other family units. This limitedness to satisfy family needs leads to the formation of a larger association, namely, a village. The village is seen as an association that will enable individual family units to get goods and services that they could not get before the association was formed. Similarly, villages form nation-states, nation-states form regional blocks and the process continues until the whole human race starts to think of itself as members of a single global village. We need to emphasize here that all these efforts to form economic units and larger associations are initiated and sustained due to human limitedness. The members are more concerned about their own needs and interests than the interests of their co-members. For instance, when families

---

[55]Aristotle, *The Politics*, 1256b 20.

43

form a village, each family seeks to satisfy its own needs and interests but not necessarily the interests of the other member families. Likewise, it is in their individual interests for nation-states to come together and form regional blocks. For example in Africa we have regional blocks such as the Economic Community of West African States (ECOWAS), the Economic Community of Eastern Africa (EAC), and the Southern African Development Community (SADC). All these communities were established because none of the member nation-states was able to meet all its interests without the assistance of the other member states.

Even social interactions are motivated by some degree of self-interest. We feel fulfilled by chatting with a friend, watching people perform on stage, doing sports together, and partying. This is because, as mentioned earlier, every human being is limited. Each one of us has a void which only *others* can fill. Thus, our so-called social instinct is catalysed more by self-interest than by altruism. We go out of our way to meet a friend not just for the friend's interests but more especially for our own interests.

Usually, community formation breeds group/collective selfishness. As Reinhold Niebuhr points out, communal existence results in parochial loyalties, for example, tribalism. Humanity is divided into 'we' and 'they'.[56] Group selfishness is when a community meets its interests at the expense of the interests of other communities. It can also mean meeting the community's interests at the expense of some of the members of that same community. This is common with communitarian societies where the individual member's interests do not matter as much as community interests do.

---

[56]Tatha, *Original Sin*, 139.

Chapter 3

Economics And Selfishness

If human beings were still living in the Garden of Eden, life would certainly be different from what it is today. Nobody would be worried about what to eat or what to wear. But something happened and so we had to leave the paradise. Since the expulsion from Eden, human beings have had to toil and labour for their welfare. The expulsion was a condemnation for us to evolve into economic animals. We cannot survive without meeting our basic needs and so since there is no Garden of Eden any more, we have to fend for those needs. Thus, Economics, which is the way people use available resources to meet their needs, is indispensable for the survival of the human race. Economics is closely linked with the human instinct for survival. In order for us to survive, we must use certain resources to meet our basic needs.

Different peoples have used different ways to meet their needs and those ways have been evolving with time. For example, some have moved from being fruit gatherers and hunters to the practice of rudimentary agriculture and eventually to modernized agriculture and industry. In other words, economics has transformed human beings into innovative and hardworking creatures and therefore, it has made life excitingly interesting. Life is certainly more interesting when people work to earn their bread compared to when everything is provided for them. There is nothing as boring as living a cost-free life. As they work for their needs, human beings actualize their potentials, make a lot of exciting discoveries, and commune with one another.[57]

However, economics has also made our life very complicated and challenging. Economics is the sphere where selfishness is actualized the most. In other words, human selfishness is more audacious in the sphere of economics than in any other sphere. This is because it is closely linked with the human instinct for survival. Every human being wants to survive and that survival is inseparably associated with the satisfaction of certain basic needs. In the process of trying to meet our needs in order to survive, we mostly think of one another as competitors rather than as companions. Resources

---

[57] E.F Schumacher. *Small is Beautiful: Economics as if People Mattered* (New York: Harper and Row Publishers, 1973), 54.

do not seem to be enough for everybody's needs and so we compete with one another for them. Each one is concerned with his needs in order to survive. Some even mistakenly think that in order for them to meet their needs, they must prevent others from meeting their interests. One person's gain is assumed to be equivalent to another's loss. Some people behave as if others had no right to life or had no interests or did not want to live a decent life. Such mistaken assumptions are nothing but symptoms of the selfishness that dominates the sphere of economics. Another symptom of our economic selfishness is the claim that human needs are endless. People keep multiplying their needs and using resources to meet those needs without considering how others are going to meet their basic needs. The so-called endlessness of human needs is a very serious problem in the sphere of economics.

Human Needs vs. Resources

In the sphere of economics, human egoism takes the extreme form of pure selfishness. Each individual thinks mainly about his own interests *only*. This is mainly because most people usually assume that resources are scarce and human needs are endless. There is a constant war between human needs and resources. Economics is usually defined as the science of how a given society of people uses *limited resources* to satisfy its people's *unlimited needs*.[58] This is one of our biggest cataclysms. Economics has become an impossible task, a paradox. How can something finite be matched with something infinite? It is similar to trying to fill a bottomless pot with water. Not even the waters of the Mediterranean Sea can fill such a pot.

The conflict between human needs and resources will never end until we critically examine the limitedness of resources and the endlessness of human needs. What do people actually mean when they say that resources are limited? Are human needs really unlimited? Is there no correlation between human selfishness and the claim that human needs are unlimited? Let us attempt to respond to these questions, although not in a systematic way.

---

[58] Hardwick, John Langmead and Bahdur Khan, *An Introduction to Modern Economics*, 3.

The Limitedness of Resources

In economics, a resource is said to be scarce when there is not enough of it to meet everybody's wants assuming it were available free of charge. Selfishness and the desire for luxuries make some resources scarce[59] and exacerbate the scarcity of others. If a resource is made available to people at zero price and they selfishly grab huge amounts of it until it can no longer suffice for their greed, then that resource becomes scarce. Scarce resources are also known as economic resources while abundant resources are called free resources, for example, oxygen is a free resource, at least in most places. Investing in scarce resources is very lucrative but if you invest in a free resource you cannot earn any profits.

In their economic activities, human beings usually think of one another as competitors. At first people might cooperate with one another thinking that the available resources will be enough for everyone's needs but with time, and especially as the population increases, they begin to compete for those resources. As the population increases, the demand for resources increases and this leads to the conviction that competition is the only weapon people can use for survival. In order to survive, each individual begins to grab resources as much as he can for the fear that other people might use all the resources for their own needs. Everyone eventually starts to believe that sooner than later resources will get finished. So, the competition becomes stiffer especially for resources whose supply is fixed, for instance land. Each individual tries as much as possible to get enough of what will presumably disappear very soon. Because of this false fear, individuals accumulate resources beyond what they actually need at the moment. The members accumulate resources not because they need them but mainly because they are afraid that other members will appropriate them. Larger and more technologically advanced societies dominate if not annihilate smaller ones.[60] This aggressiveness depletes resources and it eventually leads to the scarcity of resources that were initially abundant. Thus, it is our selfishness that is to a very large extent responsible for the scarcity of resources.

We need, however, to clarify that the scarcity of resources is in two categories: natural scarcity and artificial scarcity. Our selfishness is not absolutely responsible for natural scarcity but for artificial scarcity. Let us

---

[59] Hardwick, John Langmead and Bahdur Khan, *An Introduction to Modern Economics*, 4.

[60] Andersen and Howard F. Taylor, *Sociology: Understanding a Diverse Society*, 136.

begin by exploring what natural scarcity is and how it can be overcome before we proceed to the artificial scarcity category.

Natural Scarcity

We live on a planet that is endowed with a lot of natural resources such as lakes, rivers, seas, mountains, forests, minerals, animals, plants, etc. Most natural resources, however, are not unlimited. Some of them are non-renewable and some are available only in very small quantities. For example, water is naturally a very scarce commodity in arid places. Also, certain minerals are abundant in some places but they are scarce in others. The most unfortunate thing about natural resources is that some of them cannot be created by human beings. For instance, we cannot create minerals or mountains; at least we are not yet able to do so despite our advancement in science and technology.

Natural scarcity is worsened by the increase in population and human greed. Keeping other factors constant, increase in population exerts pressure on natural resources since the supply of natural resources is perfectly inelastic. We cannot create natural resources despite the arrogant and bullish belief of some economists who adore technology. More so, when greedy people accumulate already scarce resources, they reduce the availability of those resources to other people. Our selfishness, therefore, is not responsible for natural scarcity but for exacerbating it.

Different societies have discovered different mechanisms of dealing with natural scarcities. First, advancement in technology enables people to discover solutions to some of their scarcity problems, for example, from hydrocarbons we get fuel for our machines and vehicles. But, hydrocarbons are naturally scarce and they have even become scarcer. However, it has been discovered that jatrofer, a plant which can be cultivated, can be processed to produce fuel for similar purposes. Thus, with science and technology jatrofer becomes a substitute for hydrocarbons and therefore a way to deal with the scarcity in question. Another example here is that of irrigation schemes. Places that used to be semi arid have been transformed into agriculturally productive lands because of science and technology. Second, adaptation has been used as a mechanism to cope with the scarcity of certain natural resources in certain places. For instance, in places where water is naturally a scarce resource people use water very sparingly compared to places where water is naturally abundant. In arid places every drop of water counts and so it is guarded jealously. Human beings have a great capacity of adapting to situations as a survival mechanism. A person who was born and bred in a desert might spend three days without drinking water or a week without bathing. The body adjusts to the conditions of the place. Third, through exchange and trade, societies are able to get resources which were previously unavailable to them. What is scarce in one place is usually abundant in other places. Exchanging what is abundant for what is scarce enables societies to alleviate the challenge of natural scarcity. The resources that are required to satisfy human needs are naturally 'scattered' in the world so that societies can depend on one another. If any society tries to be selfish by refusing to trade with other societies, it will most likely not get what it lacks.

The above mechanisms cannot respond to the problem of natural scarcities unless people suspend their selfishness. Natural resources are enough if and only if we use them for our needs but not for our wants or greed. Our greed reduces resources for other people's needs and more especially for the needs of future generations. Even abundant resources can become scarce due to human selfishness. River Nile, for example, has not solved the water problem in some parts of the sub-Saharan region because of the 1929 Nile Water Agreement which was signed for selfish motives. The treaty was drawn when Egypt was a strategic British satellite. Egypt was given a lion's share of the Nile waters partly for safeguarding the interests of Britain. It "is guaranteed access to 55.5bn cubic metres of water, out of a total of 84bn cubic metres" and has "a right of veto over any work which might threaten the flow of the river."[61] The waters of the Nile can meet all the basic water needs of the entire Nile basin population if it were not for selfishness. Millions of people in Tanzania and Kenya are constantly in dire need of water because the treaty prevents the governments of Tanzania and Kenya from embarking on any water projects that might limit Lake Victoria's capacity of feeding the Nile River with waters. Likewise, some people in Uganda, Sudan, and Ethiopia have no access to water even though the world's longest river passes through their countries. Almost all the waters go to Egypt at the expense of the landlocked countries.

---

[61]Jeevan Vasagar, "Storms lie ahead over future of Nile," http://www.ntz.info/gen/n01799.html (accessed: 31st August 2011).

Artificial scarcity

There is another form of scarcity that is not natural. This is called the artificial or human-made type of scarcity. It results from human selfishness and greed. Artificial scarcity is caused by the amassing of resources by certain individuals – by the unnecessary excessive demand for commodities or resources. When selfish individuals accumulate resources, irrespective of whether those resources are abundant or naturally scarce, other people eventually get nothing. Some people are able to meet their luxurious wants while others cannot even meet their basic needs. Resources cannot be enough for everybody's needs as long as selfishness is allowed to prevail. In other words, selfishness is the surest way of creating resource scarcity in any society. It is indeed the root and sole cause of artificial scarcities.

If humans were not selfish, resources would only be limited at the natural level but not at the artificial level. Unfortunately, however, some of us have taken selfishness for a virtue and so artificial scarcities are simply an everyday occurrence. For instance, some producers and sellers create artificial scarcities by hoarding commodities in order to get abnormal profits. When a supplier of a commodity restricts the quantity supplied, he creates disequilibrium in the market. Demand exceeds supply and so the price shoots up. This is because the lower the quantity supplied, the higher the commodity price – *ceteris paribus*. By hoarding commodities, suppliers profit a lot. It pays to be selfish – to create artificial scarcities. Since scarcities are more lucrative than abundances, selfish producers will do everything possible to create scarcities however much buyers or governments might complain. People who own foreign exchange bureaux sometimes do the same thing in order to make quick and abnormal profits. They hoard foreign currencies so that the demand can be higher than the quantity supplied of those currencies. Speculators make things even worse. They create fear among the customers by pointing out that the scarcity of the hoarded currencies will only get worse. Customers who urgently need foreign currencies, especially those who are involved in international trade, are forced to rush to the bureaus to buy the few notes that are still available. The bureaus keep increasing the foreign exchange rates because of the increase in demand for the 'scarce' currencies. Huge profits are made just because the bureaus are able to create an artificial scarcity in the foreign currency market. Whenever fuel is hoarded the situation is even worse because once the price of fuel goes up all commodity prices shoot up – inflation worsens.

Another common way of creating artificial scarcities is the smuggling of goods from one country to another. For instance, it is not unusual for traders to smuggle cocoa from Ghana to Ivory Coast or Ugandan traders to smuggle food items from Uganda to Southern Sudan. Of course it is not bad to share food or any other commodity with neighbouring countries, especially during times of need. However, when traders smuggle commodities they do so not because they want to assist those who are in need but because the price of the commodities is higher in the neighbouring country than in the home country. They make a lot of profits but eventually their own country ends up experiencing shortage of the commodities that have been smuggled. Sometimes the commodities are not even smuggled; they are officially exported by greedy traders or government officials. For instance, Uganda exports hydro-electric power to Kenya and yet many Ugandans do not have electricity in their towns and homes. The profit motive is stronger than the moral obligation government has for its citizens. Nigerians who own oil refinery companies outside their country profit a lot by having the crude oil refined outside Nigeria and imported back as a finished product. Also, those who trade in generators ensure that there is no constant supply of electricity in the country to create market for their generators.

The Illusive Endlessness of Human Needs

Human needs are not endless except for our greed. We keep multiplying our so-called needs simply because we do not care about how other people will meet their needs. Needs become endless when people deliberately refuse to get satisfied with what is necessary for their existence. This hunger deprives other people from meeting their own needs. Therefore, saying that our needs are endless is another way of saying that we are selfish. Our needs fall under the following categories.

a. Basic needs

Basic needs are things without which life is either impossible or extremely difficult. They are things which we have to have - things which are absolutely necessary for our existence. It is in the interest of every human being that his basic needs be met. We can hardly do without things such as food, shelter, clothing, and basic education. These are primary or basic needs for every human being although what constitutes food, shelter, clothing, or basic education might vary from place to place or time to time. However, the

51

most crucial human need that is usually taken for granted and therefore never mentioned as a need is oxygen. No human being can survive where there is no oxygen. When a baby is born, it must be 'supplied' with oxygen even before it can be given 'food' or covered with clothes. Thus, oxygen is the most basic human need; it is hierarchically followed by food, shelter, clothing, and then basic education.

b. Contingent needs

Unlike basic human needs, certain needs can be categorized as contingent human needs. Contingent needs are things that are conditionally necessary. Their necessity is circumstantial and so they cannot be universalized to everybody or to every place or time. Certain things are needed by people who live in certain places. A person who lives in a very hot place might need a fan in his room while he who lives in a very cold place would instead need a heater. Likewise, there are things whose necessity changes from time to time, for example, people can hardly survive through the winter period without warm clothes. Warm clothes are needed during winter but surely not during summer time. Also, some things become needs for people who are experiencing physical difficulties, for instance, a person whose respiratory system is dysfunctional needs a life support machine in order for him to survive. In actual fact, medical care can generally be categorized under contingent needs although most scholars place it under basic human needs. Medical care is needed especially by those who are sick. Those who are healthy do not need a doctor.

c. Occupational requirements

People might require certain things in order to be efficient and effective in their work. Such things are often referred to as needs but they are actually not needs, they are what we might refer to as *occupational requirements*. Strictly speaking, occupational requirements are not needs because they are not absolutely necessary for anybody's existence and moreover they cannot be universalized. For example, a secretary requires a typewriter or a computer in order to do her work more effectively and efficiently but her life does not depend on that typewriter or computer. Lacking a typewriter or a computer will make the secretary's job difficult or even impossible but the secretary cannot die simply because there is no such machine in her office. Moreover, the typewriter or computer will certainly cease to be a requirement if the secretary changes her job or when a new device for secretarial work is invented.

Wants

There are situations where we find ourselves possessing or desiring to possess certain things which we do not actually need. Such things are not needs - they are wants. Wants are not absolutely necessary for our existence. For example, although we like them, we do not need toys or entertainment – we want them. Most needs can become wants when we demand them in excessive quantities or when we are influenced by changing lifestyles and fashions. For example, if one kilogram of food is enough for a couple to have dinner but the couple buys two kilograms for dinner, the second kilogram is not needed - it is wanted. Likewise, I *need* a simple mobile phone to be able to communicate but I *want* a sophisticated mobile phone which, in addition to the communication function that I need, has functions for playing music and taking photos. We want certain things in order to boost our status in society, to appear fashionable.

In economics, wants or luxuries are referred to as Veblen goods or goods of ostentation. They form an exception to the law of demand. According to the law of demand, ceteris paribus, there is an inverse relationship between the price of a commodity and the quantity demanded in the market of that commodity. Thus, keeping all factors constant, the higher the price of a commodity, the lower the quantity demanded of that commodity and vice versa. Luxurious commodities do not obey this law; other factors remaining constant, the demand for luxuries increases with increase in price and vice versa. Named after 19th century American economist Thorstein Veblen, Veblen goods are demanded for the purpose of emphasizing social status. People buy the latest and most expensive phone or vehicle brand not because they need it but because they want to prove to society that they are not ordinary men/women – they are people of 'class'. Additionally, luxuries have a positive Income Elasticity of Demand; increase in income causes an increase in the quantity demanded of luxuries. If my income increases, I will buy more luxurious commodities so that my name might appear in the Guinness book of records for rich people. However, needy people too can and do possess luxuries. A poor person who is not true to his condition is likely to buy luxuries but at the expense of his needs, for example, he might starve himself or refuse to pay school fees for his children in order to buy a phone which he does not actually need.

Another cause for the acquisition of more wants is advertisement. The advertising and sales promotion media create new wants leading to what economists refer to as contrived demand.[62] Consumers demand certain things not because they need them but because they allow themselves to be misled by business adverts. This is true not only of uneducated people but also of some of the most highly educated people. Because of the influence of adverts, many people make a lot of irrational decisions in the market. Some even buy luxuries before their basic needs are met. A poor woman might spend all her little money making her hair and therefore starve her children. The story is a bit different for rich people. The question of basic needs rarely arises for them but some end up buying a lot of unnecessary toys. Some of the things which they buy are not needed and they sometimes even forget that they have bought them because they do not use them and so they end up buying the same thing more than once.

Mahatma Gandhi rightly insists that "the world has enough resources for our needs but not for our greed"[63] - not for our selfish desire for or possession of luxuries. This is true mainly because human needs are not endless. According to the law of diminishing marginal utility, "the more an individual consumes of a good, the less utility he is likely to derive from the consumption of an additional unit of it."[64] This is true only for the satisfaction of needs but not for luxuries; the desire for luxuries increases continuously. While the satisfaction of human needs is not unlimited,[65] that of luxuries is unlimited. With needs, a point reaches when more units cannot be consumed but you can never get satisfied by the consumption of luxuries. In the process of trying to meet their personal needs, human beings are usually mindful of other people's needs or at least they do not hinder others from meeting their needs. There is nothing wrong with meeting human needs; what is problematic is meeting wants. It is in our interest to meet our needs but meeting wants makes us selfish.

In the attempt to meet their wants, individuals are likely to hinder others from meeting their needs. Some people get involved in corruption not

---

[62] Hardwick, John Langmead, and Bahadur Khan, *An Introduction to Modern Economics*, 134.

[63] Schumacher, *Small is Beautiful*, 33.

[64] Hardwick, John Langmead, and Bahadur Khan, *An Introduction to Modern Economics*, 75.

[65] Aristotle, *The Politics*, 1256b 30.

because they are struggling to meet their needs but mainly because, among other reasons, they want to buy luxurious commodities. Corruption enables some people to acquire luxuries at the expense of more people becoming poorer. Competition is stiffer in the process of meeting wants than in that of meeting human needs since wants are endless while human needs are not. And, economics (household management) remains a nightmare as long as the aim is to accumulate wealth or to meet wants but not needs[66] - to aim at something that is endless is as if to chase the wind. The resources we have in this finite universe cannot suffice to satisfy endless human wants. Moreover, the endlessness of human wants worsens the resource scarcity problem. Unfortunately, most of the things which we possess are wants not needs; we live in a world where some people luxuriously possess a lot of wants while others desperately yearn to meet their basic needs. Most of our economic entities prevail by dealing not in basic human needs but in wants. Industries that produce luxuries fetch more profits than those that produce for the satisfaction of basic needs simply because the basic needs market is limited while that of luxuries is enlarged by human selfishness.

Selfishness is when we possess something which we do not need – when we possess wants. This in one way or another prevents other people from meeting their needs. What I possess cannot be possessed by another person, at least not at the same time. If I do not need it, I reduce the likelihood of the one who actually needs it to get it. I should own only what I basically need, what I contingently need and what I occupationally require. This is what controlling human selfishness means. When I control my selfishness by keeping my needs in the rightful limits, I spare resources for other people to meet their own needs and the intensity of natural scarcity reduces or it can even vanish. More so, I am able to spare some resources for future generations. Certainly, the question of artificial scarcities does not arise if everyone is willing and able to control their selfishness.

Unlocking Private Property

People possess property in order to enjoy life. But, it is immoral to waste property by taking more than what one needs. In his *Two Treatises of Government*, John Locke (1632-1704) deals with the question of private property. His main project is to justify the appropriation of common

---

[66] Aristotle, *The Politics*, 1257b 35-40.

property for private use and how much an individual can rightly possess. For Locke, both natural reason and revelation tell us that once born, human beings have a right to their preservation and hence, as means to that end, the right to meat, drink, and such other things as nature affords for their subsistence.[67] Human beings have the responsibility of using their rational capacities and labour to make use of what has been given to them in common (i.e. resources/nature) to the best advantage of life and convenience. By reason of the labour of his body, the individual rightly possesses whatever he removes from the state of nature which initially belonged to all. However, he should not appropriate more than he needs and he should leave enough and as good in common for others.[68] He has the right to as much land as he tills, plants, improves, cultivates, and uses the product of. But, whatever is beyond what he needs is more than his share, and it belongs to others. Indeed, according to Aristotle, it is immoral to consume anything beyond the quantity that suits nature.[69]

Locke's justification for private property is appropriate for primitive economic systems but it is quite problematic for modern economic systems like ours. For primitive societies, resources are abundant and technology is poor. The individual is free to appropriate as much as he can make use of since there is still enough and as good left for others.[70] It is almost impossible for someone to be selfish because there is no way an individual can appropriate or store all the common property. Selfishness would be the situation whereby an individual appropriates more than what he needs so that things end up getting spoiled under his roof and/or when he does not leave for others what is enough and what is as good for their needs. Locke emphasizes that the most serious offence against the common law of nature is the rotting of things under someone's possession.[71]

However, Locke's justification for private property is inadequate for modern economic systems. This is because resources are scarce in modern societies and technology is advanced. Most modern societies are highly populated and so if individuals are free to appropriate as much resources as

---

[67] John Locke, *Two Treatises of Government*, ed. Thomas I. Cook (New York: Hafner Press, 1947), 133.

[68] Lock, *Two Treatises of Government*, 134.

[69] Aristotle, *Nicomachean Ethics*, 1118b 15.

[70] Locke, *Two Treatises of Government*, 137 and 146.

[71] Locke, *Two Treatises of Government*, 140.

they can improve, it is almost impossible that enough and as good will be left for others. Moreover, with advanced technology, the stipulation that an individual should not appropriate beyond the rotting limit does not suffice because it is possible for individuals to use capital machinery for appropriating huge quantities of the common property and to store their produce in form of money or with the help of preservatives. Selfishness will prevail even though nothing is getting spoilt. Modern societies therefore require a more complex justification for private property. Unfortunately, most people still justify their private property by the mere fact that they worked for it and that they are preserving it well so that nothing is getting spoilt. Private property owners hardly ask themselves whether or not they need that property, whether or not they got it through the right way, and whether or not by possessing it they prevent others from meeting their needs. Those who have the power and/or technological means privatise common property in amounts that they wish without thinking about other stakeholders. The grabbing continues until there is nothing left for others or until there is nothing as good left for others. Society becomes a jungle in which the fittest survive while the weak simply perish. There is indeed a need for a paradigm shift in the way common property is shared in modern economic systems. There is a lot of private property which can justifiably be unlocked from private ownership to common use.

Chapter 4

Economic Systems As Institutionalized Selfishness

By economic systems is meant the structure of ownership and control of important resources in a given economy. The owner of important resources determines what is to be produced in the economy, how it is to be produced and for whom it is to be produced. Because they have all these powers, the owners of the important resources in the economy tend to be domineering and selfish. Economic systems therefore are ways in which selfishness is institutionalized in societies. To know the economic system of any given society is to know how selfishness is institutionalized in that society. In other words, the selfishness within a given society is revealed by the way important resources are owned, controlled and used within that society. Every society has an economic system at any given time. However, as societies evolve, they change from one economic system to another and because of this evolution economic systems can also be called *economic regimes*. Most economic regimes are characterised by selfishness or even solipsism.

Primitive Economic Systems

Subsistence Economics

Subsistence economics is the economic system that pertains to a world which is still very primitive. The primitive world is mainly characterised by rudimentary technology and a very low population density. There are no organized leadership structures, markets or industries. People live either as individuals or as nuclear families and there is hardly any interaction among them because of the poor means of communication. People depend on natural resources for their livelihood, for example, forests, bushes, rivers, lakes, and swamps. These resources belong to no one; they are still in their natural state and so nobody possesses them except may be God. Primitive activities such as hunting, fishing and fruit gathering are the main economic activities and they are carried out using simple tools such as stones, arrows, spears, hooks, and sticks. Subsistence economies are what sociologists usually refer to as foraging societies, for example, the pygmies of Central Africa.[72]

---

[72] Andersen and Howard F. Taylor, *Sociology: Understanding a Diverse Society,* 137.

59

Certainly, all human societies have been primitive at one time or another and they have therefore practiced subsistence economics. In his *Politics*, Aristotle describes how the ancient Greeks used to depend on activities such as hunting, fishing and fruit gathering for their survival. In any subsistence economy, economic activities are carried out for the sole purpose of household consumption. Actually, the word economics is derived from a Greek word *oikonomia* which means 'household management'. The *telos* of *Oikonomia* is to provide household members with basic needs.[73] Nothing is taken to the market since there are no markets and other infrastructures in very primitive societies. Every household is able to meet the basic needs of its members without buying anything from anybody. The aim is to satisfy needs but not wants.

Because of the poor means of transport and communication, no family is aware of other families' existence. Each family utilizes only the resources that surround it. However, the family does not and indeed it cannot amass more resources than it needs for its basic necessities. This can be attributed to several factors. First of all, the technology used is very rudimentary; with a spear the hunter can only kill one animal at a time and with a hook the fisherman can only catch one fish at a time. At this rate, it is very difficult to kill more than five animals or to catch more than five fish in a single day. Second, reliable storage facilities and preservation mechanisms are not available. Even if it were possible for a family to catch a lot of fish or to kill many animals or to gather a lot of fruits, it would find it impossible to preserve the surplus. Nobody in such a world is able to imagine that fruits, fish or meat can be stored for longer periods. Moreover, there are no markets to which the surplus can be taken in order for it to be sold. Families are therefore forced to operate at the subsistence level of economics. They gather as much fruits or kill as many animals as they need for survival. The desire to accumulate resources is frustrated by poor technology and the lack of a vent for the surplus.

There is hardly any selfishness in the primitive world. Although families exist in isolation, none of them is able to amass more resources than it needs. Each family acquires resources to meet its basic needs only. It cannot intend to prevent other families from meeting their interests since it does not even know that those other families do exist. In its economic activities the family is motivated by self-interest but not selfishness. The interests of a given

---

[73] Aristotle, *The Politics*, 1256a 1.

family are met without any awareness that other families too exist. There is no competition for resources since the population is still very low and it is sparsely distributed. Moreover, resources are still abundant and they can only be used for basic needs but not for any luxuries. Meeting basic needs in a primitive world does not require a lot of hard work; working for two days in a week might suffice for the maintenance of a small household whose lifestyle is after all simple.

Communitarian Economics

As the primitive world evolves, there is a shift from subsistence to communitarian economics. With time the population increases and more so people begin to settle closer to where the means of livelihood are. Generally, society is organized around an economic base.[74] Every family wants to settle near the forest or lake on which life depends. This brings families into contact with other families that were previously unknown to them. By settling within the same locality, families form a community, a village. For some time each family continues to fend for itself as it used to do at the substance level but eventually there is the realisation that certain activities require concerted efforts. The families begin to recognize that some of their household needs can only be met by cooperating with other families. Hence, the geographical village becomes also an economic community.

Note that it is not selfless love that leads to the formation of community bonds but the challenges which are involved in meeting certain economic needs by individuals or households. Communities are formed mainly for economic reasons. Families form a village by moving closer to where the resources are located and the village is transformed into an economic community so that through joint efforts each of the families can meet its own basic needs. In other words, community comes together for individuals or families to do what one person or a single family cannot do alone.[75]

Social bonds boost human survival. "In solo combat, our ancestors were not the toughest predators. But as hunters they learned that six hands were better than two. Those who foraged in groups also gained protection from predators and enemies."[76] The community is a form of strength, social capital, which enables families to get what they can hardly produce by

---

[74] Andersen and Howard F. Taylor, *Sociology: Understanding a Diverse Society,* 454.

[75] Walzer, *Spheres of Justice*, 80.

[76] Myers, *Psychology*, 367.

themselves. "The first thing members owe one another is the communal provision of security and welfare."[77] As they work together, each family aims at meeting its own interests and needs but without necessarily intending to prevent other families from meeting their interests and needs. Additionally, at the communitarian regime families begin to exchange goods for other goods.[78] For instance, if a family has fish, it can exchange it for meat with another family that has meat and needs fish in exchange. This is known as barter trade and it creates bonds among families. However, since the community is still primitive, all economic activities, including barter trade, are carried out for subsistence purposes.

One main feature of communitarian societies is that vital resources on which families depend for their livelihood are communally owned and they are accessible to all the members of the community. Nobody can claim private ownership of a forest or lake or swamp and it is morally wrong for anyone to use such resources selfishly. Since almost all economic activities are carried out communally, the spoils are equitably shared. It is morally wrong for a family to take more than it needs while other families do not have what is enough for their upkeep. Moreover even if a family wanted to accumulate certain goods, it would find it hard to store the surplus because of poor facilities and very poor trade opportunities. This is one of the reasons why there is very little or no selfishness at all in communitarian societies. Additionally, since the member families benefit from living and working together, they try as much as possible to maintain good relations. Each family is able to meet its needs and interests without hindering other families from meeting their own needs and interests. This is possible because resources are still abundant, the population is still small, and the lifestyle is not yet sophisticated or luxurious. However, as soon as the use of money is invented, selfish interests begin to crop in; the use of money facilitates the accumulation of wealth and the erroneous assumption that there is no limit to riches.[79]

---

[77] Walzer, *Spheres of Justice*, 64.

[78] Aristotle, *The Politics*, 1257a 25-30.

[79] Aristotle, *The Politics*, 1257b 10.

Feudalism

As the population continues to increase, certain changes take place in the community. Some charismatic figures emerge to assume leadership roles and so the community is transformed into a hierarchically organized nation-state. The king assumes political, economic, religious, cultural and social roles. Also, more economic activities are invented, mostly agriculture. With the invention of agriculture, land becomes a very precious resource and given the fact that the population is on the increase, families begin to compete for land and for other resources that were previously owned communally. In order to tame that competition, the king decides to possess the land and other vital resources. The resources are placed under the control of the king even though they are still the common property of the whole society, at least in principle. The king becomes the lord of the land - a landlord. He distributes the land to his subjects who then become his vassals. This is the major characteristic of the feudal system of economics. In order to meet their needs and interests, the subjects cum vassals use the land and other communal resources but on condition that they are willing and able to pay rent/taxes to the king/landlord, for example, by giving a portion of their harvest to the king.

One of the functions of the landlord is to protect the vassals against catastrophes. For instance, when he collects taxes in terms of food items, he stores that food and distributes it back to the people when the need arises. During droughts the people turn to their landlord for relief. If there are no hazards, the food is consumed at community celebrations. However, soon or later, the landlord becomes economically rich and therefore politically powerful. The landlord begins to misappropriate some of the community resources. Instead of returning the food to the contributors, he consumes it and gives some of it to his close friends and relatives. His friends and relatives are given plenty of fertile land while other people are given smaller and infertile plots.

Feudalism is the first stage of institutionalising selfishness. The political structures are associated with a lot of economic powers and they are initially designed by charismatic people who are virtually selfish. Although the landlord might to some extent be concerned with the welfare of the vassals, he is basically motivated by his own interests. The absurd thing is that by pursuing his interest, the landlord somehow controls his vassals as they try to pursue their interests. The landlord feeds on the sweat of his vassals and this leads to some conflict between him and his vassals.

Mercantilism

Due to the conflict between the landlord and the vassals and also because of the increase in population, some of the vassals decide to seek settlement elsewhere by migrating to places that have not yet been claimed or occupied by anybody. This gradually leads to the establishment of numerous nation-states because as people migrate to different places, they form their own nation-states there and one of them becomes a king. With the establishment of numerous nation-states, the competition for resources becomes an inter-state affair. Kings mobilize their states to compete with rival states for resources. The belief is that the world's wealth is static and limited. So, the more wealth a nation-state accumulates, the less there will remain for the other nation-states. This is what Ayn Rand refers to as moral cannibalism, the delusion that one man's happiness necessitates the injury of another.[80] Economists refer to it as 'the zero-sum-theory' and it is the major feature of the mercantile economic system. According to this theory, a nation-state can only gain as much as what is lost by the other nation-states.[81] In other words, each nation-state believes that it is impossible for it to achieve economic progress without harming other nation-states. For instance, pastoralist states that have reached the mercantilist stage begin to raid animals from other pastoralist states. The Karimajong of north eastern Uganda, for example, raid cattle from neighbouring tribes because they believe that they cannot meet their interest of getting more animals without raiding from the other tribes. Actually, the Karimajong believe that all long-horned cattle belong to their tribe; the rest of the tribes that own long-horned cattle stole from them and so raiding is seen as taking back what belongs to them.

The Mercantile system or the economic theory of absolutism is sustained by what we might refer to as state selfishness and this selfishness is stimulated by the zero-sum theory. The mercantilist zero-sum-theory is very much in operation when one state colonizes another. It is as though the world has reached its Pareto efficiency point, i.e., a point at which it is not possible to increase the satisfaction/utility of one or more individuals without reducing the satisfaction of at least one other individual.[82] This false assumption compels the colonizing state to loot resources from the

---

[80] Rand and Nathaniel Branden, *The Virtue of Selfishness,* 34.

[81] Karl-Hienz Peschke, ed. *Ordo Socialis: Social Economy in the Light of Christian Faith* (Cologne: Paulinus-Verlag, 1991), 18.

[82] Hardwick, John Langmead, and Bahadur Khan, *An Introduction to Modern Economics,* 9.

colonized state. The colonizing state believes that it cannot gain anything unless the colonized state loses it. What is gained by the colonizer is equivalent to what is lost by the colonized. The colonizer eventually becomes richer and more powerful while the colonized becomes poorer and less powerful.

However, Mercantilist states eventually become unpopular because they not only exploit other states but they also oppress their own citizens by centralizing economic activities and especially by restricting the citizens from trading with citizens of other states. The citizens can only trade domestically because the state fears to lose its wealth to other states if its citizens are allowed to engage in trade with citizens of other states. Thus, only domestic trade is allowed but not inter-state (international) trade. Resources are acquired from other states through dubious ways, for example through raiding and colonialism, as opposed to fair means such as trade. More so, what matters for the Mercantilist state is not meeting the basic needs of the citizens but the accumulation of wealth which consists of precious metals such as gold, silver, and diamond. These precious metals are used as money for domestic trade. The state becomes rich and powerful but the people's standards of living either remain constant or they diminish. Of course, the king and his cohort do not experience any economic hardships. The wealth of the nation is always at their disposal and so their needs and interests are always met. The whole economic system soon collapses as the citizens decide to revolt against the king's selfishness.

Modern Economic Systems

No human society remains static. From their primitive state, societies change into modern societies. A modern society is mainly characterized by advancement in science and technology. This advancement is brought about by some individuals in the society who take the initiative to utilize their rational capacities in order to invent better and usually easier ways of doing things. In other words, freedom from the shackles of feudal restraints and social phenomenon becomes a voluntary transaction of daring individuals.[83] Those individuals gradually lead to the emancipation of all the citizens from

---

[83] Daniel M. Hausman, "Liberalism, welfare Economics, and Politics ," in *Liberalism and the Economic Order*, eds. Ellen Frankel Paul, Fred D. Miller, Jr., and Jeffrey Paul (Cambridge university press: Cambridge, 1993), 176.

the hegemony of the state. The state must loosen its grip so that individuals can make discoveries that will enable the society to advance. For example, in the seventeenth and eighteenth centuries, first Anglo-Saxon and then other European countries abhorred the notion of communal life.[84] The general conviction was that human beings needed to be liberated from the control of kinship, institutions, and the state. Modern thinkers such as Francis Bacon, René Descartes, John Locke, David Hume, Jean Jacque Rousseau and Immanuel Kant argued strongly that people needed freedom to use their rational capacities in order to discover what human nature is and how the universe operates.

Certainly, just as new wine requires new wineskins, a modern state necessitates an economic system which is appropriate to the society's clamour for liberalism. The economic systems that operate in modern societies include liberal capitalism, socialism, mixed economics, and geocentric economics. Liberal capitalism is embraced at the beginning of the modern era but eventually some societies embrace socialism and then shift to mixed economics. Some societies, however, move directly from capitalism to mixed economics. In any case, geocentric economics is the final regime in the cycle of a society's economic evolution.

Liberal Capitalism

When the citizens emancipate themselves from the control of the state, they embrace liberal capitalism as their new economic system. This is a system in which the state does not interfere with people as they pursue their interests except in very extraordinary circumstances.[85] The government's role in economics is limited to functions such as providing security for private property and enforcing laws for debt settlement[86] otherwise economic activities are freely carried out by individuals. Important resources, that is to say, the means of production which include not only land but also labour,

---

[84] MacIntyre, *After Virtue*, 229.

[85] Note that we are emphasizing the fact that the government can and does interfere with economic activities in some circumstances. This is what distinguishes liberal capitalism from pure capitalism. In a purely capitalistic economy, the government does not interfere with economic activities at all. This kind of economic regime has never and might never exist anywhere in the world.

[86] Smith, *An Inquiry into the Nature and Causes of The Wealth of Nations*, 273.

capital, machinery and technology, are owned by private individuals but not by the state. Both domestic trade and international trade are liberalized and paper money and banking services are invented to facilitate the transactions. Money is used as a medium of exchange, measure of value, and store of value. Commodity prices are not fixed by the government. They are determined by the market forces of demand and supply, by the voluntary interaction between buyers and sellers.

Adam Smith's "*An Inquiry into the Nature and Causes of the Wealth of Nations*" (1776) offers a classical description of what liberal capitalism is and how it operates. Liberal capitalism comes into being as a reaction against oppressive economic regimes that perpetuate state selfishness by for example, making laws which further their interests at the detriment of the society.[87] Additionally, liberal capitalism is a falsification of the claims and theories made as shields to protect oppressive economic regimes. Examples include: A) in a liberal capitalistic economy, wealth is defined in more wide-ranging terms; the wealth of the nation is composed not only of precious metals but also of labour. Labour is recognized as an important element of a nation's wealth. B) The Zero-sum-theory is falsified by the fact that savings can be used to create more wealth. Liberal capitalism results from the realization that if a nation saves its money and invests it productively, it creates more wealth without having to exploit other nations. In other words, one nation's gain is not necessarily equal to another nation's loss. There is a possibility of an ever increasing wealth due to savings and investment.[88] The money invested for the creation of more wealth is referred to as capital and hence the concept 'capitalism'. Therefore, individuals or business enterprises that own capital possess an important means of production. Additionally, advancement in science and technology enables a nation-state to acquire wealth without necessarily impoverishing other nation-states. Technological machines are part of an economy's capital. C) It is not true that in order for the nation-state to achieve economic progress, the government has to own the means of production and to regulate economic activities. In a liberal capitalistic economy, economic progress is propelled by the freedom with which individuals pursue their interests without unnecessary government

---

[87] Heinz Lubasz, "Adam Smith and the Free Market," in *Adam Smith's Wealth of Nations: New Interdisciplinary Essays*, eds. Stephen Copley and Kathryn Sutherland (Manchester: Manchester University Press, 1995), 53.

[88] Peschke, ed. *Ordo Socialis: Social Economy in the Light of Christian Faith*, 19.

interference. When people have the liberty to pursue their interests, they become more innovative, creative and therefore more productive. Moreover, as opposed to centralized economic systems, the beneficiaries of pure capitalism are the citizens. The purpose of economic activities is not to meet the interests of the state but to meet the interests of the citizens.[89]

Liberal capitalism is buttressed on the belief that nature is benevolent. It harmonizes economic activities.[90] The famous Smithian notion of *laissez-faire* has its roots in this belief. It alludes to the claim that the pursuit of individual interests with a government 'hands off' approach benefits the whole society. As individuals pursue their interests, other people eventually benefit from those pursuits. Smith argues that nature has an "invisible hand" which distributes the fruits of individual people's economic activities to the whole society. In all their economic activities, individuals intend to meet only their interests and to maximize their gains but they are inadvertently led by the invisible hand to promote an end which they did not initially intend, namely, meeting the interests of other people.[91] The society does not benefit from the benevolence of the butcher, the brewer or the baker but from the pursuit of their own interests and advantages.[92] Any business man is initially moved by his own interests but he ends up providing services to the rest of the society, albeit inadvertently. He neither intends to promote the public interest nor does he know how much he promotes it. For example, an industrialist benefits society by employing workers or by constructing a road that can be used by other people. His initial intention is to increase production, transport his business' raw materials and goods and services, and to make more profits. But, the rest of society does benefit from his self-love. In some cases, the individual does not have control over who should benefit from his economic activity – altruism is unavoidable in such cases. This is very true in the case of positive externalities. For instance, a florist becomes of great help to a beekeeper without intending to be generous. He can hardly prevent the beekeeper from benefiting from his flower garden. Thus, the individual's self-interest is not only economically justified but it is also morally justified.

The invisible hand of nature plays the government's role of redistributing the fruits of individual people's economic activities to the entire society.

---

[89] Peschke, ed. *Ordo Socialis: Social Economy in the Light of Christian Faith*, 18.

[90] MacIntyre, *After Virtue*, 228-34.

[91] Smith, *An Inquiry into the Nature and Causes of The Wealth of Nations*, 166.

[92] Smith, *An Inquiry into the Nature and Causes of The Wealth of Nations*, 15.

People do not need to be morally conscious in their economic activities; all that is required of them is the pursuit of their own interests since the invisible hand of nature automatically translates their self-centredness into benevolence – something that was not part of their initial intention.[93] Because of the invisible hand of nature, the benefits of economic growth automatically 'trickle down' to the entire society. Thus, there is no need for the government to interfere with people's economic activities.

In a liberal capitalistic economy individuals become more productive because of the freedom with which they pursue their interests. Since there is no government interference, people do what they are good at and what enables them to meet their interests. There is nobody to force individuals to do what they are not interested in. When people do what they are interested in, they tend to be more creative, effective, efficient, and productive. They are stakeholders and so they care about what they are doing.

With a freely operating price mechanism, both commodity prices and output levels are not fixed by the government but instead they are determined by the market forces of demand and supply. This is why liberal capitalistic economies are sometimes referred to as free market economies. Private firms supply the market with goods and services to maximise their own profits while consumers demand those goods and services to maximise their satisfaction (utility).[94] Everybody aims at maximizing his own interests. Profit-maximizing firms try as much as they can to minimize their costs of production, to make use of the most efficient methods of production, and to channel resources away from unprofitable economic activities to more profitable ones. Consumers on the other hand maximize their utilities by dictating on what should be supplied by the producers.

The power of consumers to determine what should be produced is called *consumer sovereignty*. "Consumers make their preferences known to producers through money 'votes'. In fact, there is a sort of general election every day where consumers cast their money 'votes' for the millions of different commodities on the market."[95] When the consumers' demand for a particular commodity increases, its price goes up and so producers respond by

[93] Smith, *An Inquiry into the Nature and Causes of The Wealth of Nations*, 166.

[94] Hardwick, John Langmead, and Bahadur Khan, *An Introduction to Modern Economics*, 129-130.

[95] Hardwick, John Langmead, and Bahadur Khan, *An Introduction to Modern Economics,* 130.

increasing its supply. The price of a commodity is determined by the interaction between its supply curve and its demand curve.

Since no economy can be completely self-reliant, international trade is inevitable; it is justified by the uneven distribution of natural resources. Unlike in centralized economies, trade is liberalized in liberal capitalistic economies – *laissez-passer*. Private individuals and business organizations carry out their international transactions without any unnecessary restrictions from the government. The government intervenes only when it is necessary to do so, for example, for the safety and wellbeing of the citizens, the government might put check points at the borders and in airports to stop individuals from dealing in drugs, firearms, and counterfeit products. This liberalization makes trade very profitable because of the fast movement of commodities and factors of production. Import and export taxes are reduced or even abolished completely. Therefore, private traders make a lot of profits and the citizens benefit from imported goods and services that would not have been available in their country had it not been for liberalized international trade.

In order for individuals to sufficiently benefit from foreign trade, they specialize in economic activities that they can do best.[96] This of course, depends on their skills and resources. David Ricardo emphasizes that in order to maximize profits, "it is better for people to specialise in those activities in which their advantage over other people is greatest or in which their disadvantages compared to others are the smallest."[97] Prudence dictates that it is better to buy what would cost a man more to make than to buy. This is the famous law of comparative advantage and it enables individuals to meet their interests more easily. The citizens of liberal capitalistic countries involve themselves in activities in which they have the greatest comparative advantage. This is possible partly because of the freedom they enjoy in their economic choices and activities since there is no unnecessary government interference. They specialize in activities in which they have greater advantage than citizens of other countries to meet individual interests.

We need to add that in a liberal capitalistic economy international trade is also guided by the invisible hand of nature. The invisible hand plays the government's role of distributing trade benefits to the entire society. Thus, when individuals engage in domestic or foreign trade, they are motivated by

---

[96] *An Inquiry into the Nature and Causes of The Wealth of Nations*, 116.

[97] Roy J. Ruffin and Paul R. Gregory, *Principles of Economics* (Glenview, Illinois: Scott, Foresman and Company, 1983), 46-47; Aristotle, *The Politics*, 1263b 1 -5.

their own interests but the invisible hand of nature ensures that in the process other people too benefit from those efforts. For instance, if an individual imports computers to set up an internet cafe in his home town, other people will benefit from his efforts in one way or another. His intention is to make profits from his business but he will have to employ some people to run the internet cafe for him since he cannot do everything alone. Moreover, people will benefit from having internet services in their neighbourhood. Of course, they will pay for the services but they will no longer travel to far away towns in search of those services. Thus, by intending only his interests, the trader ends up meeting the interests of other people whether he likes it or not.

Advantages of Liberal Capitalism

i.   Liberal capitalism creates a free environment in which people are at liberty to pursue their interests. When people are free to pursue their personal interests, they become innovative, hardworking, efficient and therefore more productive in their economic activities[98] as compared to when they are compelled to work for other people's interests or to engage in activities which they did not freely choose. The innovative spirit leads to improvement in technology. Generally, the freedom to pursue self-interests leads to economic growth. This is one of the major reasons why most capitalistic countries enjoy higher rates of economic growth than socialist or communist nations. In a capitalistic economy, people know that they will directly benefit from their endeavours and so they are generally motivated to work hard. "For when people know they are working on what belongs to them, they work with far greater eagerness and diligence."[99] But, in a socialist economy there is only an indirect link between the people's efforts and how individuals benefit from those efforts. In a socialist nation, people think that they are working for the government and so they are de-motivated but in a capitalistic economy people know that they are primarily working for themselves and so they are motivated to work hard. Everyone works hard to meet their interests without expecting assistance from anybody. The government is not involved in economics and so people do not expect any subsidies from it. An individual's survival depends on how he is able to work

---

[98] Hausman, "Liberalism, welfare Economics, and Politics," 174.

[99] Leo XIII, Encyclical letter *Rerum Novarum, On the Conditions of Workers*, 15 May 1891 (Nairobi: Paulines Publications Africa, 1990), 66.

hard for his needs. Thus, everybody is forced to work hard - you either work hard or you simply die. The hard work that is characteristic of capitalistic economies is what accounts for the high rates of economic growth in those economies.

ii. In a capitalistic economy producers compete with one another. This competition leads to the production of diversified and better quality products for the benefit of the consumers. Business entities that cannot compete with their rivals in terms of improving the quality of their products and charging lower prices risk closing down because survival in the market is for the fittest. Due to the stiff competition from their rivals, producers are forced to improve the quality of their products and sellers try as much as they can to charge lower prices than they would if they were monopolists. All these efforts are of benefit to the consumers. Consumers maximize their utility by choosing from a wide range of goods and services. They can negotiate for lower prices and demand higher quality goods since the producers or sellers are many.

iii. Since firms are free from government regulations and control, it is possible for them to respond very fast to changes in the market, for example, changes in consumer preferences or in relative prices of goods and raw materials.[100] As soon as consumers change their demand from one commodity to another, producers shift as fast as possible to the production of the newly demanded commodity. The shift is fast simply because producers determine where, how, and when to invest their factors of production. What to produce depends on the availability and mobility of the factors of production but not on what the government wants. The government cannot dictate on what private investors should produce. This freedom enables producers to respond to the needs and tastes of the consumers without much delay.

iv. Firms benefit by investing in profitable lines of production and using resources more efficiently or using less expensive materials. Since it is in the interest of the firm to make profits, unprofitable lines of production are avoided. The profit motive compels producers to use resources in a very economical way and hence avoiding the wastage of resources. This is very important for the conservation of natural resources and the environment.

v. Liberal capitalism creates an ambience for investment. The level of savings is usually high because of the availability of numerous investment

---

[100] Hardwick, John Langmead, and Bahadur Khan, *An Introduction to Modern Economics*, 133.

alternatives. People save some of their income and invest it in creative ventures.[101] High savings lead to increased investment and this boosts the economy. It is claimed that in liberal capitalistic economies, the marginal propensity to save is usually higher than the marginal propensity to consume. This is because individuals are interested in making more and more profits.

Disadvantages of Liberal Capitalism

Generally, critics have pointed out that liberal capitalism is the economic system in which people are most individualistic, selfish and exploitative.[102] It is also said that freeing private economic activities from the so-called unnecessary government interference is very dangerous for the economy because individuals are only concerned with prosperity irrespective of how capital is invested, what is produced, how trade is conducted, or how labour is treated.[103] These accusations can be expounded upon as follows:

i.   By putting much emphasis on the pursuit of personal interests, liberal capitalism inevitably facilitates selfishness. Capitalism is one of the surest ways of institutionalizing selfishness. Individuals are concerned with their own interests but the so-called invisible hand of nature does not distribute those interests to the rest of the community. Leaving community interests at the mercy of blind and mystical forces (the invisible hand of nature) is to give a moral justification to immoral greed and to sacrifice community interests on the altar of individual selfishness. The invisible hand argument assumes universal competition in an economy where labour is fully employed such that as every employee pursues his interests following the division of labour principle, the rest of society will benefit. But, this assumption is untenable in technologically advanced economies (where machines replace labour) or in economies that are characterized by high levels of unemployment.[104] Unemployed people can hardly pursue their interests and so the invisible hand distributes nothing from them to the rest of society. More so, the few who are employed are likely to pursue their interests at the expense of the unemployed. Their aim will not be to maximize production but to maximize profits.

---

[101] Peschke, ed. *Ordo Socialis: Social Economy in the Light of Christian Faith,* 21.

[102] Peschke, ed. *Ordo Socialis: Social Economy in the Light of Christian Faith,* 20.

[103] Lubasz, "Adam Smith and the Free Market," 62.

[104] Lubasz, "Adam Smith and the Free Market," 47 and 66.

ii. The claim that the private sector is indispensable for growth is not true of all members of the private sector. There are criminal elements in the private sector who become wealthy through unproductive rent-seeking activities, for example, speculative activities, gambling, corrupt activities, and aggressive tax avoidance behaviour. This lot are prone to colluding with equally rent-seeking politicians to break or manipulate the law.[105]

iii. In reality, the so-called trickle-down effect of economic growth does not exist or at least it is a very slow process.[106] It is common, especially in urban areas, to find people who have been flamboyantly rich for many years and yet they are surrounded by very poor people. The poor people's standards of living have remained low or have even worsened despite the fact that there are rich people in their neighbourhood. One wonders why the effects of the rich people's economic progress have not trickled down to the poor people. The rich guard their wealth jealously to the extent that the poor cannot access it since they are regarded as thieves; they employ machines instead of employing human beings.[107]

iv. There is stiff competition for resources and goods and services. Everyone begins to work against the interests of others. Business enterprises too become selfish. Each business enterprise becomes a rival of all its competitors. This leads to constant price wars. Businesses have to channel some of their resources to persuasive advertisements in order to lure customers lest they lose them to their rivals. Customers therefore end up buying goods and services even if the quality of those items is poor. Thus, stiff competition forces business entities to get involved in dubious advertisements that mislead customers.

v. Liberal capitalism gives birth to individualism. People generally prefer to live individually or as nuclear families especially in cities and industrial areas. They avoid extended kinships. This kills family ties that might have been a form of security in difficult times. The only relationships that people value are what we might refer to as market or transactional relationships. The market, more than anything else, links people with one another. People no

---

[105] From a discussion with Abugre.

[106] Ian Christie and Diane Warburton, eds, *From Here to Sustainability* (London: Earthscan publications ltd, 2001), 86.

[107] Keith Tribe, "Natural Liberty and laissez-faire: How Adam Smith became a free market ideologue" in *Adam Smith's Wealth of Nations: New Interdisciplinary Essays*, eds. Stephen Copley, and Kathryn Sutherland (Manchester: Manchester University Press, 1995), 25.

longer relate with others because of friendship or blood links but because they are doing business together. Relatives are avoided because they are seen as liabilities. To spend money on a relative without expecting some returns is to act against one's interests. Any unprofitable relationship is curtailed.

vi. Because of the stiff competition for resources and commodities, individuals and nuclear families amass a lot of private wealth. They are afraid that resources or commodities will be taken by their rivals. Selfishness becomes the order of the day and the only tool for survival. Another reason why people amass property is the question of prestige. Material prosperity or the accumulation of private property is seen as an end in itself and the standard measure for the good life. Power and status in the society depend on how much wealth a person possesses. What matters is prosperity but not how wealth is acquired. More so, since there is a lot of individualism, each nuclear household accumulates wealth in order for it to become a self-reliant entity. People are able to amass a lot of properties, even perishable ones, because of improved technology and especially because of the use of money as a store of value – certain goods and services are stored in monetary form.

vii. Liberal capitalistic economies are characterised by consumerism. Producers create a lot of wants through massive advertisements. Consumers demand certain things not because they need them but because they are enticed by the producers' adverts - contrived demand.

viii. The so-called consumer sovereignty is a false concept. The general election in the liberalized market economy "is unlike a political election of 'one man one vote' because a rich person has more money 'votes' than a poor person and so has a bigger say in what is produced."[108] Those who have more money 'votes' sometimes 'vote' for luxuries and so, because of the profit motive, producers respond by shifting resources to the production of luxuries. Markets do not reach the very poor, be it in rich countries or in poor countries.[109] The market serves the needs of the rich. The poor have nowhere to get basic goods and services since the market is saturated with luxuries whose production is lucrative. Additionally, the shifting of resources to the production of another commodity causes structural unemployment in the economy since some workers are occupationally immobile. Workers whose skills cannot be transferred to the

---

[109] Jeffrey Sachs, *Common Wealth: Economics for a Crowded Planet* (London: Penguin Books, 2008), 257.

new line of production are laid off because the producers are not ready to incur the unnecessary cost of training them in the skills that are needed by the new industry.[110]

ix. Nobody invests in non-profitable lines of production. The consequence of this is that social services such as security and sanitation are not provided as public services but as commercialized private services. Individual households, at least those who can afford, take care of their own security and sanitation but nobody takes care of the security and sanitation of common places. Some rich people begin to provide society with social amenities including medical facilities, schools, security, and sanitary services but they charge very high prices in order to get exuberant profits. These are services that need not be used as a means of making profits but capitalism transforms them into money-spinning undertakings. The poor must either pay to the rich or forget all about the services. The most unfortunate of all are people who naturally cannot fend for themselves, for example, the mentally and or physically handicapped people. The likelihood of them dying prematurely is very high if they are neglected by their own relatives. Because of the profit motive, neglected handicapped people can hardly find a charitable organisation in a purely capitalistic economy that would offer them food, clothing, shelter, education, and medical care. Running a charitable organization is simply non-lucrative and therefore non-existent in a capitalistic economy. Charitable organizations, which were formerly non-profit making organizations, transform themselves into profit making institutions in order for them to keep pace with other organizations. Thus, in order to survive, one must be strong enough to fend for himself. Only the fittest survive in a capitalistic economy.

x. Liberal capitalism exacerbates income inequalities.[111] Society is gradually divided into two major classes: the class of those who own the means of production (the aristocrats or capitalists or bourgeoisies) and those who own nothing except their labour (the proletariat). The bourgeoisies have control over resources while the proletariats must sell their labour in order for them to earn a living. The proletariats are important only as far as they are a source of labour. This makes it very easy for the bourgeoisies to exploit the proletariats and to subject them to poor working conditions. The

---

[110] Hardwick, John Langmead, and Bahadur Khan, *An Introduction to Modern Economics*, 557.
[111] Hausman, "Liberalism, welfare Economics, and Politics,"192.

exploitation is as bad as what Adam Smith criticizes in his *Wealth of Nations*.[112] As Michael Walzer clearly points out in his must-read book *The Spheres of Justice*, what is at stake is not the fact that there are rich and poor people but the fact that one group of people (the bourgeoisies) dominates its fellows (the proletariats).[113] The bourgeoisies are able to dominate the proletariats because they own the means of domination, i.e. capital, education, power, and ideologies. Moreover, some of the bourgeoisies monopolise the domestic as well as the foreign market[114] and the production of certain goods and services and so they charge very high prices for them. Sometimes the monopolists hoard their products and create artificial scarcities in the market in order to charge high prices and earn abnormal profits. Because of all these factors and tricks, the gap between the bourgeoisies and the proletariats widens; the rich become richer and greedier while the poor become more impoverished and envious or the rich.

xi. Money creates new dynamics in society; power no longer belongs to the monarchs but to the rich – even if the king remains in power he is greatly influenced by those who own the means of production. The king must ensure that the rich people's interests are met even if it means sabotaging the interests of the whole society. The rich become influential in politics, religion, and educational institutions not because they are wise or holy but simply because they have money and with that they can buy anything or anybody. This is what is referred to as Plutocracy; the rich rule the state as well as the company and the factory.[115]

xii. There is no centralized mechanism to ensure that resources can be allocated from one place to another. In the same country, people who live in less endowed areas are likely to languish in misery while their counterparts are living executive lives. Capitalistic economies are characterized by huge regional imbalances. Likewise, certain sectors of the economy are more developed than others. Regions and sectors that have something receive more while those that have nothing receive nothing or even the little that they have is taken away from them. Powerful politicians and business people have the power to decide where and how resources should be allocated.

---

[112] Lubasz, "Adam Smith and the Free Market," 66.

[113] Walzer, *Spheres of Justice*, xii.

[114] Smith, *An Inquiry into the Nature and Causes of The Wealth of Nations*, 170-73.

[115] Walzer, *Spheres of Justice*, 317.

Resource allocation is done without much consideration of what justice entails but how the rich will benefit.

xiii.   Because of the profit motive, producers engage in activities irrespective of how those activities affect the environment. The most important factor to consider is the profitability of the activity.[116] Moreover, producers evade paying for the negative externalities which are caused by their activities. In order to minimise the costs of production and therefore to maximize profits, producers do not pay for the pollution or any other ecological and social costs that are caused by their industries. It is possible to avoid paying for the 'invisible elbow' because in a liberal capitalistic economy the government has negligible powers to regulate economic activities; the government can hardly enforce taxation policies or penalties to avert negative externalities such as the dispersion of toxic chemicals in water bodies.[117] Even if the government were to be a little strict, the capitalists would bribe it instead of paying taxes. Government officials are more willing to take bribes than to enforce taxation policies because they, like everybody else, are motivated more by self-interests than by national interests.

Socialism

This economic system is basically a consequence of the shortcomings of liberal capitalism. Liberal capitalism works to the advantage of the bourgeoisies but at the expense of the proletariats.[118] As the exploitation worsens in a capitalistic economy and the number of poor people gets bigger and bigger, some activists emerge and they begin to advocate for the poor people's rights by asking the government to regulate economic activities. Alternatively, the activists might incite the proletariats to revolt and or demand that the government should protect their rights against the selfishness of the exploiters. In any case, the government then resumes intervening in economic activities in order to protect the poor from being exploited by the selfish owners of the means of production. There is indeed the need for the government to intervene in the price mechanism system in order to control monopoly profits[119] and negative externalities such as

---

[116] Schumacher, *Small is Beautiful*, 42-43; 51; 60.

[117] Hausman, "Liberalism, welfare Economics, and Politics,"192.

[118] Jerry Z. Muller, *Adam Smith in His Time and Ours: Designing the Decent Society* (Princeton: Princeton University Press, 1993), 182.

[119] Hardwick, John Langmead, and Bahadur Khan, *An Introduction to Modern Economics*, 132.

pollution. Eventually the government nationalises key business enterprises that were previously owned and run by private individuals. Important resources are also nationalised and put under the ownership and control of the government. Communism is the extreme form of socialism. In a communist economy, the government is entirely in charge of all economic endeavours. The government owns all the resources and it controls both the production and distribution of goods and services.

Advantages of Socialism

1.   Since, at least in principle, the government is more concerned about the welfare of the citizens than about making profits, it is able to provide social services such as security and sanitation which are important even though they are not lucrative. Services are generally offered at relatively low prices that are affordable even to the poor people. The little profits which the government makes by supplying social services are used to pay civil servants and more so to set up public schemes for the needs of those who are disadvantaged, for example, the physically or mentally handicapped people.

2.   The government ensures that all the citizens have their basic needs before resources can be used to produce luxuries. National resources are for all the citizens but not for a few powerful and rich people. Ideally, every citizen must have food, shelter, clothing, basic education, security, and medical care before some of the national resources can be diverted to the production of goods and services that are generally considered to be luxurious. States such as Denmark, Finland, Norway, and Sweden have extensive systems of social insurance and high levels of social expenditure as a share of their national budgets to care for the needs of the citizens.[120]

3.   Resources are planned and distributed in such a way that even people who live in less endowed areas are able to meet their needs. The resources belong to the entire nation but not just to the people who stay where they are physically located. This makes it possible for the economy to achieve regional balance in its development process. The government distributes resources to all the regions and sectors of the economy. For instance, good teachers are not commissioned to just one school or region and likewise not all scholastic materials are given to one school or region. All regions are balanced as much as possible.

---

[120] Sachs, *Common Wealth*, 259.

4. Given the fact that important resources are owned by the government, income inequalities are relatively low in socialist economies, at least in the initial stages. No group of people owns the chief means of production or exploits other people. It is almost impossible for some people to become extremely rich while others are poor. Of course, people can never be the same but there are ways by which differences can be minimized. People are culturally, religiously, politically, economically, and socially different. However, when the disparities are huge or used for exploitation, then there is something wrong with the system. Surely, there must be something wrong somewhere if in a given nation some people cannot afford the basic needs of life while others are already at the top of the ladder of luxuries.

Disadvantages of Socialism

i. Business entities that are run by the government can hardly be efficient. This is because in principle they are owned by nobody even though they belong to everybody. Each individual keeps expecting 'the government' to take care of the public facility but at the end of the day nobody actually takes care of it since the so-called 'government' is not a person. This sense of irresponsibility is exacerbated by the lack of the self-interest motive which is characteristic of facilities that are owned by the government. Thus, government owned entities end up being neglected, mismanaged and underutilized. Nobody is passionate about government facilities since they do not directly respond to anybody's personal interests.[121] An individual can benefit from such a facility even if he does not participate in taking care of it as long as other people are taking care of it – it is difficult to exclude *free riders* from the consumption of a public good. Thus, the lack of the self-interest motive, the 'I don't care' attitude, and the free rider problem make public institutions very inefficient.

ii. The sharing of publicly owned property leads to what Garrett Hardin refers to as the tragedy of the commons.[122] Some individuals grab huge shares of the common property leaving almost nothing or what is of poor

---

[121] Aristotle holds that taking care of common property is usually problematic; everyone thinks about his interests – nobody thinks about common interests; everybody neglects what he thinks others will do. (see *The Politics*, 1261b 30-35).

[122] Sachs, *Common Wealth*, 38 and 115.

quality for others. Indeed, commonly owned resources are easily depleted compared to privately owned resources in capitalistic economies.

iii. Although the state is instrumental in breaking the private monopolization of resources by a few individuals at the expense of the common good, state power itself ends up dominating and monopolizing everything in the economy.[123] Basically, through the so-called centralization process of public resources and facilities, the government monopolises all the major business enterprises and this leads to all the shortcomings that are usually associated with monopolies. For instance, monopolies have no competitors so they are not in a hurry to improve the quality of their products and services. They sometimes hoard commodities and create artificial scarcities. This leads to increase in prices and the rise of black markets. In a socialist economy, therefore, people have no choice but to consume low quality products. Moreover, the products are not diversified implying that the consumers do not have much of a choice to meet their tastes and preferences. Socialism collapsed in Eastern Europe and in the former soviet republics not because the economies did not function at all but because they did not function well.[124] They did not supply good quality and diversified products and so the people were constantly irritated by persistent shortages of goods and services.

iv. As Karl Peschke has observed, human beings are simply too bad for socialism.[125] This maxim is usually ignored by socialist nations. Some of the government officials are given the responsibility to run state owned economic and business entities without being scrutinized. It is taken for granted that all state officials have the interests of the people at heart but this is a wrong assumption. Like any other person, some of the government officials who are entrusted with public utilities are actually concerned about their own interests only and some are even selfish. Such despots begin to use public entities for their own interests while the rest of the citizens languish in abject poverty. The government officials eventually forget that the enterprises under their control actually belong to the whole state to the extent that they begin to operate them as if they were personal properties. This therefore creates a class of some privileged people who think that they have the right to manipulate and to exploit others. In other words, selfish

---

[123] Walzer, *Spheres of Justice*, 15.

[124] Hausman, "Liberalism, welfare Economics, and Politics," 174.

[125] Peschke, ed. *Ordo Socialis: Social Economy in the Light of Christian Faith,* 25.

81

and corrupt government officials are to socialism what the bourgeoisies are to liberal capitalism.

v.   Socialist governments have the tendency of becoming dictatorial. The president of a socialist nation easily becomes a solipsistic leader who determines everything for everybody. Especially when socialism reaches its extreme form, communism, the president controls everything including economics, culture, religion, and education. This hegemony kills people's freedom and innovativeness as economist Friedrich Hayek argues in his influential book *The Road to Serfdom*.[126] People's interests are determined without any consultations. The citizens are treated as ignorant people who cannot think for themselves or identify their own interests. Nobody has the freedom to pursue his interests. Sometimes what the president decides to be provided for everybody is different from what the people actually need. Individual preferences and tastes are not taken into consideration. This leads to misallocation and wastage of national resources and the citizens feel alienated from the decisions that affect their lives.

vi.   Because the government is in charge of everything, people begin to expect that it will do everything for them. In most socialist economies, "the state is above all regarded as an institution of supply service which, like a magician, should give to all from inexhaustible financial resources and, if possible, take from nobody."[127] Such unrealistic expectations cannot be met by the state. Socialist economies are usually characterized by a serious dependency syndrome.

vii. Most citizens of socialist nations are very uncreative and unproductive. This results from the above challenges. First of all, the government tends to regulate economic activities to the extent that individuals lack the freedom to pursue their interests. Secondly, people keep expecting that the government will do everything for them. The consequence is for the people to become less innovative and lazy. People's talents are either killed or frustrated. The economy suffers as its GNP remains low.

Mixed Economies
More than any other economic system, mixed economics reflects our true nature as human beings. There are two equally important players in a

---

[126] Sachs, *Common Wealth*, 257.

[127] Peschke, ed. *Ordo Socialis: Social Economy in the Light of Christian Faith,* 40.

mixed economy, private individuals (the private sector) and the state (public sector). Some of the important resources are owned by the private sector while others are owned by the public sector. Each of the two sectors is involved in the production and distribution of goods and services. Mixed economics is the middle ground between pure capitalism and pure socialism. The two major sectors of a mixed economy are actively involved in economic operations unlike in a capitalistic economy where only the private sector is active while the government sector is redundant or in a socialist economy where the public sector is active while the private sector is passive. In a mixed economy, the private sector symbolizes the fact that human beings are motivated by self-interest while the public sector symbolizes the need to transform some of our self-interest into altruism instead of transforming itself into selfishness. The two sectors complement each other. Because of the private sector, people are free to pursue their interests and to stop the government from monopolizing economic operations. The main role of the public sector is to ensure that private entrepreneurs do not become selfish as they pursue their interests and also to provide the public with certain goods and services which might not attract private investors and yet they are necessary for the people's lives.

For a society that has experienced both capitalism and socialism, mixed economics comes as a reaction against the failures of these two economic regimes. In a capitalistic economy, the proletariats are exploited by the bourgeoisies. As a consequence, the proletariats revolt and ask to be protected by the government from the selfishness of the bourgeoisies. The failure of capitalism might also be revealed by events such as an economic depression or a financial crunch. After the failure of capitalism, socialism is embraced but eventually socialism too crumbles. Socialism is said to have failed when government officials in charge of economic operations become too selfish to the extent that the basic needs of the citizens can no longer be met. The citizens cannot get what they need when the government officials are busy using public resources for their own interests. More so, socialist economies are usually inefficient, they operate below their capacities. Because of all these limitations, the citizens begin to demand that some of the economic operations should be shifted from the government to private entrepreneurs. After both capitalism and socialism have failed, the right thing to do is to establish a hybrid economic system that blends the positive elements of capitalism with those of socialism i.e. mixed economics.

Some societies embrace mixed economics immediately after the demise of capitalism without first shifting to socialism. For them, capitalism is generally good but there are certain elements within it that need to be rectified by another stakeholder. This necessitates the government to get involved in economics. The main task of the government sector is to address the failures of capitalism. What private entrepreneurs cannot do the government does or is expected to do. For instance, the government regulates market prices so that private entrepreneurs do not exploit people by unjustifiably charging high prices. It is also the role of the government sector to deal with negative externalities such as pollution through its taxation policies, subsidies and legislation.[128] The private sector cannot deal with such externalities.

Important Principles for Mixed Economies

The following principles need to be maintained if a mixed economy is to flourish.

The Principle of Subsidiarity

In order for a mixed economy to flourish, the principle of subsidiarity needs to be maintained. According to this principle, "Just as it is gravely wrong to take from individuals what they can accomplish by their own initiative and industry and give it to the community, so also it is an injustice and at the same time a grave evil and disturbance of right order to assign to a greater and higher association what lesser and subordinate organizations can do."[129] In other words, it is wrong in a mixed economy for the government sector to do what belongs to the private sector and for the private sector to do what the government sector ought to do. The two sectors should not supplant each other but they should supplement each other. If the government keeps doing what the citizens can and should do for themselves, they become *lame ducks*. The citizens might never be able to walk on their own and they are likely to remain infants forever. A government that pampers its citizens turns them into lazy and irresponsible people and its economy fails to kick-off because there is more consumption of goods and services than there is production. There is no way an economy can grow without the citizens contributing to that growth. More so, if the citizens

---

[128] Hardwick, John Langmead, and Bahadur Khan, *An Introduction to Modern Economics*, 254.

[129] Pius XI, Encyclical Letter *Quadragesimo Anno*, 15 May 1931, *AAS* 23 (1931), 528.

simply receive everything from the government, everything becomes a right. They begin to demand even what is beyond the capacity of the government to provide and they can never be grateful for whatever they receive from the government. Sadly, unless the citizens struggle to meet some of their interests, they become wasteful in the use of goods and services since the government is always there to provide.

Certain government programs fail simply because the principle of subsidiarity is not put into consideration. For instance, if a government decides to offer free education, it has to uphold this principle otherwise it is likely to fail or to do so inefficiently. The first thing is to do a survey in order to find out what the citizens can do. The government should do only what the citizens cannot do or what is extremely difficult for them to do. The government might be financially overwhelmed if it tries to pay school fees and teachers' salaries, buy scholastic materials both for the teachers and students, construct school buildings, and provide meals for students and teachers, etc. This litany of necessities requires cost-sharing between the government and the parents or guardians. How will parents be proud of their children's education if they do not do anything for that education? Parents must not be denied the chance to carry out their responsibilities, one of which is to sacrifice for the education of their children. The government subsidises education just because it is an expensive form of investment. However, subsidizing does not mean substituting. The government should never substitute the parents in the role of educating their children but it must support them. As a way of complementing the parents' efforts, the government might for example provide free university education but it does not have to take care of nursery, primary, and secondary school education levels. The principle of subsidiarity is about division of labour.

Likewise, it is against the principle of subsidiarity if what is supposed to be done by the government sector is left to the private sector. Members of the private sector who are able to do what the government is supposed to have done will exploit the society by charging high prices for it. For instance, if a private individual manages to supply the community with electricity, the bills will be higher than if the government had been the supplier. Thus, if the government neglects its responsibilities, it opens doors for the private sector to actualize its inherent selfishness. Also, using the above example about education, if the government does not subsidise education, children from poor families can never dream of university education. It is even worse if the government takes care of the less expensive level of education and leaves the most expensive level to the parents. Since parents can afford nursery, primary and secondary education, the government should supplement their efforts by offering free university education which is usually more expensive.

In order for the principle of subsidiarity to be implemented in a mixed economy, the two sectors need to be critical of each other. The private sector should ensure that the government sector has played its role and vice versa. If the government sector does not carry out its responsibilities, it is the duty and right of the private sector to demand that those responsibilities be carried out. Likewise, once the government sector has carried out its obligations, it has the right to demand that the private sector should not job-sleep. The economy will grow if and only when each of the two sectors knows its duties and is willing and able to carry out those duties and knows its rights and is able to demand for those rights from the other party.

The Common Good Principle

The common good is "the sum total of social conditions which allow people, either as groups or as individuals, to reach their fulfilment more fully and easily."[130] According to this principle, the government sector needs to adopt an attitude of enabling members of the private sector to meet their interests more fully and easily. The government sector exists because of the common good.[131] The common good principle completes that of subsidiarity. Under the principle of subsidiarity, the government sector subsidizes the private sector by doing what private individuals cannot do by themselves or what is extremely difficult for them to do. It is a division of labour principle. The common good principle goes further to insist that what the government has to do should be done with the intention of making it easy for people to meet their interests either as individuals or as groups. The assumption behind this principle is that each individual or group of citizens has something original to offer for the growth of the economy. The role of the state is to enable individuals to actualize their potentials so that they can meet their interests and contribute to the welfare of the entire society. The government is not supposed to spoon-feed the people. Thus, just as it is wrong for the government not to empower people so that they can meet their interests, so also it is immoral for the government to do everything for the people. The analogy here is, once the shepherd has led the animal to the

---

[130] Vatican II, *Gaudium et Spes*, 7 December 1965, *AAS* 58 (1966), 104.
[131] Leo XIII, *Rerum Novarum*, 133.

river, it becomes the responsibility of the animal to either drink or not to drink.

Failure to observe the common good principle might result into a serious dependency syndrome in a mixed economy. If the government keeps providing goods and services to the citizens without the intention of enabling them to reach their fulfilment on their own, they can never become self-reliant. They will perpetually depend on the government even for what they could do for themselves. This is one of the major criticisms against foreign aid that does not aim at making people to become self-reliant. Such aid cannot lead to economic growth. According to the common good principle, instead of giving fish to the people, the government should give them fishing nets and teach them how to fish. The fishing nets will enable people to fish for themselves and therefore to become self-reliant in the future.

Once the government sector plays its role, members of the private sector feel obliged and motivated to seek possible ways of meeting their interests. For example, as soon as the government provides electricity to a given locality, private individuals or groups begin to setup small-scale business enterprises such as barber shops or kiosks for selling cold drinks in order to meet their needs. Similarly, instead of embarking on an impossible task of creating jobs for everyone, all that the common good principle requires of a government is to establish a loan scheme which will enable people to create jobs for themselves either as individuals or groups.

It is very crucial for the government to provide social conditions which will enable people to meet their interests. Certain social conditions are indispensable if people are to meet their needs and yet those conditions can hardly be provided by the private sector. The most obvious example of such conditions is national security. It is impossible for an economy to develop if there is no security and peace in the country. Peace is a prerequisite for development but since it can hardly be provided by the private sector, the government sector must provide it so that people can go on with their daily activities. If there is turmoil in the country, it becomes the responsibility of the private sector to demand for peace and security from the government sector. Once peace has been restored by the government sector, individuals must take it as their responsibility to utilize the peaceful atmosphere by working for their needs. The government should not allow people to take peace for granted. They must make good use of it.

The Break-even Point Principle

One of the main roles of the government sector is to provide society with goods and services which are important for public interests but which do not attract private investors because they are not lucrative. It is the role of the government to provide society with services such as sanitation and security and goods such as roads and railway lines. If a private investor risks providing such goods or services, he will most likely incur losses because of the difficulty of ensuring that consumers pay for them. Losses accrue because it is very difficult for private investors to exclude *free riders*. Private investors will therefore shy away from investing in such public goods and services because they are not profitable; they do not meet the interests of the private investors. However, given their importance to the society, the government must provide those goods and services. First of all, the government, at least in principle, is motivated not by self-interest but by the wellbeing of the people. Secondly, the government has the mechanisms and authority to alleviate the problem of free riders. Moreover, through direct and indirect taxation policies, the government is able to retrieve its expenditure on public goods and services. However, although the government does not aim at making profits, it endeavours to avoid making losses otherwise it runs into deficits. It operates at the breakeven point. It is economically efficient for the government sector to operate at the breakeven point, the zero-profit point as long as the interests of the public are met.

The Welfare Principle

Members of the private sector who are physically and mentally fit will be able to meet their interests once the subsidiarity, breakeven point, and the common good principles have been adhered to both by the government sector and the private sector. However, not every member of the private sector is physically and mentally healthy. Some are mentally and or physically handicapped. This category of people deserves special care from the government sector because the private sector cannot cater for their needs since such a venture would not be profitable, at least not monetarily. The government sector has an added responsibility of establishing charitable schemes to assist people who cannot work for their interests, for instance, people who are severely lame, those who are insane, and the elderly people who have no relatives to take care of their needs. Government benevolent schemes should also take care of the needs of people who have serious social and or cultural difficulties, for example, orphans and widows who have nobody to look after them. People who fall victims of natural calamities such as earthquakes, floods, tornadoes, and tsunamis have a right to be assisted by the government sector. However, the government is under no obligation to provide the beneficiaries of the charitable schemes more than their basic needs. Beneficiaries of charitable schemes have no right to luxuries. Both the government and the members of the private sector should ensure that only those who qualify for assistance get it.

Requirements for a Mixed Economy to Achieve Economic Development

In addition to abiding by the above principles, the following conditions need to be fulfilled in order for a mixed economy to achieve economic development.

a. Mixed economies are established on the assumption that there are two equally strong sectors in the economy, i.e., the private sector and the government sector must be equally strong. However, this condition is hardly fulfilled by most mixed economies and hence the failure to achieve economic development. On one hand, if the private sector is extremely stronger than the government sector, the economy will be more of a capitalistic economy than a mixed economy. The government will not be able to stop the powerful and rich members of the private sector from exploiting people. Therefore, the pursuit of self-interests by the private sector will gradually lead to selfishness and the economy will inevitably be characterized by huge income disparities, negative externalities, injustices, etc. On the other hand, if the government sector is extremely stronger than the private sector, the economy will be more of a socialist economy than a mixed economy. The government sector will tend to unnecessarily restrict the weak private sector from the pursuit of self-interests. This will lead to all the disadvantages of socialism such as killing creativity and hard work among the members of the private sector. Moreover, an extremely strong government sector will tend to relax or even neglect its duties because there is no private sector that is strong enough to challenge it. The economy will therefore be characterized by lack of social amenities. Thus, in order for a mixed economy to function well, there is a need for a strong private sector that can keep the government on its toes. Likewise, the government sector needs to be strong enough in order for it to challenge the private sector to play its role without being manipulated by the selfish members of the private sector.

b. A mixed economy cannot achieve economic development without government officials who have the common good at heart. It is not enough for the government sector to exist and to be of equal strength with the private sector. In order for the government sector to be able to play its role, there is also a need for special people who are to work in that sector. The government sector should be made up of benevolent people who have the interests of the society at heart. This does not mean that they should not work for their own interests but that in addition to working for their interests, they should also be willing and able to work for the interests of the entire society. If the government sector is dominated by selfish people, the interests of the society will not be met because government resources will be used by the selfish government officials for their own interests. The economy suffers if those who work in the government sector are employed not on merit but simply because they are related to the president in one way or another. Sometimes the government sector is given to those who supported the president during the political campaigns as a way of rewarding them and ensuring that the president can always get what he wants from the government coffers.

In order for a mixed economy to prosper, those who are employed to work in the government sector should not only be professional experts but they should also have some degree of selflessness. Thus, meritocracy alone is not enough. Additionally, whether or not they are related to the president, government sector employees should have the capacity to challenge the president in case he is tempted to use national resources for personal interests. The dilemma for most mixed economies is where to get people who can faithfully work for the common good. Very few people feel attracted to the government sector with the intention of serving their society. Most want to work in the government sector in order to use national resources for their own interests. They do not have the interests of the society as part of their concerns. The only question they ask themselves before accepting to take a position within a government sector is: how will I benefit from this job? There is a need for people who in addition to asking this question will ask themselves a second question i.e. how will the society benefit from my accepting to take on this job? If this second question is not asked or if it does not make sense to the person, he should not be employed by the government sector.

Geocentric Economics

This is the final regime of any society's economic cycle. During the previous economic regimes, i.e. liberal capitalism, socialism, and mixed economics, individual economies try to operate as separate entities. Each nation-state is a *sovereign* economy preoccupied with its own interests. It is only international trade that brings them together and the main purpose of engaging in international trade is to get from other countries what a country cannot produce on its own. In other words, international trade is the only way economies express themselves as inter-dependent entities. It is the proof that no economy in the world can be self-reliant even though some might aspire to become or even claim to be independent. A nation-state must rely on others for some of its interests. The main point here is that sovereign economies, be they capitalist or socialist or mixed, engage in international trade not for altruistic reasons but for egoistic purposes. Each nation-state is motivated by self-interests and the interests of its citizens. No nation-state engages in international trade for the interests of another nation.

With time, however, it becomes obvious that there are certain challenges which cannot be dealt with by individual economies or even through mere international trade. Challenges such as climate change, extreme poverty, and international terrorism require global efforts. They are what we might refer to as global challenges. They affect all the economies of the world in one way or another. Thus, global challenges must be dealt with by all the world economies coming together to form a single economic entity. Global challenges necessitate global cooperation; the idea that nation-states need to scramble for markets, power, and resources becomes passé.[132] When nation-state economies form a single economic unit they constitute an economic system that we can refer to as geocentric economics. We call it *geocentric* because it is mainly concerned with issues which affect the whole world – the whole planet earth. Moreover, it involves all the economies of the world. All the economies are stakeholders. If global challenges are not alleviated, individual nation-state economies will find it very difficult to meet some of their interests or they can even perish. Geocentric economics is an economic system not just because it brings together all the economies of the world but mainly because the global challenges that are dealt with have serious economic implications. Global challenges do have other implications, social,

---

[132] Sachs, *Common Wealth*, 3.

political, cultural, religious, etc., but their economic implications are more acute. An economy or a world which is still challenged by climate changes, extreme poverty, international terrorism, or population pressure cannot claim to have achieved economic development.

Geocentric economics is the stage at which economies experience the highest degree of altruistic egoism. Each member state of the geocentric economic system is motivated by its own interests but it cannot meet its interests without enabling others to meet their own interests. If, for example, a given country reduces its emissions of carbon-dioxide gas or plants forests, the resulting benefits will be shared by that country and other countries – both the particular country and the whole universe will benefit. Global cooperation has found favour with people who know that it is in their interest and the interest of the whole world.[133] In other words, with geocentric economics countries are both egoistic and altruistic. The whole system collapses if individual economies are interested only in their own interests. For instance, if a country builds high industrial chimneys in order to exude obnoxious industrial gases as far away as possible from its vicinity but such gases pollute other parts of the world, this country will achieve economic growth in the short run at the expense of other countries but in the long run it too will suffer from the effects of that pollution – the whole world will suffer. As Jeffrey Sachs would put it, because of our interconnectedness, "No part of the world can be abandoned to extreme poverty, or used as a dumping ground for the toxic, without jeopardizing and diminishing all the rest."[134] This is true not only at the global level but also at every level of society. In most urban cities, for example, the rich have insulated themselves against the poor by building high electrified fences around their houses. They are not peaceful because they are always afraid of the poor coming to rob them of their wealth at any time. Thus, cooperation is not just desirable but necessary if we want to live peacefully in this world.

An important step toward the actualization of geocentric economics is the formation of regional blocks and international organisations. Groups such as the EU, AU, EAC, SADC, ECOWAS, the G8 and G20, and international organizations such as the IMF, WB, WTO, UN, RC, etc. are indications that the world is slowly becoming a global village. The formation and operations of these trans-national organizations have been facilitated by

---

[133] Sachs, *Common Wealth*, 5.

[134] Sachs, *Common Wealth*, 5.

technological progress in information and communication. With the internet and mobile phone technologies, for example, it is now possible to share any form of information with the whole world in a matter of seconds. Also, people are able to travel faster from one place to another because of improved land, water, and especially air transport. All these facilities have made it possible for people to get connected to one another. The international organizations are able to efficiently execute their operations because of the availability of good information and communication mechanisms.

Regional and global organizations enable nation-states to solve problems which they might not have managed on their own. The provision of relief aid is an immediate example here. An organisation is obliged to assist its member countries especially when they are challenged by natural disasters such as droughts, floods, tsunamis, or earthquake. Also, there are some international organizations such as the Red Cross and the World Food Program which assist any country in times of dare need. The United Nations High Commission for Refugees assists countries that are challenged by the human-made problem of refugee influx and outflow. All these examples serve to indicate that there are certain problems which cannot be solved singlehandedly. The whole world or at least a group of countries must come together to solve such problems. This is what we saw in 2010 when Haiti was seriously destroyed by an earthquake. The country was in a dilemma – it did not know what to do. But, in just a matter of seconds the world was already aware of Haiti's situation, thanks to the improvements in information technology. People from different corners of the world, nation-states, and international organisations started contributing food, clothing, medicine, tents, human labour, and money for the welfare of the victims. The process of re-constructing Haiti could only depend on global solidarity but not on Haiti alone. Such efforts remind us that humanity is indeed one family or, as Jeffrey Sachs would say, global challenges which require new forms of global cooperation point to the fact that humanity shares a *common fate*.[135]

Challenges to Global Cooperation

Although it is now obvious that the world needs to come together in order to alleviate certain problems, the date on which this will be actualized is moving at a snail's pace. Geocentric economics is taking ages to be

---

[135] Sachs, *Common Wealth*, 3.

concretized and yet the problems are already causing a lot of untold suffering. Everybody is convinced that there is no choice other than coming together but nobody is moving fast - nation-states are moving but reluctantly. The following are some of the reasons why geocentric economics is taking ages before it can be actualized:

1. Some members of international bodies are still largely pre-occupied with their own interests. Even though the reason why those bodies have been formed is to solve global problems, some of the member nation-states are more concerned about protecting their individual interests. Many countries still find it harder to fund scientific researches for global needs than researches for national economic advantage or private profits.[136] There is little or sometimes no concern for the common good. Some of the nation-states even try to work against the intended common objective. They even try to prevent the other member nation-states from achieving the intended common interest. This is what we referred to as selfishness. Also, some of the people who are employed by international bodies are more interested in their salaries and other personal benefits than in working for the common good for which the body was formed. Some even swindle the bodies' funds. Selfishness is more acute in poor countries. Some of the funds that are sent by international bodies to alleviate certain problems are diverted by local government officials. For instance, in 2008 some Ugandan government officials defrauded money that had been sent by the WHO for malaria prevention. What is even more disappointing is that some of those corrupt officials were exonerated by the Ugandan government. This kind of barbaric behaviour discourages international bodies from sustaining existing projects or embarking on new ones.

2. Some countries have been very reluctant to join international bodies for one erroneous reason or another. Actually up to now there is not even a single body that we can call 'global'. There is no body whose membership consists of all the countries of the world – not even the UN. Some nation-states have not yet joined international bodies because they think that they have nothing to contribute; others fear that they will lose the little that they have to the big body; others are sceptical – they think that global problems can never be solved by whatever means; others argue that they did not contribute to the problem, for example, the climate change problem, and so they do not see the reason why they should be part of the solution; some rich

---

[136] Sachs, *Common Wealth*, 303.

countries think that they have nothing to gain from international bodies since they are not heavily affected by the so-called global problems – they fear to lose their wealth to poor countries. We all still remember how reluctant America was to sign the Kyoto protocol! Needless to say, it is impossible for the world to form a single economic unit while some of the countries are still cynical about the need for global cooperation.

3. Many nation-states have not yet forged cooperation within their boundaries. Especially in poor countries, some regions are highly developed while others are extremely deplorable. Because of the wide disparities, the citizens do not see themselves as belonging to one country. For instance, whenever the Turkana people of the north eastern part of Kenya travel to Nairobi they usually say that they are travelling to Kenya because for them Kenya means Nairobi which to them is a foreign country altogether. The divisions and conflicts that exist in countries are symptoms of human selfishness; national resources are used for the development of the regions where influential people come from. These divisions are a challenge to global cooperation; it is almost impossible for countries that are still divided by race, income levels, religion, etc. to cooperate at the global level. Indeed, the paradox of a unified global economy and divided national economies makes impossible the cooperation required for addressing global challenges.[137] There is no global unity without local unity. Cooperation is needed at all levels, from the most micro, i.e. the household, to the most global.

4. The so-called super powers of the world tend to dominate international bodies. Sometimes they behave like solipsists. Because they have veto power, they monopolize research, management of global institutions, and all the decision making processes.[138] Consequently, they bully the smaller members whose suggestions are simply rubbished. There is an unnecessary classification of superior and powerful members versus inferior and weak members. With this kind of inequality, weak members do not feel enthusiastic about international cooperation. They feel that a lot can be done without their contribution. They think that the 'big brothers' have all it takes to solve global problems. But the reality is that those so-called super powers cannot achieve much without the support and cooperation of the weak members. No country is so poor that it cannot contribute anything and likewise no country is so rich that it can solve all the problems of this world

[137] Sachs, *Common Wealth*, 7 and 315.

[138] Andersen and Howard F. Taylor, *Sociology: Understanding a Diverse Society*, 456.

singlehandedly. Global challenges, as Jeffrey Sachs insists, require the harnessing of the energies and talents of all the countries of the world and all parts of society.[139] There is a need for a strategy that relies more on global cooperation and less on the might of the super powers.

5. Unending rhetoric is another big challenge to global cooperation. A lot of time is wasted at meetings of international organisations but very little is being done. There are more disagreements than agreements at those meetings. Instead of looking for solutions, time is wasted on blame games. For instance, irrespective of what the topic for discussion is, African countries spend most of the time at those meetings attributing its problems to colonialism and slavery. Rich countries spend huge amounts of time blaming poor countries for being lazy and corrupt. Although such issues might be important topics for discussion at global meetings, sometimes they are irrelevant to the issue at hand. Surely, discussing racial or religious or cultural differences at a global meeting that has been convened to seek solutions to the current ecological crisis is a waste of time and other resources. Unnecessary rhetoric delays decisions and action and it therefore exacerbates global challenges. The rhetoric is a form of air pollution that is contributing to the crisis instead of coming up with a remedy. As long as international meetings are still producing long documents only without any concrete actions, non-member countries will not be motivated to join international bodies and even some of the members will soon get discouraged by the prolonged sluggishness. Speeches or good grammar will not solve the contemporary global challenges.

6. We have mentioned that the success of international bodies largely depends on improvements in information and communication technology. However, there are still places in this world which have not yet enjoyed the benefits of the technologies that are taken for granted elsewhere. The internet has not yet reached some African and Asian villages and some people are so poor that they cannot buy or maintain mobile phones. This inaccessibility makes it very difficult to bring everybody on board. Some people are left out as the rest of the world share some important information and exchange views on certain crucial issues. There is still a lot to be done. The world needs to be connected by a single web before it can be declared a global village. Also, technology has been abused to create global fear and mistrust. Some countries do not trust others because of their advancement in

---

[139] Sachs, *Common Wealth*, 291.

the manufacture of weapons of mass destruction, atomic bombs, and nuclear bombs. Because of this suspension and fear, some countries hesitate to cooperate with certain countries. Surely, globalisation without trust is simply impossible.[140] Likewise, global cooperation will remain an inaccessible ideal as long as countries are still fighting against one another instead of combining efforts to fight against global problems.

7. Efforts to global cooperation are stifled by the lack of authentic global leadership. Unlike nation-states which have governments, parliaments, and judiciaries, there is no such a thing as a president or parliament for the entire world. Global institutions such as the WB, IMF, UN, and WTO have assumed some kind of leadership to a world that is moving towards becoming a global village. But, these institutions do not have the kind of power presidents have over their countries. Moreover, they sometimes lack moral authority to govern the world since they too are seldom democratic and transparent.

---

[140] Sachs, *Common Wealth*, 7-8.

Chapter 5

Development or Egoism?

Development

The term development is like the devil, or the Holy Ghost among Christians, so often mentioned but hardly understood. To give a holistic definition of development is as tasking as piercing a nail through a dry log of a Thai teak. Put differently, it is as difficult as getting a live cat to lie on its back. We all talk about development of ourselves, talents, religions, nations, and continents. Different terms such as civilization, Europeanization, evangelization, Christianization, Islamization, industrialization, urbanization, modernization, economic growth, liberalization or globalization, have been used over the years to denote development. For poor countries, the word means escape from backwardness and darkness, salvation from misery, and catching up with the enlightened world. For rich societies the word symbolizes heightened possibilities, the achievement of the affluent society, then its transcendence, a process culminating in a postindustrial world from which scarcity has been banished. The 1960s were hailed as the "Decade of Development," and the Cold War, which reached its peak during those years, was fought in the name of development. The difficulty in defining development lies in its extreme vulnerability to individual or group of individuals' manipulation in space and time; as the term migrates spatially and temporally, people twist it at will depending on their interest and social situation. Yet, we cannot give up attempting at a meaning of development since it is a fundamental goal of every human person and society.

In biology, development describes a process through which living things— plants and animals grow until they mature. This process is an imperceptible one, impossible to grasp at any moment of time yet clear enough when followed over a period, and the way the process unfolds is spontaneous and predictable.[141] Characteristically, we can say that development of a living organism involves directionality, continuity, cumulativeness and irreversibility. Growth in living organisms is not amorphous; it has a direction and a purpose. It follows well defined stages

---

[141] Rist, *The History of Development*, 26.

99

during each of which the organism metamorphosizes or transforms into another until the final stage. Often, the final stage can be imagined from the few initial stages of growth of the organism.[142] We can tell the shape of a maize plant at the first few early stages of its growth. In light of this, some scholars consider development as necessarily positive and synonymous with growth. Living organisms, for example, a lamb can change morphologically through the various stages of its growth but it essentially remains a sheep and this is the reason for insisting on continuity as a characteristic of development. Similarly, each stage an animal or a plant grows into depends on the preceding stage that is from the lower to the higher stage indicating the cumulativeness of the process. For instance, a mango plant can only flower after it has gone through a vegetative stage, and it can only fruit after it has flowered. These variations are positive and imply quantitative and qualitative additions. Once a stage is passed, it is impossible to go back; a ram cannot reverse to a lamb which is the reason why we uphold irreversibility of growth in living organisms. Sheep can however, reproduce themselves, or the seed formed at fruition of the plant can 'die' and germinate to begin another cycle of life. So in this understanding, growth or 'development' is a cyclic process.

Perceiving human society as an 'organism,' this analogy becomes a fitting metaphor to describe development of economies.[143] Development is positive, an advancement toward a desirable goal. Aristotle shares this understanding when he says that everything we do is for a *telos*— an end or a goal. Everything we do must have a limit and growth is not an exception; that which has no term or limit is by definition incomplete and imperfect.[144] This awareness of the limit, of a kind of optimum level after which the curve necessarily moves downwards to comply with the laws of 'nature' has been kept within the Western tradition from the time of Aristotle till the modern period when the barrier collapsed giving way to the perception of exponential infinite progress. Development now means growth forever especially economic growth, and technological growth (physical infrastructure, automobiles). This understanding dominated the development discourse and practice over the years especially after the Second World war

---

[142] Rist, *The History of Development*, 27.

[143] Gustavo E. Gustavo, "Development" in *The Development Dictionary: A Guide to Knowledge As Power*. ed. Wolfang Sach (London: Zed Books, 1992), 8.

[144] Rist, *The History of Development*, 31.

when the former President of the United States of America, Harry S. Truman's 'Point Four' inaugurated the 'development age.' "Greater production is the key to prosperity and peace. And the key to greater production is a wider and more vigorous application of modern scientific and technical knowledge."[145]

Undeniably, this model of development has had its positive side especially when it comes to the reality of the role of technology in smoothing life for humans. People used to travel on foot for at least one month to cover 870 kilometres. It was often a tasking, tiring, long, and a risky venture to undertake such journeys but technology has made travel now so comfortable and efficient. For example, when people travel by air, it takes them utmost fifty minutes to cover a similar distance; they sit on comfortable seats, have all kinds of services including food, drinks, and facilities such as lavatories. Therefore, denying economic and technological advancement as constituent parts of development is as good as denying the obvious. However, the economic growth model, which is a dominant development paradigm, and often called 'growth mania',[146] has many weaknesses. It is problematic to embrace economic growth as a model par excellence for measuring development.

Economic Growth or Growth mania

Economic growth is the persistent increase in the volume of goods and services produced in a country in a particular period of time as indicated by increase in GNI (Gross National Income). What matters here is the quantity of the gross national income or product; for instance, if Uganda is growing at the rate of 6.3%, this model considers the country as developing. Subscribers to this model get worried only when there is a down trend in the annual economic growth rate of a country. Whichever methods the country employs to achieve this growth and whatever the consequences to the environment or the people is a non-issue.

Central to the 'growth mania' paradigm of development are the assumptions of infinite human needs, a boundless natural resource pool, growth of Gross National Income as the best measure of human wellbeing,

---

[145] Rist, *The History of Development*, 114-5.

[146] Herman E. Daly, "Economics in a Full World." *The Scientific American* (September 2005), 78-79.

and finally, that growth in GNI as a panacea to every problem: poverty, unemployment, and environmental degradation.[147] For example, if the water table falls, dig deeper wells, or build bigger pumps. If mines are depleted, build more expensive refineries to process lower grade ore. If soil is depleted, produce more chemical fertilizer. If there are pollution and depletion of resources, we grow materially so that we will be rich enough to afford the cost of cleaning up and discovering new resources and technologies, and if it is a problem of war, we grow in technology so that we can have weapons. In short, there is no limit to growth, and production, advertisement, and consumption are its hallmarks. These mutually enforcing factors have made the contemporary human person a slave to consumerism with the consequences expressed in environmental pollution, corruption, and estrangement of social bonds.

But growth in GNI actually ignores many important indices, without which a country or people cannot really be said to be progressing. For example, corruption, income inequalities, unemployment, inflation, the content of production, and the 'health' of the environmental elements (biotic and abiotic), justice, human rights, and happiness are not considered by this model. Uganda's growth rate may be at 6.3% but the question is: where do the high incomes go? That is why a poor woman who is hungry and thirsty considers it absolute nonsense when she hears pronouncements that her country is doing very well economically. This growth remains an illusion until she is able to meet her basic needs with ease. Unless corruption makes way for the trickledown effect to work, a country cannot claim to be truly developing. If only few selfish and corrupt leaders keep the wealth and majority of Ugandans wallow in abject poverty, we cannot justifiably conclude that Uganda is developing unless the income inequalities are addressed. Similarly, a country's GNI may be growing because of foreign investment in the country. But, again the question is who are those employed by such investors? What kind of goods do they produce? Do these goods meet the basic needs of the people? To what extent are the methods used environmentally friendly? For instance, gold may be mined in Tarkwa in Ghana and in the process destroy the farms from which the local people cultivate their staple crops. These people cannot cook gold to eat if they are

---

[147] Herman E. Daly, *Toward A Steady-State Economy* (San Francisco: W. H. Freeman and Company, 1973), 150-51.

given any at all. They do not also get to be employed. If they do, they are contracted on casual basis in which case they handle the most dangerous part of the work yet with the least wage. How about the issue of inflation, the increase in prices of goods? The economic growth model does not consider any of these important qualitative variables of life. That is why the pursuit of growth in GNI is considered inadequate as far as pursuing true development is concerned. It has and continues to cause unsustainable exploitation of the environment, widens income gaps, promotes corruption, and selfishness, and it leaves many people poor, voiceless, and unhappy.

Unfortunately, this model is imposed and promoted by the powers that be and has thus, dominated global development discourse and practice. It is premised on an instrumental attitude toward the environment. The instrumentalist attitude promotes an unhealthy competition between human development and environmental sustainability. As long as we achieve economic growth, it does not matter how the environment has been exploited. Our concern is to meet only our interests— economic growth. After all, the environment is inanimate and has no intrinsic value. We are basically solipsistic in our relationship with the environment. In fact, it would not be wrong to tag the relationship between the human person in the name of development and that of the environment as warring. Deceivingly, human beings often declare themselves the victor but current experiences have proved that we are not. The current disasters both natural and human-induced and their telling negative impacts on the human person clearly attest to this point. We may claim to be shooting at the environment without missing but the environment retaliates without mercy. When it retaliates we have nowhere to hide but are left at its mercy. We are and will be the losers in the long run for engaging in a war which we are pretty sure we will not win. To use an analogy, it is like a fish fighting hard to dry up a lake in which it stays. Unfortunately, this is what growth mania has and continues to encourage us to do. As rational animals, we need to rethink our relationship with the environment and the starting point is to reconsider our understanding of what development really is. We need to accept the fact that "An attitude of life which seeks fulfillment in the single-minded pursuit of wealth – in short, materialism – does not fit into this world, because it contains within itself no limiting principle, while the environment in which it is placed is strictly limited."[148]

---

[148] Schumacher, *Small is Beautiful*, 29-30.

The worship of Economic Growth

Notwithstanding all the methodologically devastating problems associated with the economic growth or capitalistic model of pursuing human development, the model has so many disciples worldwide so much so that it is being worshipped and vigorously spread. Daniel Bell is right when he describes economic growth as "secular religion of the advanced industrial societies".[149] In fact Bell could as well be right if he extended the scope to the developing world. We do not need any philosophical tools to understand this fact; commonsensical experiences in what we see, hear, and practice daily point to our faithfulness to this "religion". As James Gustave Speth, the famous Yale University professor queries rhetorically in his *The Bridge at the Edge of the World: Capitalism, The Environment, and Crossing from Crisis to Sustainability*, "Is there anything in our society more faithfully followed than economic growth?"[150] For its movements are constantly watched, measured to the decimal place, deplored or praised, diagnosed as weak or judged as healthy and vigorous. Newspapers, magazines, and cable channels report endlessly on it. It is examined at all levels— global, national, and corporate.[151]

Yet, mania has a pathological connotation so that when we pursue growth to manic levels, then it is no longer healthy, and the environmental crisis we experience is a clear attestation. Unfortunately, the patterns of production, advertisement, and consumption are at manic levels and it is hard to tell when this phenomenon will change for better. The most worrisome reality is that underneath this unfortunate dynamic is national, corporate and individual greed for power and control. We hear of politico-economic dualistic nomenclature of the global family as third world and first world, or developing and the developed world. Everyone wants to be considered first because to be first is axiomatic of power and control. Therefore, those who are not first strive relentlessly and sometimes foolishly to achieve the first status and those who are already first devise means of making sure that they remain first. This unhealthy competition for economic, technological, and political power is the reality which we all experience, consciously or unconsciously. The competition often takes the form of 'winner takes it all'. In most of the cases the so called developing countries

---

[149] Daniel Bell, *The Cultural Contradictions of Capitalism* (New York: Basic Books, 1978), 237-38.

[150] James G. Speth, *The Bridge at the Edge of the World: Capitalism, The Environment, and Crossing from Crisis to Sustainability* (New Haven: Yale University Press, 2008), 46.

[151] Speth, *The Bridge at the Edge of the World*, 46.

succumb to the so called developed countries in matters of technological, economic, and political confrontations. But, the developing countries devise other means to catch up. One of such means is what one may call an indiscriminate and wholesale consumption of the products of the technology, economics, and political ideologies of the developed countries. For example, in an African home, it is no news that the music gadgets, kitchen utensils, even toothpick sticks are all imported. Cross check the shelves of many African professors and you will notice that almost all the books are written by foreign counterparts. The lists can go on but the idea is to emphasize the fact that across almost all spheres of life, Africans remain mere consumers of ideas and products from the developed nations.

Further Problematics

Growth mania is not the only shortcoming of the development models which we have been using in the past. The biological analogy, which we alluded to earlier on, can be used to discuss how our development models have been inadequate and problematic. According to the biological process, development is supposed to be directional, continuous, cumulative and irreversible. First, at least in Africa, most of the development processes did not take off with clear direction. Local communities and nation-states were not given the chance to identify their needs and to decide on the path to take in order to meet those needs. Both the needs and the path were dictated by the outsiders who had come to develop Africa. For example, at a banquet commemorating the abolition of slavery, Victor Hugo put it like this, "The moment has come to make Europe realize that it has Africa alongside it [...] In the 19th century, Europe will make a world of Africa. To fashion a new Africa, to make the old Africa amenable to civilization— that is the problem. And Europe will solve it."[152] Europe took it upon itself to "develop" Africa without consulting Africans. It imposed its concept of development on Africans and forced them to abandon their lifestyle. This problem did not end with the so-called independence. Some African charismatic leaders started to dictate on which path to take for their nation-states to achieve development— the so-called visionary leaders. During the cold war era, Africa's road to development was paved by the two main blocks, capitalism and socialism. Today the path to Africa's development is still dictated by outsiders, especially international bodies such as the World Bank, the

---

[152] Rist, *The History of Development*, 51.

International Monetary Fund, and the World Trade Organization, and several multinational corporations. Thus, Africa has never known where it is heading to or at least it is not familiar with the road map to development and it will not recognize the destination. It is like a blind person being led through unfamiliar path. If left on his own, he will get lost but even if he is led to the destination, he will not recognize it. Those who pave the road to Africa's development are motivated more by their own interests than by the interests of the beneficiaries— some are even selfish. For instance, Victor Hugo ordered Europe to go to Africa to make roads, ports, towns, and to grow, cultivate, and colonize with the main aim of solving Europe's social problems and changing its proletarians into property owners.[153] Thus, developing Africa was going to be of more benefit to Europe than to Africa.

Second, there was little or no planning when Africa embarked on the journey to development. The requirements, methodologies, and the eventual consequences were not clearly stated. Several projects were started but they were abandoned because of lack of materials and expertise to complete them and even those that were completed are unsustainable. Africa borrowed its development models from the West without much reflection. Nobody first sat down to calculate the cost to see if there would be enough resources to complete the whole development project.[154] Sadly, Africa too treats the environment as a mere depository of resources for selfish interest and this has caused adverse environmental changes such as climate change. With climatic hazards such as droughts, floods, and sicknesses, it is now obvious that Africa cannot continue doing business as usual. The current ecological crisis is a sufficient proof that Africa's development efforts cannot be continued. The development models which were borrowed from the West are not sustainable.

Third, Africa was denied the chance to go through all the stages of development. The development process was not cumulative. Africans were told to throw away whatever they were doing and believing in before the outsiders came. They were even forced to jump some of the stages of development. From the use of sticks for cultivation, some Africans jumped to the use of tractors without going through the stages of using hoes, and mould-board ploughs. These two stages should not have been ignored. This is because the preceding step should serve as a springboard to the next. This

---

[153] Rist, *The History of Development*, 51.

[154] The piece of advice given by Jesus Christ in Luke 14:28-31 has not been taken seriously.

is what Africa has missed in its development efforts. It was forced to jump into the use of advanced technology. Africa keeps depending on the West for its technological requirements simply because its development process has never been cumulative. Africa is like a child that has been forced to participate in the Olympics before it is able to crawl. It is like a school child that is made to jump from primary one class to high school. However intelligent that child might be, it cannot excel in high school because of lack of an integrated primary school experience.

Fourth, Africa has been moving back and forth as it tries to develop. After moving two steps forward it slides three steps backwards. For instance, several development projects have been destroyed by wars and conflicts. Countries such as Ivory Coast, Zimbabwe, Nigeria, Egypt, Tunisia, and Libya that were once flourishing have deteriorated. Political conflicts, diseases, inflation, unemployment, corruption, and income inequalities have reversed the whole process of development. More so, Africa's development will continue to move backwards because of external negative forces. Africa's development experience can be likened to a young plant that grows luxuriantly in the beginning but later starts to experience stunted growth because of lack of one or two essential soil nutrients.

Toward a Better Definition of Development

Development, in the most inclusive sense is more than technological advancement or economic growth. Development necessarily entails change that gears towards sustainable human happiness and fulfillment. We can only talk of true development of a nation or persons when there is a considerable presence of enjoyment of human dignity, freedom of economic, social and political choices by the people. It includes the process whereby the real per capita income of a country increases over a long period of time subject to the stipulation that the number of people below the poverty line does not increase and that the distribution of income does not become more unequal; real income per capita must increase both quantitatively and qualitatively, it includes improvement in general welfare e.g. standard of living, price stability, improved quality products, employment stability, leisure, wider choice of goods, narrower income gaps, improvement in social, political, moral and religious lifestyles of the people. The three basic components of development are: life sustenance (provision of basic needs), self-esteem (self-respect and relative autonomy and authenticity) and freedom (individuals can determine their own destiny).

1. The South Commission's Concept of Development

According to the report of this commission under the chairmanship of the former Tanzanian president Julius Nyerere, development is a *process* which enables human beings to realize their *potentials, build self-confidence, and lead lives of dignity and fulfillment.* It is a process which frees people from fear of want and exploitation. It is a movement away from *political, economic, or social exploitation.* Development is a process of growth, a movement essentially springing from within the society that is developing... The base for a nation's development must be its own resources, both human and material, fully used to meet its own needs... Development has therefore to be *an effort of, by, and for the people.* True development has to be people-centered.[155] The Human Development Report of 1991, published by the United Nations Development Programme, supports this definition when it states that the basic objective of human development is to *enlarge the range of people's choices* to make development more democratic and participatory. The choices should include access to income and employment opportunities, education and health, and *a clean and safe physical environment.* Each individual should also have the opportunity to *participate fully in community decisions* and to enjoy human, economic and political freedoms.[156]

2. Joe Remenyi

Development is change towards self-reliance and contentment; a process whereby individuals, groups, communities, countries, or continents obtain sustainable livelihoods.[157] The term livelihood is critical because it suggests an intergenerational dynamic and responsible attitude towards the environment.

From the above, we can say that development is both a process and an end. It is a process that optimally balances all human activities vis-à-vis environmental regenerative capacity in such a way that human beings are able to derive adequate and sustainable wellbeing. This definition calls for new

---

[155] The Challenge to the South, *The Report of the South Commission* (Oxford: Oxford University Press, 1990), 10-11.

[156] UNDP, *Human Development Report 1991* (Oxford: Oxford University Press, 1991), 1.

[157] Joe Remenyi, "What is Development?"in *Key Issues in Development* (New York: Palgrave, 2004), 24.

human consciousness that makes us more sensitive to the environment, to one another, and to the future generations. Development is intimately connected to the way we relate to the environment and how we plan for future generations.

True development is characterized by directionality, continuity, cumulativeness, and irreversibility. First, as the South Commission clearly states, development is an effort of, by, and for the people. In other words, the people own the whole process. They identify their needs and interests, decide on which direction to take and enjoy the benefits of their efforts. Second, the development process makes good use of available resources, both human and capital. The environment is used sensibly in order to ensure continuity. Before the whole process begins, there is need for a feasibility study to ensure that the technology and direction to be taken are in line with the generative capacity of the available resources. This ensures sustainability of the development process. Third, development is a cumulative process. The people need to go through certain stages and acquire certain experiences from each of those stages. None of them should be jumped. Each stage should lead to the next and subsequently to the achievement and sustenance of the final goal. Fourth, the goal of development is self-confidence, sustainable livelihoods, dignity and fulfilment. Once these goals have been achieved, it should be impossible for them to be reversed. As Kwame Nkrumah used to say, "Forward ever, backward never." The society that has achieved development should no longer be exploited by others, and relapse into extreme poverty and unhappiness. Finally, development is when people are able to pursue their own interests without being selfish.

Chapter 6

Egoism and Multinational Corporations

Multinational corporations are business firms that have their operations in more than one country. Jacques Maisonrouge in a speech once said that a corporation is a business structure whose sole reason for existence is the earning of profits by manufacturing products for as little as possible and selling them for as much as possible. It does not matter whether the product does good or evil; what counts is that it be consumed— in ever-increasing quantities.[158] Their branches or subsidiaries located outside of the country of origin are connected to the headquarters. For example, Toyota Ghana is connected to the parent company in Japan. Many of these multinational corporations are often headquartered in the developed economies such as the United States of America, Japan, and Western Europe. Others are headquartered in some of the emerging economies such as South Africa, South Korea, Singapore, India, Malaysia, and China. The headquarters controls all the branches in the world. The scope of the multinational companies is as diverse as their business activities.

Multinational corporations dominate the global economy and control world trade. They control the patents on new technologies and products. In terms of goods or services, their reach into the global economy is massive and extensive. Some extract, refine and distribute most of the oil, petrol, and diesel or jet fuel used around the world. The Royal Dutch Shell Oil Company and British Petroleum Company (BP) are only a few examples. Some multinational corporations are involved in the mining of mineral resources, for example, Anglo Gold Ghana, and in running hydroelectric and nuclear power plants. Multinational corporations have control over banks and other financial institutions and also the print and electronic media. The news that most of us hear, watch or read is mediated through the lenses of those corporations. They dominate the seed-production, processing and distribution of much of the world's food. They control the automobile industry. Here, General Motors and the Japanese Corporations (Toyota and

---

[158] Richard J. Barnet and Ronald E. Müller, *Global Reach: The Power of Multinational Corporations* (New York: Simon and Schuster, 1974), 24.

Mitsubishi) come to mind. Others like Pfizer manufacture most of the world's chemicals and drugs.

The growth of these corporations has been astronomical. They have increased in number at a twinkle of an eye. In 1970 there were around 7,000 multinational corporations globally. By 1995 that number had grown to 40,000.[159] With the increase in global population and its appetite for goods and services today, one would not be wrong to state that the number of multinational corporations globally has exceeded 40,000. These corporations have strong backing of the World Trade Organization (WTO), the International Monetary Fund (IMF), and the World Bank (WB), which underwrite the basic rules and regulations of global economic, monetary, and trade relations. They also have strong support from home countries, many of which are global economic, political, and military powers.

The Power of Multinational Corporations

The men who run the global corporations are the first in history with the organization, technology, money, and ideology to make a credible attempt at managing the world as an integrated unit.[160] The managers of the world's corporate giants proclaim that where conquest has failed, business will succeed. Aurelio Peccei, a onetime director of Fiat and organizer of the Club of Rome, states that the global corporation "is the most powerful agent for the internationalization of human society." With the technology which changes man's view of space, time, and scale, in their hands, global corporations aspire to be global managers. As the president of the IBM World Trade Corporation once said, "the boundaries that separate one nation from another are no more real than the equator. They are merely convenient demarcations of ethnic, linguistic, and cultural entities... The world outside the home country is no longer viewed as series of disconnected customers and prospects for its products, but as an extension of a single market."[161]

Many of the multinational corporations operate on the same principle that countries outside their home countries are extensions of their territories

---

[159] Joshua Karliner, *The Corporate Planet: Ecology and Politics in the Age of Globalization,(* San Francisco: Sierra Club Books, 1997), 13.

[160] Joshua Karliner, *The Corporate Planet: Ecology and Politics in the Age of Globalization*, 13.

[161] Joshua Karliner, *The Corporate Planet: Ecology and Politics in the Age of Globalization*, 13.

and markets. The resources in foreign countries are also theirs. To those who question their power, corporate statesmen like to say that the sources of their extraordinary power are to be found in their power to transform the world political economy as well as the nations in which they operate. This power comes not from the barrel of a gun but from the control of the means of creating wealth on a worldwide scale. In the process of developing a new world, the managers of firms like GM, IBM, Pfizer, Shell, Exxon, etc. are making daily business decisions which have more impact than those of the most sovereign governments. They decide on where people live, what work, if any, they will do; what they will eat, drink, and wear; what sorts of knowledge schools and universities will encourage; and what kind of society their children will inherit.[162] One of the goals of managers of the multinational corporations is to profoundly transform the human organizational system of countries in a way that enables them to transcend such countries. They see themselves as philosophers in action. "How can a national government make an economic plan with any confidence if a board of directors meeting 5,000 miles away can by altering its pattern of purchasing and production affect in a major way the country's economic life?"[163]

Corporate managers have strategized, written, commissioned studies and granted interviews in many diverse ways to justify their political and economic legitimacy and to demonstrate that the maximization of global profits is compatible with human survival.[164] Whatever the justifications may be the effects of their decisions and activities will always affect the lives of the current and future generations. The corporate men look at the entire world as a market, and as a factory site; they count customers before they count population. They structure world business to satisfy the needs and demands of the world's people and thus end up controlling the global consumer. The resources of the poor nations, including the raw materials on and under their territory, cheap labour represented by their teeming populations, and the potential customers represented by their expanding middle classes are increasingly crucial to the plans of the global corporations. What the corporate manager wants to know about undeveloped countries is this: what vital raw materials do they have and how dependent is he on them?

---

[162] Joshua Karliner, *The Corporate Planet: Ecology and Politics in the Age of Globalization*, 15.

[163] Joshua Karliner, *The Corporate Planet: Ecology and Politics in the Age of Globalization*, 20-21.

[164] Joshua Karliner, *The Corporate Planet: Ecology and Politics in the Age of Globalization*, 25.

What kind of labour force do they possess, and for what wages will they work? How many customers are there (now and in the future) with money to buy his goods?[165]

Among the factors that undergird the forward ever dominance of multi-national corporations in the global political, economic, and social spheres include their control over technology, finance capital, and ideological marketing or values that determine how people live. Global corporations are the most lavish advertisers, and TV is the most powerful communications medium. The three essential structures of power in underdeveloped societies are typically in the hands of global corporations: the control of technology, the control of finance capital, and the control of marketing and the dissemination of ideas.[166] With these sources of power firm in their grips, multi-national corporations control some of the states. African countries such as Kenya, Ghana, Zambia, and Ivory Coast can be cited as some examples. In such a situation, one wonders to what extent, in practical terms, are these countries sovereign!

The Multinational Corporations and Advertisement

Multinational corporations determine most of what people in poor countries see on the television or movie screen, hear on the radio, or read in magazines. They play a role in shaping values, tastes, and attitudes. Through TV, movie-house commercials, comic books, and magazine adverts, foreign corporations unquestionably exert more continuing influence on the minds of many people. TV has a socializing influence on all age groups especially in the developing countries. Global marketeers are not persuaded that there is anything wrong with spreading the thrill of consumption in poor countries. "The factory girl or the sales girl in Lima or Bombay (or the Harlem ghetto)," says Peter Drucker, "wants a lipstick…There is no purchase that gives her as much true value for a few cents." The fact that she is in all probability malnourished and without a decent place to live does not mean that she is spending foolishly. Altert Stridsberg, an "international advertising specialist" writing in *Advertising Age*, says that we must rid ourselves of "the conventional range of ideas about who will minister to the poor man's physical needs. The psychological significance of spending his money on a transistor radio may be more important than the physical benefit generated

---

[165] Joshua Karliner, *The Corporate Planet: Ecology and Politics in the Age of Globalization*, 125.

[166] Joshua Karliner, *The Corporate Planet: Ecology and Politics in the Age of Globalization*, 146.

by spending the same money for basic foodstuffs."[167] Creating and satisfying wants such as lipsticks and transistor radios while the basic necessities of life recede ever further perpetuates and compounds mass misery in poor countries. The global corporations have power to determine what does or does not give "psychological satisfaction".[168]

Similarly, the companies' control of ideology through advertising has helped to change the dietary habits of the poor in unfortunate ways. Beginning in 1966, the major global food companies had begun research on low-cost protein foods, baby cereals, soft drinks, imitation milk, candies, snacks, soups, and noodles, and by 1968 a dozen such products were on the market. "The food industry in developing countries has been a disaster... a minus influence," says Derrick B. Jelliffe, a leading nutrition expert. Companies are using advertising to take what Berg calls "blatant advantage of nutrition consciousness." J.K. Roy's studies in West Bengal show that poor families under the influence of advertising are buying patent baby foods "at exorbitant rates" although they could buy local cow's milk at much lower cost. They had been persuaded (falsely) that the packaged food had "extraordinary food value".[169] Since people in Africa are attracted to imported goods, local manufacturers label their products with trademarks that sound American, European, or Chinese. People believe adverts to the extent that they stop reasoning.

Global companies have used their great levers of power— finance capital, technology, organizational skills, and mass communications— to create a Global Shopping Centre in which the hungry of the world are invited to buy expensive snack. The World Manager's vision of One World turns out in fact to be two distinct worlds— one featuring rising affluence for a small transnational middle class, and the other escalating misery for the great bulk of the human family. The central strategy of the global corporation is the creation of a global economic environment that will ensure stability, expansion, and high profits for the planetary enterprise. The implementation of that strategy depends upon the control of the three basic components of corporate power: finance capital, technology, and marketplace ideology.

---

[167] Joshua Karliner, *The Corporate Planet: Ecology and Politics in the Age of Globalization*, 177.

[168] Joshua Karliner, *The Corporate Planet: Ecology and Politics in the Age of Globalization*, 177.

[169] Joshua Karliner, *The Corporate Planet: Ecology and Politics in the Age of Globalization*, 183.

Experience has shown that the global corporation has over the years used these components of power to promote its growth and profitability.[170]

Knowledge is Power, Ignorance is Impotence

The ability to manipulate, grab, and control much of the environmental resources directly determines how economically, politically, and technologically strong each of the players becomes. The question of the location of environmental resources is secondary in this context. There may be wells of oil of commercial quantities sitting in Nigeria, Chad, and Angola, tons of gold in Ghana, and tons of diamond in Botswana, and tons of silicon in the Democratic Republic of Congo but in reality, do these countries own their resources? The UN resolution of 1962 may state that by virtue of being sovereign states, they have control over these resources but in reality that is not the case since they do not have the necessary expertise and technology to utilize these resources. They will have to need the multinational corporations that trade in these different resources. This is where the power of knowledge and its accompanying consequences of corruption, arrogance, and insensitivity make inroads into issues relating to the environment. The questions of how these resources should be exploited, by who, for whose benefit and at what proportion therefore become pertinent. These are usually difficult questions and fair answers to them are hard to come by; the answers are girded by the spirit of the winner takes it all. So long as the benefits get to the winner, the loser can go to hell. That is why finding concrete solutions to environmental issues is as difficult as getting a live cat on its back. The few beneficiaries are ready to logically defend their selfishness. The question is therefore one of individual good versus the common good. It is a question of injustice and insensitivity, which is clearly portrayed in the politics of environmental issues.

A country may have oil wells or hydrocarbon fields, huge deposits of gold or diamond, vast stretches of forest land, fertile land and good climatic conditions, pools of freshwater, and human resources ready to explore these resources and yet be on the brink of starvation if it lacks the necessary expertise to explore its natural resources and create wealth out of them. This lack is the painful situation of Africa. Knowledge as we are using it means more than possessing academic certificates. If that is the case, Nigeria alone has enough to drive Africa forward. It means more than rhetoric because if

---

[170] Joshua Karliner, *The Corporate Planet: Ecology and Politics in the Age of Globalization*, 152.

116

that is the case, Africa has had more than enough conferences and workshops where participants spoke grandiose grammar yet nothing came out of them. They were often cosmetic, designed for good press and TV sound bites, and for the selfish interests and participants and multinational corporations. Knowledge also means more than just the ability to operate imported machines. If that is the case, we have more than enough in Africa; the continent has become a dumping ground for anything and Africans always look forward to consume whatever is dumped. The basic industries in many African countries are largely in the hands of foreigners. The warehouses, malls, and the streets are flooded with imported goods such as cameras, TVs, tape recorders, furniture from South Korea, China, Europe and America. Many African countries continue to have weak government institutions such as taxation, labour unions, judiciary, and legislature because of either lack of critical and creative knowledge or because of selfishness.

Africa needs sapiential techniques of socioeconomic and social organization, and instrumental reason that allow things to work and work sustainably. Sapiential knowledge encompasses creative, meritocratic, and selfless approach to organization of socioeconomic, legal, and educational institutions of a country. Education that is organized sapientially does not merely prepare graduates for multinational corporations. Rather, it prepares critical and creative citizens to help organize and serve their countries faithfully in whatever government or non-governmental institution they find themselves. Selfishness is an unwelcome guest while meritocracy is a highly cherished value. It is lack of sapiential techniques of organization in many African countries that gives multinational corporations high bargaining power. Apart from being able to use instrumental reason and technology to create, communicate, and market a set of values to Africa for their selfish ends, these corporations also take advantage of lack of proper organization in African countries. These corporations have played a key role in keeping the dependent role of Africa. Africa sees its development efforts in terms of how it conforms to the dictates of the multinational corporations. The multinational corporations and their parent countries continue to set the terms not because they possess the natural resources but because they are superior in terms of the knowledge needed to create wealth out of such resources. The most painful yet real fact is the fatalism that surrounds many African countries in terms of economics. These countries have already made the decision to emulate the economies of the developed countries through a similar process of industrialization, and therefore dependency on outside technology, finance capital, and marketing techniques, especially the diffusion of the ideology of the consuming society is built into their model of development.[171] All these work to the selfish interest of the MCs and developed countries. It is in the interest of the developed countries that the developing countries become more and more mere consumer consumers of their goods and services.

The multinational companies therefore wield unwavering economic, political and communicative knowledge or power especially in countries that are in dire need of investors. All over the world, these companies are some of the most powerful, technologically advanced and richest conglomerates. They have strong bargaining power and do influence public policies considerably to their favour. They become so invincible when they transact business with weak governments. They therefore produce, advertise, and sell their goods, exploit their local employees, manipulate governments, and pollute the environment as freely as they want. In their helplessness, many governments in the developing world especially in Africa form unholy alliances with the multinational corporations.

Unholy Alliances between African Governments and Multinational Corporations

In its simplest terms, unholy alliances between governments and multinational corporations means cooperation, agreements or memoranda of understanding whose outcomes do not benefit the average person the governments represent. The agreements between African governments and multinational corporations do not necessarily intend to achieve the common good, the good of all people exemplified in fair sharing and participation. Rather, the alliances are for the good of the individuals in government and the owners of the multinational companies. These individuals ardently believe in their welfare and that of their families but they are insensitive to the growing plight of others. For instance, selfish government officials sell national resources to foreign investors (multi-national corporations) at throw-away prices as long as they put something in their pockets. They do not care about the kind of goods that will be produced by the new industry and whether those goods will be produced for the local market or will be exported. The new industry may pollute the environment without the government officials getting concerned. Even if the economy is a labour-

---

[171] Joshua Karliner, *The Corporate Planet: Ecology and Politics in the Age of Globalization*, 140.

intensive one, the government officials do not hesitate to permit capital-intensive investors because they do not care about the creation of jobs for the unemployed citizens. Sometimes governments grant long tax holidays to foreign investors at the detriment of the domestic infant industries. Ghana is a case in point. The unholy alliance between multinational corporations and local governments makes it easy for the former to avoid or evade taxes.

Governments may occasionally undertake transactions for the sake of the citizens but because they lack the necessary technological, political, and economic expertise to command strong bargaining power, they become more of beggars than equal negotiators. The multinational corporations are so strong that they dictate to the weak governments what should be produced, how it should be produced, and for whom it should be produced. What matters is the profit-motive of the multinational corporation but not how the citizens of the host country will benefit from the production. This is an existential reality in countries such as Nigeria, Angola, Ghana and the Democratic Republic of Congo, which are well endowed with natural resources.

A Case Study of the Multinational Oil Corporations in Nigeria

Nigeria, one of the world's largest oil producers, has earned over 350 billion USD from oil exports since it began production in Oloibiri over 50 years ago. Lately gas has joined the oil and these God-given resources provide the bulk of funding for all tiers of government. Yet, with all the revenues derived from petroleum activities, living standards have plummeted to unacceptable and appalling levels so much so that well over 70% of the population lives on less than a dollar a day.[172] How come the huge wealth derived from these God-given resources has failed to foster economic development and has in effect led to a deterioration of the rest of the Nigerian economy and by implication, the lives of Nigerian people? How come these resources have not been harnessed to create long term sustainable development? To what extent have the activities in the oil and gas sector been open, transparent and accountable? What has been responsible for the enthronement of the popularly known "resource curse" on a nation so abundantly blessed by God? Why is it that petroleum activities have

---

[172] The Justice Development and Peace Commission of the Catholic Bishops Conference of Nigeria, *Nigeria: The Travesty of Oil and Gas Wealth* (Lagos: Catholic Secretariat of Nigeria, 2006), 1.

brought so much destruction and devastation to the environment and has so far remained largely unchecked? Why is it that there are many conflicts in circumstances associated with the exploration of petroleum resources? Are there legal, regulatory policy changes that need to be put in place or faithfully implemented where they exist to promote the efficient management and fair allocation of oil and gas revenues in a manner that serves the common good? Why is there so much misery amidst plenty?[173] These questions are genuine and applicable to many African countries that are endowed with precious natural resources. The questions point to the problem of resource exploration and equitable distribution of the derived benefits for a sustained national development. They show the inverse relationship that human persons have volitionally created between God's given gifts and their use. Instead of riches amidst plenty, it is rather poverty amidst plenty.

In Nigeria where crude oil is the mainstay of the economy, what the multinational oil companies do significantly determines the fortunes and misfortunes of the country in very many ways.[174] First, the abundance of oil in the economy has turned the country into an insatiable rent-seeking entity and a money spinning machine. Everyone who has the necessary strong muscles seeks to maximize profits from oil exploration at all costs. With the federal government as the principal keeper for oil revenues, the centre has necessarily become the main target of an intensive zero-sum game between and among various factions and fractions of the ruling classes, military and civilian alike. It is a winner takes all syndrome. Secondly, oil revenue has led to the creation of an elaborate and largely informal part of those in charge of political power. This concentration of power in the hands of a few elites who circulate around the corridors of power almost without an end nurtures political corruption and the excessive abuse of power. Thirdly, being a classical oil rent economy, economic development is closely tied to maintaining and increasing oil earnings.[175]

As the principal goose laying the golden egg, multinational oil companies are in a particularly vantage position to enjoy a close symbiotic and working

---

[173] The Justice Development and Peace Commission of the Catholic Bishops Conference of Nigeria, *Nigeria: The Travesty of Oil and Gas Wealth*, 2.

[174] The Justice Development and Peace Commission of the Catholic Bishops Conference of Nigeria, *Nigeria: The Travesty of Oil and Gas Wealth*, 25.

[175] The Justice Development and Peace Commission of the Catholic Bishops Conference of Nigeria, *Nigeria: The Travesty of Oil and Gas Wealth*, 25.

relationship with the government. This sometimes "unholy" alliance operates at official and unofficial levels, but it boils down to essentially the same thing in terms of their multiplier effects of fostering a mutually rewarding political and economic relationship between the State and multinational oil companies to the exclusion of oil communities. In many instances, however, this alliance has benefited multinational oil companies more than the government. It should be recalled, for instance, that during the sad and inglorious days of military rule in Nigeria, multinational oil companies were among the few openly flaunting their preference for such "stable" regimes instead of an unstable democracy.[176] Eventually, this relationship is at the root of the chronic violence which followed the allegations by minority oil communities against political alienation and domination, socio-economic marginalization and exclusion, and the massive despoliation of their environment by multinational oil companies.

Down the years especially after 1971, the government of Nigeria steadily increased its participation and regulation of the oil industry, transforming its role from being a mere collector of oil taxes and royalties to that of active participation in the oil industry. In order to gain leverage with multinational oil companies, in 1971 the government transferred rent and royalties from off-shore petroleum mines from the various states concerned to the federal government. By April 1977, the Nigerian National Oil Corporation and the Ministry of Petroleum Resource gave way to the formation of Nigerian National Petroleum Corporation (NNPC), which became the sole government agency for controlling and regulating the oil industry. The re-organization of 1988 again transformed NNPC into a fully commercial conglomerate with 12 strategic business units covering exploration and production, gas development, refining, distribution, petrochemical engineering and commercial investment. The Department of Petroleum Resources (DPR) was also created to further ensure effective regulation of the oil industry, enforce compliance with industry regulations, process applications for licenses, and to enforce environmental regulations by multinational and indigenous oil companies.

At a glance, these measures seem to point to the governments' ingenuity in setting up buffer nets against manipulation and exploitation by

---

[176] The Justice Development and Peace Commission of the Catholic Bishops Conference of Nigeria, *Nigeria: The Travesty of Oil and Gas Wealth*, 25.

multinational oil companies. One easily gets the impression that these were adequate regulatory and enforcement measures. But the existential experiences show that governments failed time and again to effectively control the affairs. More than fifty years down in the history of oil discovery in Nigeria, no government including the current one, can genuinely claim to have gained sufficient knowledge of the operations of the industry, not to speak of controlling it. Multinational companies continue to wield and enjoy a lot of economic and political leverage. In spite of the quest for control, government can neither challenge nor gain leverage over the technical capabilities of multinational oil companies. The oil companies continue to fine tune their domination of the sector.[177] The over-reliance on multinational oil companies to produce oil seriously undermines the ability of government to exercise effective control on the industry. It is this lack of technical knowledge and skills about how the oil industry operates that translates into the complex romance between it and multinational oil companies. Since government is still unable to impose a water-tight oversight and technical control over the oil industry, it is understandable that much of its relationship with oil companies should be shrouded in secrecy or conducted with enlightened ignorance.[178]

Of course, the high-profile status of multinational oil companies makes some of what they do, even in their direct line of business, to have political ramifications. The very nature of the oil business in Nigeria means that multinational oil companies sometimes act or are seen as quasi-government rather than being accountable corporations. One of the major attractions of oil revenue is the canalization of political power in such a manner that brings huge advantages and opportunities to those in power, and to generate hostility from those excluded from it. As state officials monopolize oil policy and revenue to the exclusion of others, frequent disquiet and frictions become predictable and indeed inevitable. These companies concentrate power and wealth in the hands of a tiny political, business and technocratic elite. The behind-the-scenes activities of multinational oil companies impinge

---

[177] The Justice Development and Peace Commission of the Catholic Bishops Conference of Nigeria, *Nigeria: The Travesty of Oil and Gas Wealth*, 26.

[178] The Justice Development and Peace Commission of the Catholic Bishops Conference of Nigeria, *Nigeria: The Travesty of Oil and Gas Wealth*, 27.

quite frequently on political issues, including cases of human rights abuses and environmental degradation.

Of concern is the disposition of multinational oil companies towards the pursuit of selfish-interests by cultivating intimate social, administrative, economic and political relationships with political, military and business elites. On the surface, such bonds of friendship with influential people in society seem to be normal. But closer, those bonds have proved useful only as premium insurance for the perpetuation of their interests. They service the parochial interests of oil companies (and interest parties) to the neglect of the citizens who are now assertively insisting on having their ways and a greater share of oil revenue. Greedy government officials grant the oil multinationals the latitude to feign ignorance and deflect allegations of negative social, economic, environmental, cultural and political impact of their operations on host communities. With the gusto of arrogance and contempt displayed towards host communities and the nation, the multinational oil companies in the country have clearly internalized the belief that they are above the law.[179]

The main problem in this alliance is greed or selfishness on the level of government, local elite and the multinational corporations. The consequences of this well layered and multidimensional selfishness on the local community have equally been multilayered and complex. At one level, the selfishness and insensitivity of the government, multinational corporations and local elites has deprived the local community of its basic needs such as food, and water. The methods of exploration have polluted potable waters; destroyed the fertility of the soil, the forest and other biota. The environment becomes generally degraded and the people suffer all forms of effects that go with that. At another level, the community suffers social, political, and economic divisions. The local elites have a comprehensive knowledge of the community. When they connive with the government or the multinational corporations, they know where to sow seed of division among the local citizenry. Once that is done, they are able to utilize the situation to their benefit. That is why in some of the oil rich communities, the intra divisions are as rife as that of community versus government or multinational corporations. But irrespective of what level the consequences of selfishness occur, the general consequence is that the masses are made to be entrapped in the vicious cycle of poverty, exploitation, oppression and

---

[179] The Justice Development and Peace Commission of the Catholic Bishops Conference of Nigeria, *Nigeria: The Travesty of Oil and Gas Wealth*, 29.

pain. This vicious cycle stretches the people to the inelastic point, the point at which they have only one option: to resist the oppressor, sometimes in a very unpleasant way through the gun and kidnapping. Under their watchful eye, they see God-given blessing that is meant for their fulfillment turn into a curse with pain and frustration as its sequel. This has been the reality in Nigeria for many years. How about other countries such as Ghana that have just discovered hydrocarbons? Where are they heading to? Will Ghana's story be different from Nigeria's story? In other words, will Ghana repeat the same mistakes or learn from those mistakes and make a difference?

Ghana, Discovery of Oil and Multinational Corporations

Ghana is not a newcomer in the equation of multinational corporations and extraction of natural resources. It was once called the Gold Coast because of its rich deposits of gold. For many years, its foreign exchange has largely come from Gold mines and cocoa plantations. Over the years, different governments, mining communities, mining companies, human rights activists, and environmentalists engage in unending tussles over what could be the most beneficial, just, and environmentally friendly ways of mining and sharing the benefits of the mineral resources in the country.

Ghana discovered offshore oil fields of commercial quantities in 2007. This expands the scope of the country's experiences with multinational gold mining companies to oil extraction companies. The first oil field to be discovered is called Jubilee Field, which is estimated to have 1.5billion- barrel oil capacity. Another oil field called Owo-Tweneboa was discovered by the UK's Tullow Oil PLC in September 2010. The field is said to have 1.4 billion-barrel oil capacity.[180] The discovery of crude oil has brought smiles to the faces of Ghanaians and their well-wishers. It has blown a wind of hope across the country. Ghanaians have largely considered the oil discovery as good news laden with hope for a better Ghana. This is particularly so considering the fact that the discovery has come at a time when the country enjoys reasonable political and economic stability. On one hand, many citizens hope that the oil revenues will be shared equitably. However, on the other hand, some Ghanaians have not forgotten how the revenues from gold mining found their way to the pockets of the multinational corporations,

---

[180]Ghana   News Agency:http://www.ghanaweb.com/GhanaHomePage/NewsArchive/artikel.php?ID=1994 75 (access date:14th December 2010)

government officials, and the local elites/tycoons. Although, the oil was discovered exactly at the time when Ghana turned fifty as a sovereign state, there is no guarantee that government officials can no longer be selfish or that the selfishness of multinational corporations can no longer render the government of Ghana powerless to use the proceeds of the oil to the full benefit of all.

The international law concept of sovereignty clothes states with an immense amount of independence and control over their territorial jurisdictions and whatever falls within them, including any natural resources found within the geographically defined territory of the sovereign state. The exercise of sovereignty over natural resources would ordinarily be expected to translate into vast wealth to a state upon the discovery of a resource within its sovereign jurisdiction. However, this is not always the case. The reality is that there are many states that do not possess adequate capital, technology and know-how to tap into these resources and generate income in a self-sufficient way and Ghana is one of these. This calls for partnership between Ghana and strategic foreign investors; an interdependence which is fraught with many tensions over the long term duration of these relationships.[181]

The recent peaceful political and economic ambience and the proximity of the oil fields to Europe and United States of America have won investor confidence, attracted many investors and created a fierce competition among them over the oil fields. The 1.5 billion-barrel Jubilee field has for instance drawn interest from Western and Chinese multinational oil corporations. At least $4 billion has been invested in the offshore field by various partners. The field is operated by the U.K's Tullow Oil PLC, which has a 34.7% stake, Dallas-based Kosmos Energy LLC, which is backed by private-equity firms Blackstone Group LP and Warburg Pincus LLC. Another operator is Houston-based Anadarko Petroleum Corp, which owns 23.49% apiece. The State-run Ghana National Petroleum Corporation is the other major shareholder with 13.75%.[182] The partnership has placed the government and investors at opposite ends of this swinging pendulum called "bargaining

---

[181] Nana Adjoa Hackman, *Ghana's Oil Policy Debate: Stabilization Clauses and the Freedom of Parliament to impose new Taxes or Royalty*, http://opinion.myjoyonline.com/pages/feature/200912/39405.php (Accessed: 13th October 2011).

[182] Ghana News Agency (24th December 2010)

power". Depending on whose side it swings, that party determines which way things should go.

Who is Who on the Swinging Pendulum of Bargaining Power?

The whole idea is about who gets a better share of the benefits of the oil that is discovered in Ghana. Is it Ghana or the multinational oil corporations? It is a question of power interests. International law provides each party with tools that will enable them to balance their interests. It provides the government with the concept of sovereignty, and stabilization clauses to the multinational oil companies. The question however is, can Ghana ensure that the stabilisation clauses in oil contracts strike a proper balance between investor interest and national interest?

State Sovereignty versus Stabilization Clause

By a UN General Assembly Resolution in 1962, the principle of permanent sovereignty of states over natural resource wealth within their territorial jurisdiction was recognised and strengthened. Under this principle, "the right of peoples and nations to permanent sovereignty over their natural wealth and resources must be exercised in the interest of their national development and of the well-being of the people of the state concerned."[183] All activities regarding the exploration, extraction and sale of the natural resources are to be done according to the national laws of the sovereign state. Section 4 of the UN resolution allows for nationalisation, expropriation or requisitioning by a state, provided that it is done for "reasons of public utility, security or the national interest" and "appropriate compensation" is paid. Section 8, further highlights the limitation on sovereignty by placing a responsibility for foreign investment agreements entered into by or between sovereign states to be observed in good faith. By a subsequent resolution dated 26th July, 1974, the UN General Assembly reaffirmed the above provisos.

The principle of permanent sovereignty grants sovereign states significant control in the management of these resources. It serves as a good basis for governments to negotiate a higher take in petroleum agreements to satisfy the nationalistic sentiments that the ownership of natural resources breeds in the citizens of a country. Owing to the usually long duration of petroleum agreements, some lasting on an average between 20 to 30 years, the

---

[183] http://www2.ohchr.org/english/law/resources.htm (Accessed: 17th June, 2010).

126

temptation for the host nation to make changes to the original agreement governing petroleum operations is great. Such changes are usually very likely upon the discovery of petroleum when the previously strong position of the International Oil Companies begins to diminish and there is an immediate shift in bargaining power in favour of the host country. This is known as the concept of "obsolescing bargain".[184] Governments may also seek a renegotiation in times of rising oil prices, when they feel that the economic projections upon which they negotiated and signed the agreement initially have changed. Governments may feel and indeed may be under pressure from their citizens to obtain greater share of the profits being generated. The government of Ghana is already feeling this heat from the populace. Again, governments may be influenced by emerging concepts around the world such as the imposition of taxes on obnoxious environmental practices, taxes to finance modern health and safety measures, the provision of security, and as compensation for local communities among others, to change the fiscal regime of the agreement.

There are a variety of actions that host governments may take to alter the existing arrangements. The government may pass new laws and regulations that indirectly have negative effects on the performance of the agreement by varying the existing legal and economic environment. In recent times, this has been termed "creeping expropriation".[185] The host state's action may also be direct in the form of increments in tax and royalty rates, imposition of new taxes and royalties, increasing the percentage of participation of the State Owned Companies, as well as imposing restrictions on the International Oil Company's (IOC) right to export or to repatriate its profits. All these are meant to enable the government meet national interests as far as benefits from the oil are concerned.

However, the multinational oil companies also have a stabilizing clause that counteracts or neutralizes the actions of the government. The use of stabilization clauses is a direct response to unilateral actions of host governments that altered the positions of foreign companies under previously concluded long term investment agreements. Investors rely on stabilization clauses to ensure relative stability of the main investment conditions needed for the successful performance of their investment ventures. For the foreign investors and their bankers, stabilization has to do

[184] Hackman, *Ghana's Oil Policy Debate: Stabilization Clauses*

[185] Hackman, *Ghana's Oil Policy Debate: Stabilization Clauses*

with, among other things, the stability of the fiscal regime to ensure investment recovery, security of tenure over property and title, the ability to sell, the ability to retain and repatriate foreign exchange earned and the ability to operate the project under reasonably foreseeable conditions.[186] Foreign Investors would also be concerned about non-financial matters like changes in labour and environmental law or changes in the interpretation of the existing law to the extent that it affects their interests adversely.

The 'Freezing' Clause is the traditional form of stabilization clause. What this clause did was to state specifically that the governing law of the contract was the law of the host state at the time of the execution of the contract. By so doing, the clause sought to 'freeze' the parties' rights and obligations agreed in the contract such that subsequent changes to the law of the host state would not be applicable to the particular contract for the duration of its term. In practice it is rare especially in recent times for host governments to agree to an absolute 'freezing' of contract terms which permanently protects the parties' rights and obligations agreed in the contract. More moderate forms of the clause can be found in petroleum contracts in Angola, Iraq, Malta, Cambodia, Kazakhstan, Poland, Tunisia and Ghana.[187]

From the above presentation, we can say that the checks and balances that the concepts of sovereignty and the stabilization clause seek to achieve are in themselves very good and have the tendency to protect the interests of all parties. However, in reality, this does not seem to be the case. Outside of these tools there are other realities that form part of the bargaining equation. These include expertise and finance capital.

Developing countries like Ghana usually agree to the use of stabilization clauses in petroleum contracts because of their perceived low bargaining power at the time of entering into these agreements. Ghana is so desperate to attract International Oil Companies (IOCs) with the needed investment and expertise to conduct exploration and production. This already puts the fifty-year old plus sovereign state at a disadvantaged position. The government of Ghana has no choice but to agree to many of the conditions that are set by these investors including the insertion of stabilization clauses. Where the country's level of proven reserves is low, like Ghana's was until recently, its bargaining power is even lower and there is increased pressure to accept

---

[186] Hackman, *Ghana's Oil Policy Debate: Stabilization Clauses*
[187] Hackman, *Ghana's Oil Policy Debate: Stabilization Clauses*

terms from IOCs that they would otherwise not accept, given a stronger bargaining position. The IOCs do not command the same power when they deal with developed countries such as Canada, United States of America or Germany over resource exploration and production. In fact, they do not have room to insert stabilization clauses no matter how mild or moderate they are. The developed countries have the expertise, finance capital and so the IOCs have nothing unique upon which they can stand to dictate. Unfortunately for developing countries such as Ghana, lack of expertise, finance capital and market makes them weak before the IOCs and thus they often succumb to the dictates of the IOCs.

Of course, one can argue that since there is a fierce competition among IOCs for the hydrocarbons in Ghana that should increase the government's bargaining power. This argument is cogent because a competition for an economic good often gives the owner of the resource a better bargaining power. It also ensures efficiency and effectiveness on the part of the company that gets the contract. But we should not forget that what drives the competition is the selfishness of each company. The multinational oil companies and other parties crave for their share in the hydrocarbons because they want to achieve their selfish interests. No company will hesitate pulling out if it becomes clear that they will not achieve their interest eventually. So there may be competition but what inspires the competition is greed. In that case, the company that wins the contract still will not compromise this primary goal of achieving its interest such as maximization of profit. Consequently, with the IOCs' absolute control over the technology, market, and finance capital, it is and will continue to be an uphill task for the government of Ghana to wield any reasonable bargaining power over the multinational corporations. The task of reaping fair benefits from the oil is going to be even more difficult for average Ghanaians. This is because there are some government officials and local elites who are and will always be ready to connive with the multinational oil companies for the sake of their selfish interests.

Before pumping its initial consignment on Wednesday, the 15th of December 2010 and coming online as Africa's newest oil producer, Ghana government, oil companies, and the oil communities had already been involved in what one can call the 'sorting out' processes. The aim is for each party to get its fair share of the proceeds. All the arguments that ensued during the sorting out processes centre on the question of interests. Every party guises itself in the rhetoric of equitable sharing of the benefits from the oil but in actual fact, each party thinks of how to claim a disproportionate share of the benefits. Reinhold Niebuhr reminds us that in some sense the assertion of a final identity of the particular with the common interest is correct, but it is never perfectly realized in a concrete situation. It is correct as an abstract ideal of reason, but the actual state of social and economic affairs is dominated by the image of conflicting interests, of repression, and rebellion. This is because it is so difficult in the midst of conflicting interests to tell what precisely the requirements of justice are and, consequently, where the point of coincidence of the common interest with the true interest of the individual is located. The difficulty is in balancing in concrete situations the individual and the common good, cooperation and competition.[188]

The situation is often one of competition where different parties crave for their selfish interests. These interests can take the form of dirty capital flights through different unethical channels into private individual pockets. It can be through corruption of public officials, criminal, and commercial activities. Charles Abugre insists, for instance, that dirty or illicit money takes 3 main forms out of a nation's coffers: bribery and corruption of public officials, criminal (drugs, counterfeit, theft of minerals, terrorism financing, other forms of organized criminal activities etc.) and commercial.[189] It is estimated that the proportion of global dirty money flows that can be attributed to bribery and corruption is a mere 3%. The second largest component, criminal activities constitute between 30-35%. The rest (60%+) are the result of commercial activities – largely international/multinational companies using different means to evade and avoid tax by concealing and moving profits abroad.[190]

Niebuhr's emphasis on the complexity of balancing must be given its due appreciation. In some societies where governments, the average citizen and multinational corporations each command reasonable knowledge and power in economic matters, things turn to be a bit more balanced. But in countries like Ghana where the average Ghanaian has little or no knowledge about how the country's resources are explored and used, it becomes easy for their interests to be ignored by the other stakeholders. Actually, the citizens are

---

[188] Wolfhart Pannenberg, *Human Nature, Election, and History* (Philadelphia: The Westminster Press, 1977), 20.

[189] From a discussion with Abugre.

[190] Raymond Baker: Global Financial Integrity Project. www.gfip.org (Accessed: 14th February 2011).

not even consulted on how their resources need to be used; they do not go to the negotiation table. They are therefore left at the mercy of the government and the IOCs.

But, even if the government genuinely wants to serve the interests of its citizens, it finds itself also handicapped. This is because the journey from the discovery of oil up to the time it impacts positively on the people of that nation is a difficult and a complicated one. Oil discovery or exploration, its exploitation and marketing require expertise, technology, and proper communication to avert it from turning into a curse. The multinational corporations own this expertise and that scores them more than half of the bargaining power even before all the other parties say a word.

Since the discovery of the oil, the government of Ghana has worked tirelessly to strategize, plan and put certain modalities in place to help it reap the benefits of this God-given gift. But the truth is that the government has been unable to put in place adequate regulatory and exploratory measures because it lacks the expertise comparable to that of the multinational corporations. The painful thing is that it may never achieve these requirements in many years to come. Even if that happens, the problem of exploitation may simply shift hands from multinational corporations to selfish and corrupt government officials and local business elites. So, well aware as government of Ghana and its citizens may be of the exploitative spirit of the multinational corporations, at least based on the experiences of countries such as Nigeria and Angola, they remain to some extent at the mercy of the multinational corporations. The manner in which multinational corporations lord it over the government is majorly based on the weakness of the government. The weakness can be moral such as corruption, greed, selfishness or it can be technical incapability such as lack of technology and financial capital. While states may want to guard firmly their sovereign rights over natural resources, contractual stabilization clauses continue to be relied on by foreign investors as a tool for ensuring the stability of long term investment contracts.

On paper, it is quite relieving to understand that all these measures including international laws and national laws are in place to protect the economic, social, and environmental safety interests of sovereign states. In the case of Ghana, it feels even better to realize that the country's constitution gives Parliament the freedom to introduce new levies on the operations of foreign investors when the need arises. Nevertheless, these measures do not give ordinary Ghanaians, directly or indirectly, a sufficient guarantee of their social, economic, and environmental safety. This is because many parliamentarians are not in the parliament for the sake of their constituencies but for their own interests. This can be extended to many of the politicians who are supposed to make decisions for the sake of the common good but they do not. This can even extend further to heads of government departments. What has been the experience of many Africans is their leaders' compromise of the common good in favour of their individual interests. How many politicians have the courage to say 'no' to a selfish multinational company as long as it promises them a handshake? The phenomenon of unholy alliances among politicians, the local business elites and multinational corporations remains a painful reality. Engrained in their hearts are desires to perpetuate inequalities and misery but with their lips they deceive the masses with copious enticing vocabulary of love, sacrifice, selfless service, and care. Beneath the veneer of the unholy alliances is a storm of dissatisfaction and frustration. The victims feel overstretched and so they explode, if not now, later. They thus tell themselves that they have to wake up lest they are crushed under the wheels of greedy political elites and insensitive MCs.

Certainly, one might say that it is too early in Ghana to point accusing fingers because the country has just started exporting oil. That is a fact one cannot justifiably refuse but as mentioned earlier, Ghana has dealt with MCs on mineral exploration for years. The experiences of Ghanaians that stem from such relational dynamics convince them especially the poor masses that nothing better will come from the politicians as far as the benefits of the oil are concerned.

The poor masses are usually vulnerable to the devastating consequences of the sins of politicians and multinational companies. The victims often lack safety nets and sometimes bear irreversible effects of the actions of the politicians and multinational corporations who often claim that they are environmentally sensitive. The deplorable environmental and economic situations in mining towns in Ghana remain a known fact of the failure of MCs and politicians. If we are to cite some few examples outside of Ghana, the1984 Bhopal tragedy in India, the 1986 nuclear plant steam explosion at Chernobyl in the former Soviet Union, and most recently the Gulf of Mexico Oil leak come to mind. After twenty six years of leak of the methyl isocyanate (MIC) gas from the Union Carbide India Limited plant in Bhopal, many residents of Madhya Pradesh region still mourn the death of thousands upon thousands of their relatives. Probably the most painful experience for them is the constant reminder of this disaster by the permanent and partial disabilities that many survivors are bearing. As David Weir rightly states the chronic poisoning from industrial pollution has caused irreversible pain, suffering, and death.[191] The same can be said of the then Soviet Union incident several years ago. This disaster spread harmful radiation to thousands of people.[192] How about the Gulf of Mexico disaster? Can BP adequately clean up this mess? Can it revive the eleven people who died following the explosion? How about the many flora and fauna that died in the process? It is a fallacy to think that after destroying the physical environment and human lives we can clean up the mess later. Yet as long as Ghana government remains weak technologically and morally, it cannot escape this devastating philosophy of the MCs which is deeply rooted in human egoism.

---

[191]David Weir, *The Bhopal Syndrome: Pesticides, Environment, And Health* (San Francesco: Sierra Club Books, 1987), 11-12.

[192] Louis P. Pojman, ed. *Environmental Ethics: Readings in Theory and Application* (Boston: Jones and Bartlet Publishers, 1994), 1.

Chapter 7

Egoism and the Environment

According to the Random House Dictionary, environment is the aggregate of surrounding things, conditions, or influences. The roots of the term lay in the French word *environ*, which means "to surround", "to envelop", or "to enclose".[193] Cognate term is "milieu", which means the same as environment but D. Cooper nuances that environment as milieu is not something a creature is merely *in*, but something it *has*.[194] Cooper's interpretation suggests that the environment is an active and possessed context within which something exists. An environment becomes part of what a creature is so that we cannot adequately identify a creature without its environment. It is the creature's extended-self. In this book, environment is understood as an active milieu within which living and non-living creatures exist. Each creature possesses the other in a mutual relationship. The environment is a system in which each component affects and is affected by the others. The system is so interconnected that whatever happens even to the minutest of the components affects the rest. It is just like the human body. If one part is affected, as St. Paul says in 1Cor 12:14-26, the whole body is affected. For example, if a person gets a cut at the tip of his finger, the reflex action is felt immediately by the whole body. Similarly, when a person has a stomach pain, he cannot go to play soccer even if his legs are in a good condition.

However, in some, especially Western civilizations, the environment simply means the physical nonhuman surroundings, which include biotic (forests, animals, birds, insects) and abiotic (rivers, waters, soil, minerals, hydrocarbons, and climatic factors such as temperature, humidity, and rainfall). In other cultures, the environment includes physical and the metaphysical things such as spirits. In African ontology for instance, the living dead, the spirits, the ancestors, and the unborn are all part of the environment. In short, without some specified thing to refer or relate to, say a species such as humans, or a culture or a place, the term environment can mean everything that surrounds everything that exists. Environment

---

[193] John Barry, *Environment and Social Theory* (London: Routledge, 1999), 12.

[194] D. Cooper, ed., *The Environment in Question: Ethics and Global Issues* (London: Routledge, 1992), 169.

understood as such is vague and needs clarification. In common usage, environment is synonymous with the "natural world" or "nature". The environment is often thought of as an objective reality; an abstract, almost neutral, non-human world that is out there.[195] Such a view of environment is inadequate because it limits the scope of the environment to non-human components such as plants, animals, and inanimate resources such as minerals and fossil fuels. This worldview portrays the environment as an objective reality which is devoid of intrinsic value. The environment is also a subjective reality. This means that whatever happens to and in the environment happens to all its subjects including human beings. If the environment warms up, animals, human beings and plants all feel the heat. If the waters are polluted, human beings as well as other animals feel the effect. If the environment is in a good state, again all of its biotic components feel it. That is why understanding the environment only as an objective reality is inadequate and relating to it accordingly is dangerous. Unfortunately, this seems to be the tradition for many years especially from the period of the Enlightenment and Industrial Revolution. This conventional understanding has led to an instrumental valuation of the environment. Instrumental valuation of the environment promotes unsustainable use of environmental resources.

The Anthropological Error

Ranking next to the sin of Adam and Eve against God is the human arrogance of conceptually and practically instilling an inverse relationship between development and the environment. This means that as human beings 'progress' economically, technologically, and politically, the environment has continued to degenerate. Human beings have unsustainably exploited the environment. The anthropological error lies in the fact that as they rationally justify this trend of behavior, they bear untold consequences. They have decided to engage in an unrealistic war against all the elements of the environment (air, water, plants, and animals) either by exploitation or pollution. This unholy war against the environment has historical roots, which different people attribute to different causes. We shall attempt to examine the conceptual roots of this war that set human development and the environment at opposite poles.

---

[195] Barry, *Environment and Social Theory*, 15.

136

The Conceptual Roots of Anthropocentrism

Lynn White Jr. (1907-1987), a scholar of medieval history, says that our ecological crisis originates in the Judeo-Christian conception that humanity is made in the image of God and is commanded to dominate nature.[196] White's claim is based on the creation story of Genesis 1: 26-29, which states that God made man in his own image, and asked him to dominate or subdue the whole of creation. For White, this implies that nature is alien, a mere pool of resources to be exploited, and is purposeless except that it serves the needs of human beings. White therefore accused Christianity of bearing a huge burden of the guilt for our present ecological crisis because of its advocacy of a spirit of conquest in regard to the natural environment. Though White certainly over-exaggerated his case, it is undeniable that some Christians tore out of its biblical context the divine command to humanity to have dominion over the earth and twisted it into an ideology of mastery. This creation story seemingly justifies an instrumental valuation of the nonhuman environment. Considering the great influence of Western Christianity on inter-human and human to environment relationships, it is tenable to agree with White's claim to some extent. Despite contestations, in *The Protestant Ethic and the Spirit of Capitalism*, Max Weber, a German sociologist attributes much economic and industrial growth in Western Europe and North America to capitalism, which he argued was an economic form that developed as a result of the religious teachings of John Calvin.[197] Besides, the Christian notion of afterlife or transcendence also seems to orchestrate a negative attitude toward the nonhuman environment, resulting in an instrumental relationship to the natural world since this world is just a transit into our permanent home. Gospel musicians such as Jim Reeves have aptly promoted this notion far and wide over the years. Locked up in this dangerous arrogance, human beings strayed; they left their responsibility as caretakers of God's creation. They charged on plants, animals, birds, and the waters in a manner that can be likened to lions devouring a prey. Thus, one is tempted to agree with White and Weber's claims as wholly true.

---

[196] Lynn White Jr. "The Historical Roots of our Ecological Crisis" in *Environmental Ethics: Readings in Theory and Application*. ed. Louis P. Pojman. (London: Jones and Bartlett Publishers, 1994), 9.

[197] Pojman, ed. *Environmental Ethics: Readings in Theory and Application*, 15.

However, the current environmental problems are so complex with multi-dimensional causes. Realistically, we cannot hold Western Christianity as the only primary cause, if at all. It seems that White's claim results partly from a hermeneutical lapse regarding the text in Genesis. For example, to the question who owns the environment, the Judeo-Christian response is that God does. When God asks man to dominate creation, God wants him to be a steward, a "manager", or caretaker of God's property. As a "manager" man owes God a responsibility of sustainable care of God's property. The human person is and should be aware of God's appreciation of creation; Whenever God finishes creating each creature, God says, "And this is good." This means that every creature has an intrinsic value. The human person who is made in the image of God ought to also appreciate God's creation. One way of doing this is to reverence and praise God through the sustainable use of the various elements of the environment. God gifts us with free and clean air for respiration. We are given clean water for drinking and other uses. Plants and animals abound so that we can have the necessary nutrients for proper biological development. The birds teach us how to sing, the oceans show us the wonders of God. The ants and bees teach us the importance of community life. Each member of the ecological system contributes to the benefit of all and that is exactly what is expected of the human person; to marvel at God's love through each of the members of the ecological system (Ps 8). Therefore, to destroy this beautiful ecological network cannot be the will of God but rather a deviation, an anthropological error. This anthropological deviation is commonplace not only in human to environment relationships but also in human to human relations. It is rife in economic and political spheres where sharing of God's gifts is marked by greed and selfishness.

Christians are part of this error but not solely responsible for it. In fact, Protagoras, one of the pre-Socratic Greek philosophers, had already asserted that man is the measure of everything. The guilt of Christians probably comes in the many ways their lifestyles affirmed this view. If the environmental crisis emanates solely from the Judeo-Christian tradition, one wonders why other parts of the world – China, India, and Indonesia, just to mention a few, which historically have been predominantly non-Christian, experience similar environmental crisis. Can we reasonably convince anyone that if non-Judeo-Christian cultures practice unsustainable levels of economic productivity, urbanization and consumption, these cultures will not destroy the environment? Are there fewer tendencies for those who control the resources of non-Christian cultures to live in extravagant affluence without the attendant high negative effects on the environment? For example, Indonesia, the most Muslim dominated country in the world has lost about 40 percent of its forest in the past fifty years. About nine thousand square miles of rain forest are cleared each year, and at current rates of loss, almost all the lowland forests on Sumatra and Borneo will be gone in a matter of years.[198] Indonesia's deforestation, forest fires, and peat land degradation have made it the world's number three greenhouse gas emitter, after the United States and China.[199] These examples show that the Judeo-Christian legacy is not at the root of conceptual separation of development and environment.

What is responsible for the separation? It is difficult to systematically trace the root of this anthropological error because greed, ignorance, and arrogance which have and continue to govern human attitude and behavior play a role here. Every human being consciously or unconsciously has contributed to the anthropological error. However, the contribution to this error differs both in kind and in degree depending on the epoch and influence of each person or community. In light of this, certain intellectuals, consciously or unconsciously through the influence of their thought patterns have strongly encouraged this anthropological error. Deserving a mention here are Francis Bacon and René Descartes. It seems that the thoughts of Francis Bacon and René Descartes are largely at the root of modern conceptual separation of the natural environment and development. According to Francis Bacon (1561-1626), the natural environment is meant for human experimentation and use.[200] If so, it means human beings have power over the environment and can exploit it at will. As such, human beings developed an instrumental attitude towards the environment, and thus conceptually separated environment and development. Similarly, René Descartes (1596-1650), says *cogito ergo sum*; I think, therefore I am.[201] This dictum suggests that anything that does not think exists less perfectly if at all because what is important is the thinking thing, the human person. The

---

[198] Speth, *The Bridge at the Edge of the World,* 31-2.

[199] Speth, *The Bridge at the Edge of the World,* 31-2.

[200] Francis Bacon, *The New Organon and Related Writings*, ed. Fulton H. Anderson (New York: The Liberal Arts Press, 1960), 279.

[201] J. L. Walting, "Descartes" in *A Critical History of Western Philosophy*, ed. D. J. O'Connor (New York: The Free Press, 1965), 175.

thinking thing is therefore justified to separate the *non-thinking thing* from itself including activities that lead to the welfare of the *thinking-thing*. These conceptions informed European economic practice during the Enlightenment and the Industrial Revolution leading to a separation between development and environment in practice.

The Enlightenment and the Omni-Competence of Human Reason

The enlightenment represented an important turning point in the place of environment within development paradigms. Enlightenment is understood as the series of interconnected and sometimes radical social and religious changes that took place within Europe in the mid to late eighteenth century.[202] During the enlightenment, the use of the environment, particularly in agriculture, commerce, manufacturing, landscaping, waterways, had largely ceased to be legitimated by the idea of "God's Creation". The environment became increasingly vulnerable to human manipulation and exploitation with less moral consideration.[203] At the heart of the enlightenment period was the belief that overexploitation of the natural environment through science and technology could lead to progress.[204] Reason, which is necessarily part of man, with which he claims superiority to other creatures, became his new 'god'. The human person saw himself as an absolute epistemologist, and claimed the power to determine what does and does not qualify to exist. The human person now became the supreme arbiter of life. Arrogating to himself this authority has blocked him from remembering that he is merely a creature whose rational capacity is limited and also is a gift from God but not a god in itself. In recent times, it is important to admit however, that some scientists and technologists have tried to create technological innovations that are efficient and environmentally friendly. Examples include recycling of waste or by-products, use of solar energy for generating electricity, and production of bio-fuel to power machines. This is a positive transformation of the enlightenment mind.

---

[202] Barry, *Environment and Social Theory*, 21.

[203] Barry, *Environment and Social Theory*, 45.

[204] Roy Porter, "The Enlightenment." *The Hutchinson Dictionary of Ideas* (Oxford: Helicon, 1994), 174.

The Industrial Revolution

The industrial revolution brought about changes in European economic and social life between the sixteenth and nineteenth centuries. This was a period during which people migrated aggressively from countryside and aggregated into towns and cities. Vast stretches of virgin lands were cleared to pave way for the construction of roads, houses, and industries. In other words, the environment was seen as a repository of raw materials for factories, machines and new productive technologies, which were being invented. Human beings saw themselves not as a part of nature but as an outside force destined to dominate and conquer it.[205] Science was a vehicle for taming the environment through technology. The natural environment became "disenchanted" – eroded of its resources.[206] These changes were the bases for the emergence and development of modern industrial society.[207] Urbanization, production, and consumerism became both causes and consequences of the industrial revolution. In an environment that was axiomatic of productionism and consumerism, capitalism found its most appropriate "nutrients" for growth. Since the period of the industrial revolution, capitalism has grown luxuriantly like a wet season plant. Underneath the exploitative spirit during both the enlightenment and the industrial revolution is selfish interest. This interest serves a justification for looting of the environment. But the looting and the exploitation are not directed only toward the environment but to fellow human beings as well. The same selfish spirit inspired slave trade and colonialism. Today, in our materialistic and consumerist society, human relationships, in many ways are not different from the way people relate to objects. Relationships are no longer for mutual benefit; they are about ownership similar to the way we own objects. This is because most of the time individual self-interests take precedence. Of course, we are not saying that everyone in the world behaves exactly the same way but what we are emphasizing is that self-interests largely determine the way people relate to one another economically, politically, and socially. Self-interests also determine how people relate to the nonhuman environment and we can decipher these interests in the debates about the environment.

---

[205] Schumacher, *Small is Beautiful*, 14.

[206] Barry, *Environment and Social Theory*, 44-45.

[207] Barry, *Environment and Social Theory*, 44.

Contemporary Politics of Environmental Degradation

In our world today more than ever before, environmental degradation has become a matter of great concern. Environmental degradation means reducing the quality of the atmosphere (gaseous medium), hydrosphere (water medium), lithosphere (the hard upper crust of the earth, and the biosphere (where life is possible). Environmental degradation takes various forms such as soil erosion, desertification, pollution (air, water, soil), and loss of biological diversity exemplified in depletion of terrestrial and marine life. Terrestrially, deforestation is a case in point, and for aquatic life, examples can be mentioned of depletion of phytoplankton and fishes. Industrial activities including mining, oil exploration and extraction, and agriculture degrade the environment.

But even with the obvious signs of environmental degradation exemplified in climate change, loss of biodiversity, forests, pollution and loss of productive lands, fresh waters, and marine life, there are still contestations from certain quarters of human society. Certain corporations and politicians have invincibly resisted the existence of these realities. They consider them as myths or fables. If these are accepted as realities, certain corporations and individuals often insist that they will not stop or readjust their production activities. They prefer to first hit their growth targets and then, if necessary, clean-up the environmental mess later. Corporations are therefore often ready to spend their last penny or to argue to the last atom of their energy to win the war in any forum that calls for positive attitudes toward environmental sustainability. Frighteningly, though not in any way discouraging, is the fact that most of these selfish politicians and corporations wield unwavering amount of political, technological and economic power and they are able to influence decisions at the global level. The failure of the 2009 Copenhagen Conference on the Environment is a typical case in point.

Fables about the Environment

A characteristic of politics of environmental degradation are certain fables about the environment. Certain facts about the environment are considered by some selfish politicians and corporations as myths. For instance, "The notion that human beings depend on physical resources is [said to be] an illusion; depletion of resources is a *non-issue*; substitutes can be found for any and all physical substances."[208] "For practical purposes, the supply of natural resources on earth is infinite."[209] "There is little or no evidence that global warming is real. Even if there is any, it is not a major environmental problem and certainly is not an environmental crisis."[210] "If the average mean temperature of the world rises, we can offset it with better air conditioning."[211]

In 2004, the United States Chamber of Commerce published the following as the top ten environmental myths with what are considered to be their counteractive "facts":

Myth 1: Forests are in rapid decline.
Fact: Forest acreage is increasing.

Myth 2: Air quality is getting worse.
Fact: Air quality is getting significantly better.

Myth 3: The Kyoto Protocol will successfully reduce levels of CO_2 in the atmosphere.
Fact: Even if the Kyoto Protocol was ratified and implemented, CO_2 would continue to increase.

Myth 4: All environmentalists are motivated by altruistic concern for the planet.
Fact: Environmentalists hype scare tactics to raise money.

Myth 5: Environmentalists are all penniless college students, backed by overwhelming scientific opinion.
Fact: Environmental groups have enormous wealth, cry wolf to raise billions of dollars, and their most serious claims have been proven wrong.

---

[208] Ronald Bailey, *Eco-Scam: The False Prophets of Ecological Apocalypse* (New York: St. Martins Press, 1993), 69.

[209] G. Reisman, "The Toxicity of Environmentalism" in *Rational Readings on Environmental Concerns*. Ed. J. Lehr. (New York: Van Nostrand Reinhold, 1992), 623.

[210] Bailey, *Eco-Scam: The False Prophets of Ecological Apocalypse*, 2.

[211] Reisman, "The Toxicity of Environmentalism" in *Rational Readings on Environmental Concerns*, 831.

Myth 6: All environmentalists are peace loving and engage in traditional forms of civil disobedience.

Fact: Some environmentalists are responsible for widespread criminal attacks both here and abroad.

Myth 7: Businesses are not hurt by onerous environmental regulations.

Fact: Businesses are hurt by such regulations and small businesses are hit particularly hard.

Myth 8: Oil can easily be replaced by renewable energy.

Fact: Oil is absolutely essential to all aspects of the American economy.

Myth 9: Genetically modified (GM) crops are "bad."

Fact: Enormous human benefit derives from GM crops.

Myth 10: We are running out of fresh water.

Fact: We have plenty of fresh water; the issue is access to it.

There is no need for a philosophical head-on collision with people of the aforementioned views because it is clear that every sane person can notice the greed, insensitivity, and irresponsibility imbedded in these views. First of all shifting the argument from environmental concerns to the lifestyle of the environmentalists is an *ad hominum* fallacy. Second, and more importantly, Paul Ehrlich, a renowned American ecologist insists that the claims of these corporations are baseless and fallacious and only aim to create public confusion about the character and magnitude of environmental problems.[212] Ehrlich is right because these views in many ways contradict our existential experiences. People do not quite need any scientific proofs to tell of environmental problems, for example, to realize that the airs and waters are polluted; fishes are dying; vegetations are depleting, wildlife are getting endangered, and the soils are depleted of their fertility. The effects are obvious and depending on peoples' social and economic statuses, some are more vulnerable to them than others.

In March 2010, Benjamin, a driver of Hekima College, Jesuit School of Theology, Peace and International Relations— Catholic University of

---

[212] Paul R. Ehrlich and Anne H. Ehrlich, *The Population Explosion* (New York: Simon & Schuster Inc., 1990), 19.

Eastern Africa visited the Rift Valley of Kenya. One sunny afternoon, he was perspiring and so coming to a pool of water, he washed his face and head in an attempt to cool down his temperature. Benjamin only realized a day later that the water was polluted by pollutants from a nearby industrial plant when the dermis of his face was burnt because of the concentration of the chemical pollutants. Had it not been for a timely intervention of some able health staff in a hospital in Nairobi, this driver could have lost his sight too. Benjamin is probably one case among many victims of pollution. If this is not enough to convince the greedy sophists, let them visit any of the mining towns in Ghana such as Obuasi, Tarkwa, and Prestea and see things for themselves or hear for themselves truths about environmental crisis. The land and the forests are degraded, and the water bodies are polluted by the mining activities. Another example is the oil-rich region of the Niger Delta in Nigeria where potable water is polluted from oil extraction.

Furthermore, let these sophists tell a Pokot of northern Kenya, or a seven-year old Egyptian child that there is abundant freshwater in the world. Let them talk to anyone in the Upper East and West Regions of Ghana about the effects of climate change. The common sign of climate change here has been the erratic rainfall patterns and this continues to get worse; droughts and floods alternate each year. Each of these extremes has had debilitating effects on the people to the extent that they are alarmed that an environmental spell has visited them. Hunger, thirst, excruciating heat, and destruction of properties have become their new faithful companions. Unless the selfish rhetoricians calculatedly choose to ignore what is obvious, the most recent environmental disaster (the oil leakage) in the Gulf of Mexico is a sufficient case to open their eyes to the reality. This human-made disaster has released several millions of gallons of oil into the ocean destroying not only marine life but depriving many residents of Louisiana and other States of their livelihoods.

The negative effects of environmental degradation such as diseases (cancer, cholera), thirst, and hunger are borne more by the numerous poor and vulnerable people. As these few examples illustrate, the growth mania model of development has the tendency to estrange people not only from their environment but also from one another. This is because as the economic gap widens between the rich and the poor amidst plenty to the extent that the former live as if they are less human, they either resign to the situation or seek alternatives by whatever means that will correct this trend. Sometimes the poor are left with no option but to respond to environmental challenges in socially destructive ways. For example, today nobody in the Niger Delta Region of Nigeria is safe. From a very genuine fight for social and economic justice, the anti-socioeconomic injustice groups have turned into criminal militia who indiscriminately kidnap people. At a very surface level, their activities stand for condemnation but when we dig deeper into the root causes, it becomes clear that these people have failed to get the right response at the right time. The people of the Niger Delta have been fighting against the oil companies for polluting their land but their cry has landed on death ears. Consequently, they have lost the initial inspiration of seeking justice because of the selfishness of politicians, business elites, and foreign investors. Thus, they have resorted to criminality. They have developed an estranged relationship with their fellow human beings.

In spite of these problems, few but influential people who drive huge short-term benefits from the current economic activities still come out with all sorts of excuses to justify environmentally unfriendly activities. It therefore comes as no surprise when they use political gymnastics to hide the reality of environmental degradation. These people, especially owners of oil companies and chemical manufacturing industries, bribe or pay scholars or researchers handsome sums of money to research on literature that contradict the obvious, media to publicize these pieces of information to every corner of the consuming society, and politicians to speak on their behalf in congress meetings. Their aim is to convince everyone that environmental degradation is an illusion. Unfortunately, environmental degradation is a reality. Environmental crisis is a reality; it is a global, regional, and a local problem.

Chapter 8

Contemporary Environmental Crisis and Responses

State of the Environment: the Global Perspective

The idea of the "global environment" has its origins in debates about "environmental crisis" in the 1960s and 1970s.[213] The concept emerged against a background of vulnerability and threat. Threats to the global environment became an object of public and political interest. Of particular importance was Neil Armstrong. Armstrong photographed the earth from the moon, which brought home to people the beauty and vulnerability of the earth and the fact that we all share the same fragile planet earth.[214] This backdrop serves as the basis for all the environmental issues that are raised. Even a ten-year-old child is able to notice some negative environmental changes. The changes might be different in rate, degree and in kind depending upon where one grew up but the unpalatable truth is that there have been more negative changes than positive ones to the environment.

We do not deny that the changes come through both natural and human activities. Human beings do not have much control if at all, for instance, over natural disasters including earthquakes, volcanoes, landslides, and floods when they strike but our activities can directly or indirectly facilitate their frequency and severity. For example, we may not be able to stop incessant torrential rains when the sky opens up but choking drains with solid wastes especially non-biodegradable ones, building houses on waterways, and clearing vegetation indiscriminately can contribute to the severity of rainfall effects. Human selfishness exacerbates natural calamities. Pertaining to climatic changes, loss of biodiversity in terrestrial and aquatic environments through pollution and over-harvest, the human person has contributed significantly. Human activities in pursuit of economic and technological developments have greatly increased the vulnerability of both the environment and human beings. Continuing with this attitude can only leave humanity with ecological and social "bads". The 2007 Nobel Peace Laureate and chairman of the Intergovernmental Panel on Climate Change, Rajendra

---

[213] Barry, *Environment and Social Theory*, 28.

[214] Barry, *Environment and Social Theory*, 27.

147

Pachauri, fittingly captures this view when he states that if the world does not take action early and in adequate measure, the impacts of climate change could prove extremely harmful and overwhelm our capacity to adapt.[215]

For example, statistics show that each year about six billion hectares of productive land turn into worthless desert; more than eleven million hectares of forests are destroyed; burning fossil fuels emit carbon dioxide leading to global warming; the "greenhouse effect" is increasing average global temperatures enough to shift agricultural production areas, raise sea levels to flood coastal cities and disrupt national economies; industry and agriculture put toxic substances into the human food chain and into underground water tables beyond reach of cleansing.[216] The Millennium Ecosystem Assessment (MEA) report of 2005 states that half of the world's tropical and temperate forests are destroyed.[217] The rate of deforestation in the tropics continues at about an acre a second.[218] About 90 percent of the large predator fish are gone, and 75 percent of marine fisheries are now overfished or fished to capacity.[219] Species are disappearing at rates about a thousand times faster than normal.[220] Human activities have pushed atmospheric carbon dioxide up by more than a third and have started in earnest the dangerous process of warming the planet and disrupting climate. Human actions already consume or destroy each year about 40 percent of nature's photosynthetic output, leaving too little for other species.[221] Fresh water withdrawals doubled globally between 1960 and 2000, and are now over half of accessible runoff.[222]

---

[215] State of the World 2009: *Into a Warming World*, http://www.worldwatch.org (Accessed: 15th June 2010).

[216] Brundtland Commission, *Our Common Future: The World Commission on Environment and Development* (Oxford: Oxford University Press, 1987), 3.

[217] Millennium Ecosystem Assessment, *Ecosystems and Human Well-Being: Synthesis* (Washington, D.C.: Island Press, 2005), 31-32.

[218] Food and Agricultural organization, *Global Forest Resources Assessment 2005* (Rome: FAO, 2006), 20.

[219] Food and Agricultural Organization, World Review of Fisheries and Aquaculture (Rome: FAO, 2006), 29.

[220] Millennium Ecosystem Assessment, *Ecosystems and Human Well-Being: Synthesis*, 36.

[221] The Proceedings of the United States National Academy of Arts and Sciences, 2007.

[222] United Nations Environmental Programme, "At a Glance: The World's Water Crisis," http://www.ourplanet.com/imgversn/141/glance.html (Accessed: 20th March 2011).

About two and half decades ago, birds used to migrate every evening between the months of March and May from probably Burkina Faso or beyond through northern Ghana to southern Ghana and returned somewhere in December. As young children, we used to assemble every evening to watch in admiration the beautiful layers created in the sky by the different birds as they migrated side by side. Today that is history. These birds are either hunted to extinction or human activities have created environments so unfavourable that led to their death or complete migration to other parts of the world. This fits into the feelings of Speth when he reechoes the words of William MacLeish about an English man who in 1602 noted in his journal that the fish schooled so thickly that he thought their backs were the sea bottom.[223] If this Englishman were alive today, he would be dumbfounded and may lament as Rachel Carson did in the 1960s. In 1962, Rachel Carson had observed that pesticides such as Dichloro-Diphenyl-Trichloroethane (DDT) were causing widespread cancer and genetic mutation, as well as wreaking a wholesale havoc on birds, fish, and wildlife. Carson says that in spring, the birds sang sweetly in the vegetation, the foxes barked in the hills, the deer silently crossed the fields, and the wildflowers blossomed.[224] Then a strange blight (DDT) crept over the area and everything began to change. Some evil spell settled on the community: mysterious maladies swept the flocks of chickens, the birds were gone; the roadsides once so attractive were now lined up with brown and withered vegetation. The farmers spoke of much illness among their families. The doctors became more and more puzzled by new kinds of sicknesses appearing among their patients; there were several sudden and unexplained deaths among children and adults. There was strange stillness; there was a "Silent Spring".

Today, so many ecological problems in the form of strange diseases such as Severe Acute Respiratory Syndrome, Ebola, and Avian flu have brought untold pain, fear, and suffering to many people. Are not the pains caused by volcanic ashes, landslides, hurricanes, and floods enough? Do we need to add more human-made disasters or to accelerate the frequency of the natural ones? We are sure the poor employees of flower and vegetable farms in Kenya or Zambia and many others whose daily bread is tied to the daily

---

[223] Speth, *The Bridge at the Edge of the World: Capitalism, The Environment, and Crossing from Crisis to Sustainability* , 2.

[224] Pojman, ed. *Environmental Ethics: Readings in Theory and Application*, 356-7.

twists of the environment will say they already have enough of the disasters and will not need more of them. When the volcanic ash of April 2010 halted the operations of many airlines, millions of tonnes of Kenyan flowers and vegetables meant for export to Europe spoilt. The consequence of this was a temporary or permanent laying off of some of the staff. This forced such families to go to bed hungry. Some of these workers from Nyahururu, we recall when recounting their stories wondered painfully how local environmental problems could be global problems. Many Pakistanis, we believe, will frown at any human activity that will facilitate floods.

Global Dispositions and Responses to Environmental Issues

The experiences of environmental crisis are global in nature but they may differ in kind and degree depending on the type and intensity of economic, industrial, and agricultural activities of an area. The responses to the crisis have been varied because of the hydra-headed nature of the environmental issues. Since environmental degradation became a topical issue, different people, individually or as economic, social, religious, corporate and humanitarian (international or local) institutions and organizations assumed different dispositions and attitudes toward the human development-environment relationship. These attitudes and dispositions inform the different peoples' responses to the environmental issues. Speth ably and craftily identifies seven different ways through which people respond to polemics about the development-environment relationship. These include the solutionist, resignation, divine providence, denial, paralysis, muddling through, and deflection.[225]

For people who assumed the disposition of resignation, all is lost as far as environmental health is concerned. There is nothing that can be done to rectify the problem. The philosophy is to eat today for tomorrow we shall be dead because of the overwhelming environmental disasters. They have been making efforts to avert the environmental problems but their efforts seem not to be getting the desired results. Some are influenced by the doomsayers who associate the current environmental crisis with the unstoppable end of the world. Those who look up to divine providence say that we do not have to be worried because all the environmental problems are in God's hands

---

[225] Speth, *The Bridge at the Edge of the World: Capitalism, The Environment, and Crossing from Crisis to Sustainability*, 42.

and so He will provide the solution. These are people who seek refuge in spiritualizing every reality. They have forgotten that by virtue of our rational capacity as humans, God respects our freedom and the choices we make. The denial group asks: "what problem?" For them, there are no environmental problems but environmental myths. Environmental fabulists especially selfish politicians and owners of multinational corporations such as chemical manufacturing and oil companies belong here. Some people consider the environmental crisis as so overwhelming that they are simply over frightened by them. These assume the disposition of paralysis. They have always been overwhelmed by the environmental problems and have given in to fatalism from the onset. Yet, there is another group, which believes that the environmental problems are going to be all right, somehow. Thus, muddling through is the way forward. These are people who are unhealthily confident. They believe that human beings in one way or another will gradually adapt to the changing environmental patterns. Taking precautionary measures or curative measures has never been part of their understanding of life. Some others, especially those who have the means to be comfortable amidst the crisis say that the environmental problems are not their problems, and, therefore, they deflect from them. These are people who are often caught in the delusion that they are prepared for eventualities. Subscribers to these dispositions do nothing to solve the problem. The last group, to which we belong and we hope many people do, is the solutionist group.

The Solutionists and their proposed solutions to environmental problems

The solutionists say that answers can and must be found for environmental problems especially the human induced ones.[226] The solutions sought for environmental problems are many and varied, traversing across international and local conferences to environmental ethical theories such as extreme anthropocentrism, biocentrism, and ecocentrism. Some of these solutions impress people and raise their hopes but others actually depress rather than impress.

---

[226] Speth, *The Bridge at the Edge of the World: Capitalism, The Environment, and Crossing from Crisis to Sustainability*, 42.

International Summits

Upon acknowledgement of the environmental crises mentioned earlier and their merciless telling effects on humanity, governments and other stakeholders have pooled efforts to redress the situation. This led to the first UN Conference on Human Environment, held in Stockholm in June 1972.[227] The Stockholm conference was a prelude to series of large global meetings, conferences, protocols, and summits that aim at environmental sustainability. These include the World Commission on Environment and Development or Brundtland Commission (1987), the Earth Summit in Rio de Janeiro (1992), the Kyoto Protocol (1997), the Johannesburg World Summit on Sustainable Development (2002), the UN Climate Change Conference, commonly known as the Copenhagen Summit (2009), and the most recent one, UN Climate Change Conference held in Durban South Africa (2011). The Brundtland Commission, headed by Gro Harlem Brundtland, a former Norwegian Prime minister, concluded that development and environment are inextricably linked, yet the processes that human beings use to pursue development have become too heavy for the carrying capacity of the environment; the environment can no longer provide adequately for and absorb waste of our untamed appetites. The commission, therefore, coined and recommended sustainable development. Sustainable development is development that "meets the needs [interests] of the present without compromising the ability of future generations to meet their own needs."[228]

The Earth Summit in Rio de Janeiro dealt with a variety of issues about the earth and issued several recommendations to help sustain the health of our planet earth. The Kyoto Protocol dealt with climate change and called on world governments to ratify the treaty that will bind them to reduce carbon dioxide emissions. The United States of America and Australia refused to ratify this document for reasons that are rooted in selfishness. The World Summit on Sustainable Development was a follow up on the previously held summits especially the Brundtland one. The Copenhagen summit was a failure, a clear sign that governments are not ready to sacrifice their selfish interests for the health of the environment. The 2011 Durban conference came up with a package of decisions known as the Durban platform but it actually ended with mixed feelings. After back and forth debates on cutting

---

[227] Sachs, "Environment" in *The Development Dictionary*, 26.

[228] Brundtland Commission, *Our Common Future*, 43.

down carbon dioxide, some of the players finally hesitantly agreed to reduce carbon emissions but that was said verbally. As a result the Russian representative insisted that these agreements should be written and signed. Russia's request did not materialize; human selfishness had once again won the debate.

Why the Failure?

All environmental summits have one basic goal: to wake humanity up from its slumber of business as usual to the catastrophe we are deliberately and selfishly creating for ourselves and future generations. Unfortunately, this call never got real action-laden receptivity. All these efforts have somehow been a failure.

i. Rhetoric, no action

The perennial rhetoric regarding environmental issues is informed by two factors. First, no one accepts responsibility and is ready for any commitment. Second, the developed world has largely not, and may never relent on continuing their development activities using conventional technology, or change their consumption patterns. Pitifully, the developing countries are becoming more aggressive in their consumption patterns and are not leaving the minutest opportunity to follow the developed world. The reigning ethic of operation is that I produce therefore I am; I consume therefore I am; I own many ultra-modern houses therefore I am; I ride in the most expensive and modern car therefore I am. I am because of these not because I think of the common good; not because I stick to my basic needs; not because my simplicity and sharing spirit put smiles on the faces of others and assures the future generations of their share in the resources with which God has blessed all of us. Amidst such operational logic of contemporary society, the international environmental summits only become moments for environmental mockery and for participants to enjoy themselves and grab more travel and sitting allowances. The good documents produced at those summits never get to implementation stage. Thanks to the excellent rhetoricians who coin beautiful and attractive phrases such as 'our common future'! But that 'our' does not include you and me. From the intellectual world, there are people who have poisoned and continue to poison many with their theories that are supposed to prescribe the best sustainable way of relating with the environment.

ii. Poisoning environmental ethical theories

Environmental ethics deals with issues of human relationship to the environment, right conduct, moral obligation, responsibility, and respect for attainment of good life. However, the ambiguity of the term "good life" provokes certain intriguing questions, for example, good life for who, human beings or the environment, or both? Are human beings and the environment equal? If not, who is, or should be, at the centre of attention? These questions have led to the proposition of some poisonous theories that claim to show how to co-habit the environment. These include: extreme anthropocentrism, biocentrism, and ecocentrism.

Extreme Anthropocentrism

According to Elisa K. Campbell, the word 'anthropocentrism' was coined in the 1860s in the context of the first debates about Darwin's theory of evolution and the implications for humans of this theory. The term describes the prevalent assumption that humans occupy the centre of the universe.[229] The prefix 'extreme' is intended to show that the centrality of the human beings in the relational equation has been unhealthily emphasized.

Extreme anthropocentrism claims that the nonhuman world and/or its parts have value only insofar as they directly or indirectly serve human interests. In other words, the earth and all its nonhuman contents exist or are available for human benefit and to serve their interests. Hence, human beings are entitled to manipulate the nature and its systems as they want, that is, in their interests.[230] They are valuable only to the extent that they are means or instruments which may serve human beings. Most policy makers and social scientists belong here, and anthropocentric assumptions underlie most of the work that they do. This unfortunately dominated human-environmental relations since the periods of the Enlightenment and Industrial revolution and has created a dualism between humans and the environment; the two became alien to each other. This type of ethic which does not promote harmonious co-habitation with the environment is wanting as optimal ethic. What this ethic seems to be proposing is that we can hide behind a tree and

---

[229] http://sh.diva-portal.org/smash/get/diva2:273605/FULLTEXT01 (Accessed: May 30th 2012).

[230] Bryan G. Norton, "Environmental Ethics and Weak Anthropocentrism" in *Environmental Ethics: Divergence and Convergence*, eds. Susan J. Armstrong and Richard G. Botzler (New York: McGraw-Hill, 1993), 136.

be taller than it. In other words, we can hide within the environment and still colonize it. The human selfishness behind this ethic has engineered the proposition of biocentrism.

Biocentrism

Biocentrism is a life-centred ethic whereby the well-being of each living thing is considered to be all that matters.[231] Albert Schweitzer, in his book *Civilization and Ethics,* proposed that values be extended to all life. Schweitzer calls this position "Reverence for Life".[232] Every living thing – "every-will-to live" in nature is endowed with something intrinsically valuable and should be respected as such. For instance, "Just as in my own will-to-live there is a yearning for more life, so the same obtains in all the will-to-live around me, whether it can express itself to my comprehension or whether it remains unvoiced."[233] This means that each living individual has a teleological centre of life, which pursues its own good in its own way. In short, the central message of biocentrism goes as follows: 1. Human beings are not more intrinsically valuable than any other living beings; they are *equal members* of Earth's community, that is, bio-egalitarianism. 2. Each individual organism is a teleological centre of life. 3. Human beings have *prima facie* moral obligation to protect and promote trees and animals for their own sake.[234]

The bio-egalitarianism, which biocentrists advocate, poses difficulties for Christian anthropology that puts humans above other creatures. Christian anthropology states that humans are the only creatures created in the image and likeness of God, and they alone are given a mandate to order the rest of creation.[235]Even though the non-human creatures are extremely important and respect for their sustained generatability is for the supreme interests of human beings, the latter can still be given a higher ontological status and at the same time be challenged to respect their stewardship role towards the rest of creation. It is also the same issue about human beings who might have superior skills and talents; this does not give them license to oppress or exploit others.

---

[231] http://cstl-cla.semo.edu/hill/ui429/eeglossary.htm_(Accessed: May 30th 2012).

[232] Pojman, ed. *Environmental Ethics,* 64.

[233] Pojman, ed. *Environmental Ethics,* 64.

[234] Pojman, ed. *Environmental Ethics,* 71.

[235] Genesis Gen 1:26-28

One problem with biocentrism is what one might call "Schweitzer's dilemma." In his reverence for life philosophy, Schweitzer considered each organism as an individual whose suffering and death were to be avoided. If one supports this philosophy, that it is the organism's discomfort, or welfare that should be our primal concern and not the effect upon the human causing it, one is confronted with the perplexing situation of having to regard pain that occurs "in the wild" as bad. One is, as Schweitzer was, forced to regard predators as evil. However, predators avoid the pains of starvation and eventual death by causing pain and death to other organisms. This relationship is an inherent part of the ecosystem where energy is transferred from one trophic level to the next. Failure to have reverence for the predator's life is itself a contradiction of the basic tenet of Schweitzer's philosophy, yet to have reverence for the predator's life is to revere those processes which result in pain and death.[236] If we go by this ethic, it means that no living organisms: herbivores, carnivores, and omnivores should be allowed to live. Not even plants will be allowed to live because they also, apart from depending on sunlight, carbon dioxide, water, and minerals to survive, are parasitic in the case of some of them. In other words, some plants feed on other plants. This ethic cannot best serve as an environmental ethic for three reasons: first, it is reductionistic because it excludes the non-living part of the environment, which is very important for all forms of life. Second, biocentrism contradicts the laws of nature, which allow interdependence in terms of feeding and self-defence. Third, it is inherently self-contradictory, and therefore, does not allow for praxis. A good example of the third point is Schweitzer's own medical efforts in French Equatorial Africa to help lepers at the expense of pathogens. Thus, although theoretically one might argue for equality among the members of the earth, in real life the other members are sacrificed on the altar of human interests. Likewise, animals too, although not to the same extent, depend on humans, at least for some of their interests. Notwithstanding, scientists have made efforts to preserve endangered species of plants and animals, for example, the African walnut, African mahogany, the African elephant, and leopard. An ethic of interdependence is key. In other words, interdependence is

---

[236] Dale R. Guthrie, "The Ethical Relationship between Humans and Other Organisms" in *Environmental Ethics: Divergence and Convergence*, eds. Susan J. Armstrong, Richard G. Botzler (New York: McGraw-Hill, 1993), 293.

inevitable. The ethical question we need to keep in mind is how can we meet our interests without being extravagant

Ecocentrism

Ecocentrism is a term coined and developed by Timothy O'Riordan in 1989 to define a radical trend in contemporary environmentalism.[237] This ethic is based on the philosophical premise that the natural world has inherent or intrinsic value.[238] Two versions of ecocentrism are: the Land Ethic and Deep Ecology. The land ethic was propounded by Aldo Leopold, a professor of wildlife management, in 1949.[239] It values nature in and of itself, rather than only in relation to its significance for the survival and well-being of humans. Leopold's land ethic encourages us to perceive the ecosystem not merely as a breadbasket but as a community of which we are only *plain* members and not conquerors. Being a plain member seems to imply eco-egalitarianism. The golden rule of the land ethic is: "A thing is right when it tends to preserve the integrity, stability, and beauty of the biotic community. It is wrong when it tends otherwise."[240]

Arne Naess, a Norwegian philosopher in 1973, coined the term "Deep Ecology." Deep ecology or ecosophy is a movement that calls for a deeper questioning and a deeper set of answers to our environmental concerns. It questions consumerism and materialism and challenges us to live more simply. Its motto is, "simple in means, rich in ends." For Naess, "live and let live" is a more powerful ecological principle than "either you or me".[241] Dave Foreman and Mike Roselle, co-founders of *Earth First!,* a group espousing deep ecology, continue ecocentric philosophy. For them, human beings are inherently and contagiously destructive. According to a metaphor they used to describe human relationship to the environment, humans play the role of a virus that gives the earth a rash and a fever, threatening the environment's vital functions. Human species are a global cancer, spreading uncontrollably

---

[237] Natalia Mirovitskaya, and William Ascher, eds., *Guide To Sustainable Development and Environmental Policy* (Durham, North Carolina: Duke University Press, 2001), 122.

[238] Susan J. Armstrong, and Richard G. Botzler, eds., *Environmental Ethics: Divergence and Convergence* (New York: McGraw-Hill, 1993), 265.

[239] Joy A. Palmer, ed. *Fifty Key Environmental Thinkers on the Environment* (London: Routledge, 2001), 179.

[240] Pojman, ed. *Environmental Ethics*, 96.

[241] Pojman, ed. *Environmental Ethics,* 102.

and taking for their nourishment and expansion the resources needed by the environment to maintain its health. Foreman tells us that the earth should be placed first in all decisions, even ahead of human welfare, if necessary.[242]

As can be seen, the two versions of ecocentrism primarily hold that the non-human environment has intrinsic value. In the land ethic, the human being is just a plain member of the biotic community. In the case of deep ecology, the human being is in fact, inferior to the biotic community.

Although the ecocentric ethic has commendable insights, it has a number of inherent weaknesses too. Like the biocentric ethic, the ecocentric ethic does not resolve the conflicting needs between human beings and the environment. Feeding starving people through agriculture may lead to the disruption of healthy ecosystems, but ceasing these agricultural efforts may lead to immoral consequences. The deep ecologists only preach ethics that they cannot practice, and we know that theory without practice is sterile. When Foreman makes the environment a no go area but he goes ahead to wear clothes made from plants, and eat food and meat, this amounts to self-contradiction. He also goes ahead to write books that use paper made out of wood! Such extremes need to be questioned. Another problem with this ethic is its inability to explain in a way that is either accurate or convincing who humans are and how they can create solutions for the crisis this ethic describes. Ironically, just as the extreme anthropocentric ethic separates humanity from the physical world, so do the deep ecologists; both of these seem to define human beings as an alien presence in the environment, except that the deep ecologists make the environment the centre.

Therefore, the biocentric and ecocentric ethical positions make the natural environment a "no-go area" for humans. These views are inconsistent with the practical view that human beings need the nonhuman world in order to survive. They defeat the law of solidarity with the whole created world. These deficiencies show the inapplicability of biocentrism and ecocentrism. Since the tenets of these ethical positions cannot be put into practice, they cannot best serve as environmental ethics.

Altruistic Egoism as an Environmental Ethic

As an environmental ethic, altruistic egoism would mean human beings taking care of their interests by taking care of the interests of the non-human members of the environment. Thus, unlike biocentrism and ecocentrism,

---

[242] Armstrong, Susan and Botzler, eds. *Environmental*, 422.

altruistic egoism does not require humans to be purely altruistic in their dealing with the non-human members of the environment since that is impossible. Also, unlike extreme anthropocentrism, altruistic egoism does not mean being purely egoistic or self-centred. Altruistic egoism means moderate anthropocentrism which involves less rhetoric, is practical, and involves you and me. Central to this ethic are the following acknowledgements: 1. Human beings though members of the ecological community – living and non-living, can contribute towards a healthy ecological community. We are aware that human beings do not have the ability to preserve all species from extinction because some species existed and disappeared long before humans came on the scene. We also know that there are millions of flora and fauna that humans do not know yet, which are daily fighting for survival among themselves. We do not know about everything that lies in the oceans nor on other planets. We do not equally know what lies ahead of us in the next million years. Yet still, these observations do not take away the fact that we have a role to play towards the preservation of the non-human members of the ecological community. The fact that humans have what it takes to daily destroy some of the non-human entities means that they can also preserve some of them. 2. Human beings should not deprive themselves of their livelihood by radically refusing to use resources because their survival depends on what the environment provides. The only problem here is how human beings can find a way of defining what is reasonable as regards to consumption. Who will decide? Do we know how many more years the planet will be around and how many more people are yet to come so that we gauge what to leave for those yet to come? It may be difficult to gauge accurately what is reasonable but the very reality of dependence is sufficient to warrant a good care for the environment. It is actually for the good of humans that they should take good care of the interests of the non-human members of the environment. Our so-called superiority over other creatures is no claim that we should ill-treat them; is an invitation to care for them, feel compassion for them, and be good to them in every way we can.[243] Thus, this ethic supports a kind of a symbiotic mode of relationship. Symbiosis or mutuality ushers in some sustainable use of the nonhuman creatures, hence, leading to sustainable human progress in a sustainable environment.

---

[243] Schumacher, *Small is Beautiful*, 108.

The ethic of altruistic egoism or moderate anthropocentrism advocates solidarity in the created world, judgment of what is essential to humans through reason and empathy, and detachment from what is superfluous. This is important in pursuing the path of human perfection, peace, security, and happiness, which do not exclusively reside in the realm of materiality. It rejects any proposal that alienates human beings from the environment. Rather, it advocates and promotes a respectful lifestyle for co-habitation with the natural environment. Even though this cosmological humanism will no doubt require a lot of pedagogy to make it clearer and easily applicable, its mention can serve as a catalyst for people to explore it.

Additionally, the ethic provides an adequate basis from which to criticize destructive environmental practices, to acknowledge human affinity to nature, and to account for the distinctive non-individualistic nature of environmental ethics. It stands on the principle that the natural environment has an intrinsic value. If humans have a strong consumptive value system, their interests dictate that the natural environment is for exploitation. Moderate anthropocentrism recognizes that a felt need can either be rational or not because such a need can be judged not consonant with the rational worldview. Hence, it provides a basis for criticism of value systems, which are purely exploitative of nature.

In the above way, moderate anthropocentrism makes available two ethical resources of crucial importance to all of us: first, to the extent that we can make a case for a worldview that emphasizes harmonious relationship between human beings and the environment. Second, it places value on human experiences that provide the basis for value formation. It emphasizes that values are formed and informed by contact with nature in which case nature no longer is seen as a mere satisfier of fixed and often consumptive values.[244] In short, moderate anthropocentrism acknowledges the freedom, power, and knowledge of humanity but it does not accept that human beings are conquerors of nature.

Of course, it is contestable to assert that human beings are not conquerors of nature. Some people claim that humans have conquered nature and they actually assert that this is the basic tenet of science and technology. This view has been held since the industrial revolution and the enlightenment period. However, it is not true that human beings have

---

[244] Norton, "Environmental Ethics and Weak Anthropocentrism" in *Environmental Ethics: Divergence and Convergence,* 288.

conquered nature. This view of human beings as conquerors often easily appears to be the case but in actual fact, it is not. For instance, if we take the field of medicine to illustrate our point, there are self-declared victorious and near-victorious drums that scientists have sounded over the years concerning certain pathogens such as viruses, bacteria, protozoa, just to mention a few. For some years back, the World Health Organization has been singing melodies on human victory over the viruses that cause polio. In recent times, the same organization is acknowledging that the virus was in resurgence.[245] How about the malaria parasites which continue to cause havoc to millions of human lives across the globe? The HIV virus remains a mystery to all of us for the past three decades since it was first detected. Scientists have failed to win the war against this virus. How can we claim to have conquered nature? In fact, as Don Marquis satirically puts it, "A man thinks he amounts to a great deal but to a flea or a mosquito a human being is merely something good to eat."[246]

Similarly, we can fell trees and make beautiful products out of them, mine the gold and diamonds, and we can extract the crude oil. We can kill the animals, harvest the fish, and kill the birds, and think we have conquered nature. But that is not true because when someone conquers another, it means the conquered is subdued and subjugated. The conquered cannot hit back but rather obliges to the dictates of the conqueror. This is not the case with regard to human beings and the environment. When we fell the trees, pollute the air, we suffer the immediate effects of heat and medium to long term effects of global warming, floods, and droughts. Therefore, the worldview that human beings have conquered nature is not true. Perhaps both humans and nature are losers as well as winners in the battle. In any case, appropriating the tenets of altruistic egoism can be a good starting step toward solving environmental crises.

---

[245] http://www.cdc.gov/mmwr/preview/mmwrhtml/mm5506a1.htm (Accessed: May 30th 2012).

[246] http://thinkexist.com/quotation/a-man-thinks-he-amounts-to-a-great-deal-but-to-a/348891.html (Accessed: June 30th 2012).

Chapter 9

Industrialized Countries' Development and Environment Experiences

The terms industrialized, advanced, or developed countries are often used interchangeably to describe countries that command strong technological and economic power. In economic terms, the World Bank describes them as countries with at least Gross National Income per capita of $ US 9, 206. We find these countries in almost all the continents except Africa and South America. Most of them are found in Western Europe and North America. Sometimes, the term 'Western world' is used loosely to embrace all the developed countries.

We cannot claim that all the developed countries have the same type of relationship and perceptions about the environment and expectations from it because each has had its own unique cultural, political, and economic experiences. The United States of America, for instance, is in many ways different from the United Kingdom, Germany, or France culturally and politically; it was once colonized but Great Britain was never colonized. However, certain experiences seem common to most industrialized nations. The most notable experience is what Ulrich Beck calls "risk society".[247] Risk society is concerned with health, socio-economic, cultural and environmental effects of "social progresses" in general and scientific and technologically based production in particular.[248] Beck's "risk society" thesis views the Western world as one in which people and politics are more worried about the distribution of "bads"(such as environmental and other risks) rather than "goods" (such as food security, income and jobs).[249] All the industrialized countries pursued development using the economic growth model, industrialization, and technology. They perceived the nonhuman environment as a mere pool of resources out there for human use. Their approach was that of the zero sum game and therefore driven by human selfishness. In the family set up, the nuclear family became much preferred over and above the extended family system. This, with time, degenerated

---

[247] Barry, *Environment and Social Theory*, 3.

[248] Barry, *Environment and Social Theory*, 3.

[249] Barry, *Environment and Social Theory*, 174.

largely into an extreme form of individualism, or capitalism, as economists would call it. This individualism estranged social bonds. The positive side of this attitude is that it kept everyone on their feet in terms of personal planning, instrumental use of reason, and skills acquisition. Notwithstanding, it has brought a range of possible "bads", which include: increase in crime; a decrease in personal safety, risk of contracting diseases or illnesses, lack of empathy for the significant other, and rising pollution levels.[250] One can witness the growing risk sensitivity of Western public through their experiences of one 'scare' or 'risk' after another: such as the 'mad cow' disease (BSE) in the UK, environmental dangers such as global warming and ozone depletion, and environmental-related illness such as the dramatic rise in childhood asthma, linked to the increase in air pollution,[251]obesity, and recently, outbreak of *Eschericia coli* (a strange strain of bacteria) in cucumbers that killed many people in Germany in May-June 2011. The advent of "risk society" marks the threshold beyond which ecological, health, and social costs outweigh the benefits of further economic growth in modern Western societies.[252]

Beck proposes "reflexive modernization" as a way of creating a risk-free society. Reflexive modernization states that society as a whole should reflect upon its own development and the institutions which further that development.[253] Society should critically and constantly reflect upon the social, ecological, and economic costs of any development path that it follows. The precautionary principle is important for this reflexivity. The precautionary principle states that in a context of uncertainty it is rational to be prudent and not to implement a particular action if there is a risk of it resulting in future significant danger or harm.[254] Core aspects of the principle include a willingness to act in advance of scientific proof and hold back from certain forms of development on precautionary grounds.[255] The precautionary principle is in many respects simply common-sense prudence and caution, a virtue that is all the more needed in our complex and uncertain world of development-environment relations.

---

[250] Barry, *Environment and Social Theory*, 154.

[251] Barry, *Environment and Social Theory*, 154.

[252] Barry, *Environment and Social Theory*, 156.

[253] Ulrich Beck, *Risk Society: Towards a New Modernity*, (London: Sage, 1992), 10.

[254] Barry, *Environment and Social Theory*, 159.

[255] Barry, *Environment and Social Theory*, 161.

Responses of Industrial Societies to the Environmental Crisis

Many industrialized societies have started making efforts towards risk-free societies by using environmentally friendly methods in agriculture, industry, and transportation. Countries such as the United Kingdom, Denmark, and Sweden offer some few cases in point. These countries have realized that pursuing development at the expense of the environment is simply being pigheaded. There is a need to respect a health relationship between development and environment.

Paul Hawken suggests as environmental friendly the term "eco-industry". This term was coined by Robert Frosch and Nicholas Gallopoulos.[256] In contrast to the conventional industrial processes which take a one-way production line: raw materials plus energy leading to production of finished products and waste products, which are thrown away into the environment, eco-industry integrates the manufacturing processes in such a way that the by-products become raw materials for another industry. A practical example of an eco-industry is found in Kalundborg, Denmark. Here a number of local industries have formed a synergy, comprising a coal-fired power plant, an oil refinery, a pharmaceutical company, a sheetrock plant, concrete producers, sulphuric acid producers, a municipal heating authority, a fish farm, some greenhouses and local farms. The power plant, instead of releasing its excess heat into the atmosphere, converts it into steam and supplies the steam to Statoil refinery, the pharmaceutical company, and the fish farm. It also supplies its excess heat to residents of the town, enabling 3500 oil-burning heating systems to be turned off. The Statoil installed equipment that enabled it to remove sulphur contained in its surplus gas. It sells this gas to the Sheetrock factory and the power plant. This helps to save up to 30 000 tons of coal per annum. The sulphur, which was removed, is sold to the chemical company. The process that removes the sulphur also produces calcium sulphate, which then is sold to the sheetrock factory as a substitute for mined gypsum. The fly ash that is generated by burning coal at the plant is used in road construction and in making concrete. The fish farm gives its fish sludge to local farmers as fertilizers. At the same time the pharmaceutical company developed a technique to make the sludge generated in its fermentation processes useful to farmers through addition of chalk lime.[257]

---

[256] Paul Hawken, *The Ecology of Commerce* (New York: Harper Business, 1993), 61.

[257] Paul Hawken, *The Ecology of Commerce*, 62-63.

Apropos of the above, Van der Ploeg *et al* tell us that the European Union (EU) is promoting a new rural development paradigm among its member states.[258] This paradigm was a response to the modernization paradigm that characterized European agricultural practices. The old modernization paradigm was associated with the heavy use of external inputs and with new destructive and more expensive technologies. It also involved clearing of large tracts of land for farming, often for mono-cropping. Thus, it reduced forest cover and consequently raised concerns about animal welfare and food safety.

The new rural development paradigm outlines a multi-faceted process that EU employed to help its members reorganize their agricultural systems. It is multi-faceted because it unfolds into a wide array of different and sometimes interconnected practices. Among them are landscape management, the conservation of new nature values, agric-tourism, organic farming and the production of high quality and regional specific products. In this paradigm, professional organizations claim conservation as their prerogative and they set out to create "wild life reserves" whilst farmer organizations strive for farmer managed landscape and nature values.[259] Particularly important are synergies between local and regional eco-systems, specific farming styles, specific goods and services, and localized food chains.[260] Conservation laws have been emphasized and reinforced. If, motivated by selfishness, an individual or industry does not abide by the established laws, the produce will not be bought – people will vote by their backs.

In terms of transportation, many westerners no longer associate development with driving a private car; development has to be sensitive to environmental concerns. This is achieved by insisting on walking, riding bicycles, or using public trains and buses instead of each person driving a private car. The public transport vehicles or trains are fuel-efficient.

---

[258] Van der Ploeg, *et al*. "Rural Development: From Practices and Policies Towards Theory" in *Sociologia Ruralis*. 40:4 (2000), 391.

[259] Van der Ploeg, *et al*. "Rural Development: From Practices and Policies Towards Theory," 393.

[260] Saccomandi, V., and J. D. van der Ploeg. "On impact of endogenous development in agriculture" in *Beyond Modernisation: The Impact of Endogenous Rural Developmen* (Amsterdam: Van Gorcum, 1995), 27-28.

The foregoing discussion has shown that the industrialized societies used economic growth model as development path. This model used modern technology for agricultural and industrial production, which has led to economic progress and food security. However, untamed capitalism characterized their intra and inter-social, economic, and industrial relations. In industrial plants, for example, it is common to see chimneys as high as one metre or more. The goal is to exude the industrial gases as far away from the locality as possible. This path of development has thus caused serious ecological, health and social costs in industrialized societies. The experiences of industrialized nations can be described as paradoxes of economic and technological successes versus ecological and health risks. These paradoxes have necessitated a change in attitude toward the development-environment relationship in terms of industry, agriculture, and transportation; more so, the "reconciliation of man [sic] with the natural world is no longer merely desirable, it has become necessary."[261]

---

[261] Schumacher, *Small is Beautiful*, 114.

Chapter 10

African Development and Environment Experiences

Strong Aspirations amidst Many Dilemmas

When we talk of African development and environment experiences, we are aware that these are not homogeneous everywhere. We know of the yawning inter country and intra country differences. These differences are culturally, socially, economically, geographically, and environmentally informed. In Kenya, the way a Masai child is enculturated to relate to the environment is different from a Kikuyu child. Whereas a Masai highly esteems shepherding of animals and spends most of the time in the bush with the animals both domestic and wild, a Kikuyu prizes trade or commerce. Similarly, in Nigeria, whereas a Fulani nomad is content with a simple temporary tent for accommodation, some herds of cattle and trekking for long distances, an Igbo person is content when he owns a big spare parts shop, a fleet of transport companies, modern houses, and rides in the latest model of cars. From inter-country experiences, differences also abound. In Addis Ababa, Ethiopia, donkeys and horses are used alongside motor vehicles in the buzzing city as means of transport, while in many other African cities such as Johannesburg, Accra, Kampala, Nairobi, Lagos, and Harare, vehicles are strictly used for same purpose. Furthermore, environmental resources that constitute the major sources of foreign exchange of each country determine the country's pattern of relationship with the environment. In countries like Ghana and Nigeria whose economies are anchored on mineral and hydrocarbon exploration and extraction, the physical environment, the flora and fauna suffer devastating human activities compared to countries like Kenya whose economies rely heavily on tourism. The latter countries tend to invest more energies and resources to conserve the flora, fauna, and ecosystems (rivers, lakes, etc.). Peoples' perceptions of non-human aspects of the environment, their consumption patterns, and the weight of their ecological footprint differ from country to country, and sometimes from one part of a country to another. We therefore acknowledge these differences.

Nevertheless, it is equally true that there are overwhelming similarities among Africans. Many African countries have similar historical, environmental and development experiences. For instance, many African countries south of the Sahara have experienced colonialism, have low agricultural productivity, low level of technology, have been misgoverned, and are poor or developing[3] by WB standards. Therefore, we can consider the continent as an entity as we rummage its development story vis-à-vis its environmental relationships.

Like people of other continents, Africans aspire for development, good and fulfilling life. The dream of Africans is that they are developed economically, politically, and technologically. They aspire to demystify the centuries-old tagging of their continent as inferior, weak, dark, evil, and poor. They want to break the fetters of oppression (internal and external), stop the looting of their resources and be a strong voice in global development discourses and decisions. Unfortunately, these aspirations are bedeviled by numerous challenges such as poverty, lack of technological advancement, conflicts, diseases, corruption, nepotism, spirit of servility or inferiority complex, reactivity, ignorance, and global economic and political forces. The continent's inability to adequately deal with these challenges has left it at crossroads or in dilemmas as far as its development aspirations are concerned.

Poverty: the Persistent but Unwelcomed Guest

Mass poverty seems a "norm" in Africa. As Agbonkhianmeghe E. Orobator cleverly insists, poverty remains an old but frustratingly volatile enemy to humanity, partly because it continues to evolve new characteristics, one of which is the phenomenon of mass or collective poverty in many parts of the world, especially Africa.[262] It has had serious negative influence not only on Africa's human development efforts but also on their aspirations, creativity, migration dynamics, values, and type of development and environment relationships. The most vexing feature of poverty is that it can be both the effect as well as the cause of the economic and technological woes, and conflicts that characterize the continent. It is in light of this that we think it is utterly important to carefully analyse the issue of poverty. This will enable honest understanding of where Africa is coming from, where it is, where it is going and where it should go in view of its development pursuits.

---

[262] Agbonkhianmeghe E. Orobator, *From Crisis to Kairos: The Mission of the Church in the Time of HIV/AIDS, Refugees, and Poverty* (Nairobi: Pauline Publications, 2005), 180.

Conceptualizing poverty: Definitions, Dimensions or Nature and Measurement

Poverty is a multi-dimensional and complex concept. It is essentially a contested or an elusive concept because of its vulnerability to different ideological interpretations. Consequently, arguments about its primary or deep level causes are inevitably also contested. Yet, much as proximate or easily discernible causes can help us understand poverty, these are only manifestations of the primary causes. It is therefore pertinent to get to the primary or the root cause(s) of poverty if we are to adequately understand why there is poverty in Africa. Poverty, especially penury, it must be out rightly noted, is not an accident of nature; it has "structural" and "conjunctural" causes. Both subjective and scientific evidence confirm that Africa has become the primary place of poverty in the world, and the ideal setting to understand features of poverty. In order to understand the features of poverty, Tirfe Mammo thinks there is no better continent than Africa.[263] In fact, for Anthony O'Connor, to think Africa is to think poverty.[264] This is the feeling many people including those from other poor countries like Haiti, Philippines, India, and Guyana have about Africans as the poorest and the most backward human beings. This is how reductionistic some peoples' views about Africa have become. Even within Africa, citizens of some countries perceive others as backward. In June 2010, a Cameroonian Jesuit friend of ours was in Cairo, Egypt for interreligious internship programme. One day in the course of his interaction with the people, an adult Egyptian said to our friend that he [the Egyptian] heard that in Africa, people live in trees and the whole environment is littered with wild animals such as lions. In other words, Africa is synonymous with poverty and backwardness in the understanding of some people even in the 21st century.

However, there is a perennial debate over how to conceptualize poverty. This debate has engendered a paradox: a sophisticated discourse on poverty, replete with disagreements over meaning, definition, measurement, scope, categorization, policies and strategies. As Majid Rahnema ingeniously asserts,

---

[263] Tirfe Mammo, *The Paradox of Africa's Poverty: The Role of Indigenous Knowledge, Traditional Practices, and Local Institutions— The Case of Ethiopia* (Asmara, Eritrea: The Red Sea Press, 1999), Xiv.

[264] Anthony O'Connor, *Poverty in Africa: A Geographical Approach* (London: Belhaven Press, 1991), 1.

poverty is a term that attracts many perceptions and countless words.[265] In Persian, for instance, there are more than thirty words for naming those who for one reason or another, are perceived as poor, and in most African languages, at least three to five words have been identified for poverty.[266] This view is true, at least among the Kasenas of northern Ghana. Terms such as *yiniga tu, nabom, looru, kabaga, kadam, badam,* among others variously denote the concept of poverty. And among the Bakonzo people of Uganda, concepts such as *abanaku, abasege, abathayithoka, abathawitheki* are used for poor people.

In many cultures of the world, poverty was not always the opposite of riches as it seems to be the case nowadays. What we need to know is that poverty means different things to different people even within the same country, and sometimes within the same locality. For some people, the loss of one's status or the marks of one's profession, being deprived of one's instruments of labour, lack of protection, children, exclusion from one's community, abandonment, infirmity, or public humiliation define poverty. A Tswana friend of ours from South Africa once said that the Tswana recognized their poor by their reactions to the appearance of locusts; whereas the rich were appalled lest the locusts ate the grass needed by their cattle, the poor who had no cattle rejoiced because they could themselves eat the locusts. In contemporary times, a neo-liberal development economist sees poverty in terms of low income, which limits consumption, whereas a Masai pastoralist would see it as lack of livestock. Perhaps an average American or Japanese would see poverty in terms of crime and depression. A Somali may see it as lack of peace. A Turkana or Pokot of Kenya may understand poverty as drought or lack of rain or water. Based on these diverse perceptions about poverty, it becomes rather difficult if not altogether impossible to have a single, precise, standardized or an all-embracing usable definition of poverty. In other words, as we stated before, because poverty eludes definition, its solution is also elusive. Something that one has failed to comprehend theoretically, one will not easily find its practical solutions. Different authors have produced variety of terms and abstractions to explain

---

[265]Majid Rahnema. "Poverty" in *The Development Dictionary: A Guide to Knowledge As Power.* ed. Wolfang Sachs (London: Zed Books, 1992), 158.

[266]John Iliffe, *The African Poor: A History* (Cambridge: Cambridge University Press, 1987), 7.

poverty. They include deprivation, destitution, social exclusion, powerlessness, vulnerability, and lack of freedom.[267]

Yet, for Howard and his colleagues, it could be argued that these categories do not really exist but are simply notions created for the purpose of arguing a case. They "do not represent a real kind of poverty as it is experienced and can be studied."[268] This is a good insight but what we cannot deny is that poverty exists and is a complex concept even if we do not have the right vocabulary to define it. In light of this complexity, some authors have distinguished material, non-material, and evangelical dimensions of poverty. Material poverty which denotes "lack", "deficiency" or "deprivation" is further sub-distinguished as chronic or structural, and temporary or transitory. People are said to be chronically or habitually poor when they are entrapped in self-enforcing conditions, also known as poverty trap. These self-enforcing conditions such as selfishness, conflicts, bad policies, droughts, to mention but a few, keep people perpetually poor. Transitory poverty designates temporary misfortunes such as harvest failures, locust invasions and price fluctuations. This shows that much as poverty can be said to be a common phenomenon in Africa, it is also particular in manifestation from one country to the other and from one part of a country to another. It is the multi-dimensionality and relativity of poverty that makes its measurement difficult and problematic.

The most familiar benchmark for measurement remains the World Bank's US$1 per person per day as the international standard for gauging the degree of poverty in developing countries. This standard has recently faced growing criticism for being too positivistic or descriptive, and arbitrary; it fails to account for differences within and between countries and regions, and within and between households. It does not take other non-monetary needs into account, and it makes it difficult to identify who is really poor. For example, a family may not have cash of one dollar per day to buy their needs from the market but they may have a farm or garden from which they simply harvest what is worth or more than one dollar for their upkeep throughout the year. In southern Ghana, a household can have on one farm cassava, cocoyam, banana or plantain, and maize, which it appropriately harvests to meet its daily needs all year round. Similarly, one wonders to what extent this

---

[267] Orobator, *From Crisis to Kairos: The Mission of the Church in the Time of HIV/AIDS, Refugees, and Poverty*, 181.

[268] Marilyn Howard et al. *Poverty: The Facts*. 4th ed. (London: CPAG, 2001), 19.

173

standard for measuring poverty takes into account herbal medicines, and firewood, which is fetched from the forest as source of fuel. Of course, one can, with rigorous economics, counter this criticism by working out the monetary equivalents for these items: cocoyam, plantain, maize, and a bundle of firewood. But, can it be realistically the case that the total monetary worth of all these fail to add up to a dollar per day? Besides, how do the economists find monetary equivalents for herbal medicines that families know and use from ages past?

Notwithstanding the contested definitions and measurements of poverty, from an experiential point of view, a variety of criteria or indices can be assembled to permit a recognizable description of poverty. These would include material deprivation, insufficient access to basic services (education, health, and transport), constraint of choices relative to basic amenities, poor nutrition, political instability, unfavourable climatic conditions, low incomes, unemployment, and poor housing.[269] In light of this, it seems that mass poverty is a "norm" in Africa and serves as a point of convergence for the different analyses, perceptions and features of poverty. If and when we adopt international standards of measurement, such as the WB's income-based method, or the United Nations Development Programme's Human Development Index (HDI), sub-Saharan Africa may emerge, compared with other regions of the world, as the region with the largest number of poor people. This is clearly indicated in the UN's Millennium Development Goals (MDG) Report of 2010. In the UN's analyses of regional progresses made in regards to its MDG goal one: eradication of extreme poverty and hunger, the MDG's report show that sub-Saharan Africa is lagging behind other regions in most of the indices. For instance, in terms of proportion of people living below $ US 1.25 a day, proportion of employed people living below $1.25 a day, and proportion of undernourished population, sub-Saharan Africa scores the highest percentages.[270]

Though John Iliffe observes that poverty in Africa has evolved both diachronically (through historical time) and synchronically (within a given space in time) and therefore might defy proper understanding of its mechanisms,[271] poverty does not escape recognition. If one cannot travel to

---

[269] Orobator, *From Crisis to Kairos: The Mission of the Church in the Time of HIV/AIDS, Refugees, and Poverty*, 182.

[270] *The Millennium Development Goals Report 2010* (New York: United Nations, 2010), 6-12.

[271] Iliffe, *The African Poor: A History*, 259-60.

the shanty towns or rural areas to understand that poverty is a serious problem in Africa, one only needs to tune his radio to any local, national, or international channels, or listen to any conversation about Africa to realize that many Africans are poor. Richard J. Barnet and Ronald E. Muller give a typical underdeveloped country as follows: "What a curious contradiction of rags and riches! One out of every ten thousand persons lives in a palace with high walls and gardens a Cadillac in the driveway. A few blocks away hundreds are sleeping in the street, which they share with beggars, chewing-gum hawkers, prostitutes, and shoeshine boys. Around the corner tens of thousands are jammed in huts without electricity or plumbing. Outside the city most of the population scratches out a bare subsistence on small plots, owned by the few who lived behind the high walls. Even where the soil is rich and the climate agreeable many people go to sleep hungry. The stock market is booming, but babies die and children with distended bellies and spindly legs are everywhere. There are luxurious restaurants and stinking open sewers. The capital boasts of late-model computers and receives jumbo jets every day, but more than half of the people cannot read."[272]

This picture may be a bit exaggerated and not completely appropriate in describing some African countries because of the strides they have made in reducing poverty, illiteracy, child and maternal mortality, and improving economic development. But, it may still capture the reality exactly as it describes it in some of the African countries. Here, our minds go to cities such as Addis Ababa in Ethiopia, Nairobi in Kenya, and Juba in Southern Sudan. Poverty in many African countries may mean going to bed hungry night after night; "bed" in this case actually means nothing more than sleeping on a mat on the floor along roads in towns and cities or in rooms that should appropriately be called death traps. In many rural areas poverty means walking about a 15-kilometre round trip to fetch water each day, often water that is far from being pure. It means spending two days on the road to a weekly-gathered market to exchange grains of turf for wheat grains, which have multipurpose use and spending another day back to the village. The most fortunate poor students who find themselves in school will have to have ten of them share one textbook. Anyone who has the opportunity to visit Lalibela in the Amhara nation of Ethiopia would appreciate this latter example. Formal education is for the reserved few. These are the experiences of many men, women, and youth at Lalibela, the site of Ethiopian monolithic

---

[272] Barnet and Ronald E. Müller, *Global Reach*, 134

churches about six hundred and forty two kilometers north of Addis Ababa, Ethiopia. In most cities, poverty means living as a family of eight people in one small room, fearing eviction from there when the family cannot put together the rent. It means having male and female teenagers sleep together on a small space night after night. This experience is a commonplace among poor tenants in Idimu, a suburb of Lagos, Mbare, a suburb of Harare in Zimbabwe, and Aboabo, a suburb in Kumasi, Ghana, and the famous Kibera in Nairobi. These seem common phenomenon in many parts of Africa; the differences may only be in degree but not necessarily in kind. Generally, a person is said to be "rich or poor according to the degree in which he can afford to enjoy the necessities, conveniences, and amusements of human life."[273]

Anyone who has ever been poor or at least has seen poor people will accept that poverty, especially in its extreme form – the lack of basic needs-- is a big problem and a challenge to humanity. It dehumanizes, stifles freedom, and makes people feel deprived of the basic needs for a decent life because it makes them unable to develop their potentials to enable them profitably tap into the resources that God or nature endowed their countries with. Poverty makes people powerless, voiceless, and vulnerable to all kinds of risks and shocks. It is for these reasons that questions regarding the root(s) of poverty in Africa cannot be overemphasized if any realistic understanding of Africa's agenda for sustainable development is to be achieved. One may ask whether the natural or physical environment, which provides Africans with the context and the resources for development, is not favourable. Or is African poverty a consequence of lack of imagination? Might some people or some institutions be responsible for poverty in Africa? Is it possible that African poverty results from a combination of several interacting factors as stated earlier?

These questions are pertinent and shall be explored subsequently. However, before that, we would like to emphasize that there are many good things that Africa celebrates. The continent is not synonymous with poverty; a good number of Africans share their resources with others including non-Africans. Positive changes have been recorded in many African countries in areas of governance, economic development, maternal and infant mortality rate reduction, basic school enrolment, to mention but a few. We are well

---

[273] Smith, *An Inquiry into the Nature and Causes of The Wealth of Nations*, 31.

aware of the many good human experiences on the continent. However, poverty is a reality and Africa can do better when it is able to understand it and what accounts for such an unwelcome guest.

Who or What Factors are Responsible for Poverty in Africa?

Our ideas and views here can be contested but our goal is to establish as honestly and objectively as possible the root causes of poverty in Africa. These views are not and will not by any means be exhaustive as far as establishing the deep seated causes of poverty is concerned. In his book *The End of Poverty*, Jeffrey Sachs, the director of the Earth Institute at Columbia University, one time advisor of Kofi Annan on the Millennium Development Goals as UN Secretary General, argues that geography—including natural resources, climate, topography, and proximity to trade routes and major markets is an important factor to consider when diagnosing deeper causes of poverty in Africa.[274] Using some kind of comparative approach, Sachs contends that in the 1950s, tropical Africa was roughly as rich as subtropical and tropical Asia. Countries such as Singapore and Malaysia were at par with countries such as Nigeria, Ghana, and Kenya in economic development. In the 21st century, the Asian countries are far ahead of their African counterparts. Today, Asia booms while Africa stagnates or is trapped in untold poverty, Sachs insists, because Asia has far more favourable geographical factors than Africa. For example, in his article "Can Extreme Poverty be Eliminated?" in the September 2005 edition of *Scientific American* magazine, Sachs asserts that the existence of the Himalaya Mountains produces southern Asia's monsoon climate and vast river systems. These allow for well-watered farmlands so that when the Green Revolution of the 1960s and 1970s introduced high yielding grains, irrigation and fertilizer, this served as the starting point for Asia's escape from extreme poverty.[275] However, tropical Africa lacks the massive floodplains that facilitate the large scale and low cost irrigation found in Asia. Africa's rainfall is not only highly variable, but also unreliable in many countries thus leading to droughts and sometimes floods. These features lead to low production of food per person resulting in rampant food insecurity in Africa.

---

[274] Sachs, *The End of Poverty* (New York: Penguin books, 2005), 192.

[275] Sachs, "Can Extreme Poverty be Eliminated?" *Scientific American* (August 22, 2005), 38.

Besides the agricultural woes, Africa bears an overwhelming burden of tropical diseases. For instance, because of climate and the endemic mosquito species, malaria is more intensively transmitted in Africa than anywhere else; these impact negatively on the continent's human capital. Additionally, high transport costs isolate Africa economically.[276] The areas where crops are produced are far from ports and international trade routes and this, coupled with bad roads, leads to high transport cost. This dissuades investors and consequently leads to lack of employment and productivity, which in turn cause poverty.[277] Therefore, for Sachs, the root of Africa's poverty is geographical. This view corresponds with Adam Smith's observation in *The Wealth of Nations* that Africa had been poor from time immemorial because it lacked navigable rivers and natural inlets that would afford the benefits of low-cost sea-based trade.[278] Sachs has some good insights here regarding the geography, including the topography, natural resources and climatic patterns about Africa. For instance, the countries of the Sahel belt — Mauritius, Mali, Chad and Niger have experienced and continue to experience persistent droughts. Zimbabwe and some parts of Kenya also have a similar problem. Droughts have become the most faithful companions of the Pokots, Turkanas, and the Samburus of Kenya for the past three years. They have lost their animals – their only means of livelihood. Countries in the horn of Africa — Somalia, Eritrea and Ethiopia have also been experiencing persistent climatic extremes; at one point they suffer from floods and at another they suffer droughts. Somalia for instance, has been hit with severe floods between June-July 2011 that displaced many people and killed many others. These bad conditions, no doubt, lead to poverty. Besides, some countries are simply not naturally endowed with adequate resources that people can utilize for their well-being. Therefore, one can say that geographical or environmental factors contribute to poverty in Africa.

However, geography is not the root cause of poverty in Africa. Many African countries are not only well endowed with agriculture and mineral resources, but also with the right climate yet they remain poor. Nigeria, Uganda, Angola, Ghana, Ivory Coast and the Democratic Republic of Congo are few cases in point here. How come that at one time Africa and Asia were

---

[276] Sachs, "Can Extreme Poverty be Eliminated?" *Scientific American* (August 22, 2005), 39.

[277] Sachs, "Can Extreme Poverty be Eliminated?" *Scientific American* (August 22, 2005), 39.

[278] Edwin Cannan, ed. *Adam Smith: The Wealth of Nations* (New York: Pelican Books, 1937), 690.

at par economically in the 1950s? Why did not geographical factor right from the beginning keep Africa behind Asia? Desert places such as the Middle East are wealthy despite their dry bare areas. Turkana land has oil as Kenya has recently discovered. What does it take to discover oil under ground and utilize it? It takes knowledge and scientific investigation. Natural disasters such as floods, earthquakes, landslides hit Asia with higher frequency than are experienced in Africa. China is an example yet it is one of the fastest emerging global economic powers. In recent years, the United States of America gets very severe tornadoes every year, yet these never bring the country to its knees. Australia is largely a rock yet Australians are able to maximize the productive portions putting themselves on the same ladder with other developed countries. Japan does not have the luxury of huge land mass yet it has managed so well the little it has to emerge as a global economic power. The truth lies in the inability of African countries to harness the forces of nature to their advantage. Geographical factors only affect, but they do not decide a country's economic, political and technological fate. If Africa had the appropriate technology, it could offset, albeit at a higher cost, some of the factors Sachs cited: drought can be fought with irrigation systems, isolation can be solved by roads or railways and mobile telephones, diseases can be fought against by preventable and therapeutic measures. In other words, the proximate or easily discernible cause of poverty in Africa in this case might be lack of imagination and its profitable application — failure to use our skills to solve our problems or sustainably explore the environment for our well-being. We do not pretend to be blind to the fact that some Africans, in fact, many, have fertile imagination as manifested in the numerous African novelists and artists. But the issue still remains that as far as using this imagination to meet our day scientific and technological needs is concerned, Africans have not yet succeeded. Actually, one of the reasons why imagination has remained stunted in Africa is because Africa has been relatively spared by serious geographical challenges. For example, winter forced Europeans think of heating systems for their houses while Africans were comfortably sleeping in trees.

It was against this background that Robert Guest, a former BBC reporter for Africa insisted on lack of imagination as the factor that underlies poverty in Africa. He asserts that "Africans hardly produce anything that the rest of the world wants to buy."[279] This assertion is an exaggeration because many African countries export raw materials and some finished products to Europe and America. Kenya and Ethiopia export flowers to Europe. Ivory Coast and Ghana export cocoa beans and pineapples especially in the case of the latter to Europe and America. These are few examples that point to the untrue nature of Guest's claim but we equally can find some iota of truth in his claims because Africans have not adequately utilized their natural capital to build strong physical and financial capitals that are necessary for economic development. What Africans export are largely raw materials and not finished goods. The term natural capital which we have mentioned above denotes land, minerals, hydrocarbons, water, forests, and animals, which can be tapped through agriculture to produce food, or which can be harvested directly for consumption, and also for all manner of construction, energy, foreign exchange, tools and art. Physical capital refers to machines, tools, irrigation systems, and all infrastructure including buildings, roads, dams, communication, market, transport, which derive from human endeavours. Financial capital refers to monetary and associated means of exchange that serve as instruments of investment. Human capital, which covers health, nutrition, education, knowledge and skills, leadership, organizational capabilities and services of human persons, has not been productive in terms of utilizing the other capitals. For example, it is clear that Africans have not been able to manufacture cars, airplanes, and modern medicines as their colleagues in the industrialized countries like the USA, Japan, and Germany are doing. There is also food insecurity in Africa because of low technology. These facts show that one can have great imagination but this remains at the level of a dream and a vision unless that imagination is translated into scientific and technological skills. Hence, to some extent, lack of imagination in terms of technology and productivity can be seen as a cause of poverty in Africa.

However, to assert that Africans lack imagination or technological skills and on the basis of that conclude that imagination is the root cause of poverty in Africa is problematic. There are many African scientists, technologists, engineers, economists, and intellectuals whose ingenuity has proved that Africa's problems do not result from lack of imagination. Philip

---

[279] Robert Guest, *The Shackled Continent: Africa's Past, Present and Future* (London: Macmillan Press, 2000), 15.

Emeagwali, a Nigerian super computer scientist, who was voted as the 35th greatest African in all times is an example. Emeagwali is a great mathematician, inventor, and a contemporary scientist on internet search engines. A winner of the coveted Gordon Bell Prize, he is undoubtedly a computer genius with forty-one patents to his credit. Based in the Unites States of America, he played a major role in the development of the internet. In 1989, he built a computer system, which became the first system to perform 3.1 billion calculations per second. This record even surpassed the expensive super computers in the United States of America.[280] This is just one example that attests to the fact that Africans do not lack imagination. Therefore, imagination cannot be the primary cause of poverty in Africa. The following questions give us a sense of direction to where the root of poverty in Africa lays: why are Emeagwali and many other African geniuses not able to break Africa from its present vicious cycle of poverty? Why are they staying and working in other countries, mostly the advanced ones and not in Africa? The most talented Africans even in humanities are teaching in Western universities where they can do research and publish while those in Africa are perishing in poverty!

Answers to these questions are likely to be many and varied. It is possible that some people will attribute it to poor leadership in Africa, which does not encourage the brilliant ideas of geniuses like Emeagwali. Others might attribute it to geopolitical manipulations whereby the countries of the West present the most attractive packages in order to woo these people to work for them. Yet, others might say it is because Western education by its very nature trains African geniuses for the West. We look at these responses with the aim of getting to the root of the problem.

In his article "Leadership for the New Era", Emmanuel Idike argues that though leadership is the soul of any community and lifeblood of any nation, it is a great problem in Africa.[281] For Idike, poor leadership underlies African penury. He argues that the citizens of many African states have not enjoyed the fruits of independence since the early 1960s because of poor leadership. Poor leadership led to rampant political upheavals and political instability, socio-economic mismanagement, oppression, the denial of fundamental

---

[280] Ankoma Baffour, ed. "100 Greatest Africans of all Time," in *New African* (August/September 2004), 21.

[281] Emmanuel E. Idike, "Leadership for the New Era." *Africa: Philosophy and Public Affairs*, ed. Obi J. Oguajiofor (Enugu: Delta Publications Limited, 1998), 139.

human rights, dictatorship, corruption and ethnic chauvinism.[282] Since leadership is an important element for order and progress in any human undertaking, it is extremely vital and indeed central to the control, motivation, and direction of every human society towards development and meaningful achievement in all human affairs. Sharing a similar view with Idike, William Kumuyi asserts that unless we have the right leaders doing the right things, Africa may never emerge from the cocoon of misery. For him, leadership is not only about who to be; it is also about what to be; a leader is a seer, seeker, servant, strategist, shepherd, sustainer, steward, and spokesperson.[283] In other words, leadership is a critical variable in the development calculus, and its dearth is the sole restrictive force that has barred Africa and its people from economic development. In short, Africa is awash with selfish leaders who misruled their nations, misled their people and misused their resources and have thus subjected Africans to poverty. The selfishness of Africa's corrupt leaders is at the root of poverty in Africa. Africa lacks not resources but the political will to use public resources for the common good.

Considering the pain and fear that many Africans are experiencing today because of poor leadership, it makes sense for one to agree with Idike and Kumuyi's emphatic assertion that leadership is central to the development of every human society. Any human society without proper leadership, be it political, economic or religious, heads for disaster. Somalia, which has existed for over two decades without proper political leadership, has created nothing but chaos, pain, fear, and poverty for the Somalis and many people of the neighbouring countries. Most African countries are patrimonial democracies; the resources of the state are treated as the patrimony of the leaders but not as common property.[284]

Nevertheless, it is again problematic to tag leadership as the only root cause of poverty in Africa. Why do Africans allow corrupt and selfish leaders to lead them time and again? Do the few countries that have good leaders show that they are technologically advanced? Botswana has had excellent

---

[282] Emmanuel E. Idike, "Leadership for the New Era." *Africa: Philosophy and Public Affairs,* 139.

[283] William F. Kumuyi, *Leadership: The Perfect Picture.* 1st ed (Lagos, Yaba: Life Press Ltd, 2009), 5-7.

[284] Booth David, ed. *Fighting Poverty in Africa: Are PRSPs making a difference?* (London: Overseas development institute, 2003), 9.

leaders and a good economy as a country yet its citizens are the most demotivated as regard education. How far has South Africa gone as far as technological innovation is concerned with its relatively good political system? Ghana can be added to the equation as far as good leadership is concerned especially for the past twenty years. But how much can it boast of technological innovation? It can only boast of having its market choked by imported inferior goods from China. Did the United States of America decline technologically under George Walter Bush (not a great leader by any estimation)? Developed societies seem not to rely on visionary leaders, but on private individuals who make things happen regardless of who is in power.

Besides, the underlying problems of leadership in Africa are historical factors — slavery and colonialism. Many Africans continue to see themselves as inferior to other races especially the Whites. The effects of slavery and colonialism cause this inferior attitude, an attitude of servility, which affects the imagination and leadership style of Africans. Colonialism is often understood as an event but it is actually a process that is named differently as it evolves; it is cloaked in different terminologies to suit different times. Nowadays, African neo-colonizers seem to be economic and political globalism, and capitalism or free market. The institutions of neo-colonization are World Trade Organization (WTO), International Monetary Fund (IMF), World Bank (WB), and the Multinational corporations. For instance, the draconian budget policies— Structural Adjustment Programmes imposed by the IMF/ WB in the 1980s and 1990s left many African countries poorer than they were before.[285] The methods the capitalists use to produce goods and services also pollute the environment in Africa. Capitalism or free market has allowed dumping of inferior goods on the African markets. However, the imposition of tariffs and non-tariffs on African finished goods by the West, with the support of the WTO does not allow Africans to access the rich markets in the West. Those who manage to access these markets are always at a comparative disadvantage with their counterparts from the West because of the subsidies the latter enjoy.

Effects of Slave Trade and Colonialism on Africa

One of the most enduring problems slave trade in Africa and the subsequent colonial rule have left in their wake is conditioning, or what Steve

---

[285] Sachs, *The End of Poverty,* 189.

Biko calls "colonization of the mind".[286] The colonialists did this by the legal, political, educational, and economic structures they left behind. The effect of this conditioning is that many Africans have accepted themselves as inferior to Westerners, and have believed that the "best" things— ideas, lifestyles, technologies, etc. always come from the West. Sometimes, these things do not simply fit the African reality and consuming them is like matching a round-shaped object into a square-shaped object. Notwithstanding, the colonized mind and attitude of servility continue to inform the worldview of life of many Africans.

Walter Rodney tells us that the processes involved in the four centuries of slave trade were terrible. The captives were obtained in Africa through warfare, trickery, banditry and kidnapping. These captives especially those obtained in the hinterlands by African collaborators, were sold and resold as they were led for hundreds of miles from the hinterlands to the port of embarkation at the coast.[287] This social violence as a means of recruiting captives in Africa points to its destructive effect on Africans. Healthy and able-bodied young men and women were the target group for such trade. Many of these died on their way to the port of embarkation; others died in the airless dungeons in castles such as the Elmina and Cape Coast castles in Ghana. Others died while on board, and those who survived were taken to new plantations in the New Indies where they worked laboriously for the plantation owners. As mentioned earlier, human capital is very important in socio-economic development. Now, considering the large numbers of African human capital flight through this activity, it shows that the slave trade has contributed to poverty in Africa.

Some people, nevertheless, argue that in spite of the large numbers of the African labour force taken out of the continent through slave trade, Africa is still one of the most populous continents in the world hence; slavery is not the cause of African poverty. It might also be argued that since the slave trade took place about six centuries ago, attributing the current state of poverty in Africa to slave trade is anachronistic. Furthermore, some people argue that since slave trade did not affect all the nation states in Africa, slave trade cannot be the sole cause of poverty in Africa.

---

[286]Steve Biko, "Some African Cultural Concepts" in *Philosophy from Africa: A Text with Readings*, eds. Coetze and A. P. J. Roux (Johannesburg: International Thomson, 1998), 23.

[287] Walter Rodney, *How Europe Underdeveloped Africa* (Harare: Zimbabwe Publishing House, 1972), 103.

Remarkably, there is apparent failure to acknowledge the moral consequence, physical and psychological trauma, and depreciatory or demeaning image of this activity. It is true that the slave trade took place many years ago but its effects were so traumatic that they remained indelible in the minds of many Africans to date. Besides it should be noted that though slave trade did not directly take place in all regions of Africa, its effects affected the others. For example, there was no port of embarkation for slave trade in Burkina Faso. However, the nature of the trade routes was such that many Burkinabes were obtained by African collaborators and brought for sale at a slave market at Paga, a Ghanaian village bordering Burkina Faso. These captives were then resold to the coastal chiefs who in turn sold them to the Europeans. Undeniably, the effects of slave trade left Africa poor.

Colonialism, which came later, exacerbated this poverty in Africa. The colonial masters undermined African culture, promoted tribalism, divided and ruled, assimilated, and exploited natural resources found in Africa. In Ghana, for instance, the colonialists deprived the northern ethnic groups of formal education for almost a century. They declared the northern territory a pool of labour good enough for physical labourers in the plantations and mines in the south. Two serious problems come with this deprivation. First, it created a big literacy gap between northerners and southerners. Second, it created the phenomenon of inferiority and superiority complex. Southerners consider their northern counterparts as inferior. The question of centre-peripheral divide became inevitable. Similarly, Uganda was also divided between north and south, military from the north, civil servants from the south, and cheap labour from the west. In addition to these intra-country divisions, there was also the arbitrary division of countries that left tribes divided across borders, that would later be a cause of conflicts.

In many ways the educational, legal, economic, and political legacies divided rather than knitted many African countries. They depressed rather than impressed on values such as unity, peace, and cooperation. Few African leaders attempted to deconstruct most of these legacies but they were eliminated. In Ghana in the early 1960s, the then Education Trust under the creative leadership of Nkrumah established standardized boarding schools throughout Ghana which allowed students to study in any part of the country. Students from the deprived north could study in the rich south and vice versa. Additionally, students from the deprived north had free education. These strategies have helped the country in two major ways. The first is that

185

it helped to reduce and in some cases eradicate the prejudices people from the north and south held about each other. Students lived, ate, worked, and studied together for as many as seven years. Northerners were perceived by their southern counterparts and the colonial masters as good only for physical labours in plantations and mines. The northern regions were therefore considered as a pool of labour. They were considered intellectually inferior even though history and existential experiences prove this mentality wrong. For example, up to the mid-1970s, it was extremely difficult for a student to score distinction in all the subjects in which students were examined at ordinary level certificate examinations. However, Kofi Morna, from the then upper region of Ghana set a record by scoring distinctions in all the subjects he was examined. Experiences of students who studied in other parts of the country other than their own localities showed that not all southerners nursed unhealthy superiority complexes against northerners and vice versa. Parents and their children across the country had healthy and good interactions on visiting days in the schools. These experiences impressed reasonably on uniting Ghanaians for a common purpose. The second benefit is that the free education for northerners helped to bridge reasonably the literacy, political, and economic gaps between the south and the north. Today, many Ghanaians remain grateful to Kwame Nkrumah for his brilliant and an all-embracing vision for better Ghana. If Africa had such leaders who are not self-centred or western-controlled, it would be a developed continent.

Many of Africa's visionary figures were hardly given the chance and support to fully actualize their visions. We are told that as soon as the colonial period ended, Africa became a pawn in the Cold War. Operatives in the Central Intelligence Agency (CIA) and their counterpart agencies in Europe opposed African leaders who preached nationalism, tried to deconstruct the Western systems, sought aid from the Soviet Union, or demanded better terms on Western investments in African minerals and energy deposits.[288] In 1960, as a demonstration of Western approaches to African independence, the CIA and Belgian operatives assassinated the charismatic first prime minister of the Democratic Republic of Congo, Patrice Lumumba, and installed the tyrant and selfish Mobutu Sese Seko as leader. Similarly, the CIA contributed to the violent overthrow of President

---

[288] Sachs, *The End of Poverty*, 189.

186

Kwame Nkrumah of Ghana in 1966.[289] Osei Boateng, in the June 2004 edition of the *New African*, gave a more detailed account of this incident when he said that USA and UK jointly helped to overthrow Nkrumah. With Nkrumah's overthrow on 24th February 1966, Robert W. Komer, the then special assistant to president Johnson of USA congratulated his boss as follows: "The coup in Ghana is another example of a windfall; Nkrumah was doing more to undermine our interests than any other black man."[290] To date, almost every African political crisis — Sudan, Somalia, the Democratic Republic of Congo, La Cote D'Ivoire, and a host of other countries continues to have Western meddling among its many causes. This meddling of the West in the political, economic and social affairs of the African continent for its own self-interests is what is at the root of the African poverty, and this meddling is historically traceable to colonialism and slavery. Many contemporary political leaders are compelled to subscribe to the dictates of the West lest they risk economic sanctions, or violent opposition from Western-sponsored rebels or even direct Western invasions.

Furthermore, like leadership, education is crucial in any type of society for the preservation of the lives of its members and the maintenance of the social structure. The most crucial aspect of pre-colonial education in Africa was its relevance to Africans, their environment and social life, in both its material and spiritual dimensions. Its collective nature, its many-sidedness, and its progressive development in conformity with the successive stages of the physical, emotional and mental development of the African were emphasized. For example, among the Bemba of what was then pre-colonial northern Rhodesia, children by the age of six could name fifty to sixty species of plants without hesitation. There was no separation of education and productive activity or any division between manual and intellectual education. Though this was mainly through informal education, pre-colonial education matched the realities of the society at the time.[291] However, the colonial educational system introduced in Africa was not designed to give young people confidence and pride as members of African societies but to create mental confusion, to shift the minds of Africans away from their realities. For example, Rodney quotes Kofi Busia, one of the Ghanaian scholars who received his secondary and university education during the

---

[289] Sachs, *The End of Poverty*, 190.

[290] Osei Boateng "A Guest is a Stranger After all" (*New African* June 2004), 48.

[291] Rodney, *How Europe Underdeveloped Africa*, 262.

187

period of colonial rule as follows: "I felt increasingly that the education I received taught me more and more about Europe and less and less about my own society."[292] This is the kind of educational structure in which many Africans were and continue to be educated. This Western type of education targets an elite group and as a result it perpetuates inequality. Therefore, Africa's poverty is caused and sustained by multi-dimensional factors including history, type of education, and global economic and political forces. The tap root cause of Africa's poverty is human selfishness whose branch roots are the corruption of contemporary leaders, the solipsism of the colonizers and slave traders, the shrewdness of the neo-colonizers, and lack of self-confidence among most Africans. Africa's poverty is not due to the lack of material factors but the prevalence of *immaterial* pathologies whose tap root is human selfishness.

Global Forces and Lack of Technology

As has been mentioned earlier, no one wants to be poor, weak, and vulnerable. Every person or country wants to attain what Abraham Maslow, the 20th century American psychologist, describes as self-actualization. But, how do African countries pursue that goal? Is there any development path that is purely African, which they can follow? Or should they follow wild capitalism/economic growth model, which the west has marketed to them? Should they continue to pursue quantitative index such as Gross National Income or the rather broader index of Gross national Fulfillment? How is that achievable? Is it possible to have a middle way that taps on the good side of the different development paths? What model is Africa using for its development aspirations and what have been the implications? Up to now, there is nothing like a purely African model of development and there may never be any considering the rate at which cultural, economic, moral, and political boundaries are broken because of the sweeping tidal waves of globalization. What is obvious is that Africa has embraced the economic growth model of development perhaps in a more vigorous and unreflective way. This is not necessarily because Africans perceive it as the best model but because they are at a dilemma. The dilemma revolves around the following vexing questions: how do Africans eliminate poverty? Even if Africans invent a new development model appropriate to their situation, how practical will that be amidst the unwavering waves of global economic forces which most

---

[292] Rodney, *How Europe Underdeveloped Africa*, 270.

of the time are anti-African? How about appropriate technology? Appropriate technology is inevitable if any development model that is identified is to be successful. Africa may have the potential for technology but the inconvenient truth is that this gift is still at the level of potentiality.

Imagine a scenario where International Monetary Fund (IMF), the World Bank (WB), World Trade Organization (WTO), and direct foreign investors (individuals or corporations) openly oppose a strategy Africa considers beneficial to its sustainable development-environment relationship. What do you think is the likely fate of that strategy? It will definitely fail, for Africa does not have the necessary funds and expertise to start and sustain to fruition what they consider theirs. It does not have the will, the honesty, and common-good spirit to achieve its goals. Thus, fear of poverty aggravation, lack of technology to explore the natural resources, selfishness, and helplessness amidst the uncompromising global forces leave the continent as a mere consumer of whatever is presented to it. This painfully, but rightly so, is what many Africans consider as development: to consume, dress, sing, speak, drive, and live like North Americans or Europeans. In short, to be developed is to behave like the aforementioned. This attitudinal assimilation has had many serious implications on the African development-environment relations, which if nothing is done, Africans are heading blindly to doom.

Economic growth: Africa's new god

One of the strongest defining marks of Africans is their hospitality to strangers. This mark was stronger among pre-colonial Africans. They shared everything and the environment was sacred. People were socialized to respect one another, the natural environment, share their material and non-material gifts with others. Though open to contestation, the arrivals of missionaries and colonialists capitalized on the African hospitality to inflict on their psyche, culture, and institutions the damage that Africans experience to date. They are conditioned to believe that whatever is presented to them by the west is the best. Today, many Africans consciously or unconsciously believe unwaveringly that consuming everything that comes from the west is the best way to becoming developed. For the inventors of economic growth, production, advertisement, consumption, and profit are the hallmarks of the model.

The *comprador bourgeoisie's* culture of consumerism is highly valued. Today, in Africa, more than ever before, a person's humanity is measured by the quantity of material wealth s/he possesses. Abraham, a high school colleague of ours came from a wealthy home. In our pen-ultimate year in high school, Abraham took to drinking, womanizing, and smoking. Being a friend, we talked to Abraham to reconsider the new habits he was forming. In response, he asked us the following questions: "Have you ever eaten meat for the sixteen years you have been on earth? Have you slept under a tile-roofed room and have you ever drunk bottled water? Have you ever sat in a saloon car? Have you forgotten that whereas at home I study under electrically lit room, you do the same with kerosene lanterns? That is the difference between you and I; we are not at the same level as human beings. So never ever try telling me what is good for me." This experience spells out clearly the requirements a person must meet in order to become fully human. This trend has painfully been a commonplace among many contemporary Africans. People's humanity and social status today, more than ever before, is measured by not only how many mansions or cars they have but what type those mansions and cars are. Achieving these tastes is what is commonly understood as development in Africa.

Human relationships in our world are largely determined by this criterion into the haves and the have-nots. The have-nots are less human and those who have are fully human. Using Kenya as a microcosm of what pertains in Africa, we find a yawning chasm between the rich and the poor. The rich and the poor live in parallel 'universes' within the same country, interacting with each other only occasionally and usually uncomfortably. They do not date each other, eat with each other, go to games with each other, and entertain each other. The popular Kibera and Kangemi slums in Nairobi are surrounded by fabulously rich neighbourhoods. Whereas the rich neighbours have resources more than they need, the exact opposite is the case of the slums. This experience often brings to mind the Parable of Lazarus and the Richman in the Gospel of Luke 16:19-31. One of the interpretations of this parable is that it points to the tough and painful realities of the effects of wealth disparity. Since recognition is a social need for every human person, and is marked by wealth and power, people explore any means to attain this recognition.

For many years in Africa, one government after another tried to pursue development largely through the same route as the industrialized nations. Put differently, African governments and the citizenry have been attitudinally slaves to economic growth. Development means mass production but not the production of the masses. One only needs to listen to *state of nations addresses* given by African presidents and they are about how much the economy has grown, how GNI has increased, and how inflation has decreased. Nothing is said about how much sanitation has been improved, how many trees have been planted after others were cut, how much the non-renewable resources have been effectively managed, how many people have access to three good meals and shelter, how inter personal relationships and morality have improved. The unfortunate experience of environmental degradation and its alienating effects on people does not matter to many African governments.

Waste management is poor especially in urban areas. Some farmers and game poachers also burn vegetation in order to farm or hunt. Forests are destroyed by many rural households for domestic fuel. Lands are cleared to build cities and industries. That is the reason why Africa's natural environment is not devoid of problems such as pollution, global warming and deforestation. We should however, emphasize that these symptoms of environmental degradation are caused by both African citizenry and the externals such as industrialized countries and multinational corporations whose industrial and agricultural activities degrade the environment. Africa shares effects that spill over from activities of industrialized nations.

In a word, the tap root cause of Africa's poverty has penetrated its tentacles to Africa's efforts in trying to eliminate poverty. Africa wants to get out of poverty at any cost. However, the economic growth model has exacerbated the poverty situation; some people have become poorer despite the deceptive quantitative figures; tyrants have become selfishly rich. Everybody wants to get out of poverty but nobody cares about fellow human beings and the non-human environment. Africa is repeating the mistakes of the western world at a time when the west has hit a rock-bottom and is making a U-turn. The west has realized that economic growth does not solve income inequalities, insecurities, crime, stress and strain (even though machines do most of the work), and environmental risks[293] and some economists are beginning to wonder how much infinite economic growth is possible in a strictly finite environment.[294] Indeed, as Aristotle argues, wealth does not necessarily lead to happiness.[295] Africa still equates development with the establishment of huge industries regardless of the pollution

[293] Ian Christie and Diane Warburton, eds. *From here to sustainability*, 6.

[294] Schumacher, *Small is Beautiful*, 48 and 263.

[295] Aristotle, *Nicomachean Ethics*, 1095a 20-25; 1095b 16-20.

problem, the heavy use of external inputs such as chemical fertilizers, herbicides, and pesticides is seen as the modernization of agriculture and many Africans want to own private cars that are moreover fuel-inefficient and destructive to the environment

Nonetheless, it is tenable to acknowledge that some African countries have made efforts to conserve their natural environments. Kakum national park in Ghana, Serengeti national park in Tanzania, Nairobi National Park and Lake Nakuru National Park, both in Kenya, and Hwange national park in Zimbabwe are a few among numerous conservation efforts that can be cited. These conservation efforts have been largely successful. Brian T. B. Jones and Marshall W. Murphree state that the Community-Based Natural Resources Management (CBNRM) conservation programme in southern Africa has made considerable positive ecological impacts in the sub-region.[296] CBNRM defines those principles and practices that argue that sustainable multi-stakeholder conservation goals should be pursued by strategies that emphasize the role of local residents in decision-making about natural resources. It helps in capacity building, resource monitoring and management.[297]

One of the impacts of CBNRM is that it has made conservation a legitimate and attractive form of land use. By recognizing the value of wildlife and increasing benefits to landholders, it enables wildlife to be able to compete more favourably with other forms of land use such as livestock. Wild life has become more attractive to residents of communal areas. In Botswana, the actual and perceived value of wildlife has tremendously increased.[298] Another impact is that habitats for conservation increased. As a result of placing a value on wildlife, CBNRM has added some hectares of conservation areas in Namibia, and CBNRM projects cover nearly 3.9 million

---

[296]T. B Jones, and Marshall W. Murphree "Community-Based Natural Resources Management as a Conservation Mechanism: Lessons and Directions" in *Biodiversity, Rural Development and the Bottom Line: Parks in Transition*, ed. Brian Child (London: Earthscan, 2004), 72.

[297] Jones, and Marshall W. Murphree, *Biodiversity, Rural Development and the Bottom Line: Parks in Transition*, 60.

[298] Jones, and Marshall W. Murphree, *Biodiversity, Rural Development and the Bottom Line: Parks in Transition*, 72.

hectares of forest resources in Mozambique.[299] Other impacts include reduced poaching and unsustainable harvesting of wildlife, and game re-introductions. Even though many of the conservation programmes rely on external funding for their success, the point is that Africa has made some progress in terms of environmental conservation.

---

[299] Jones, and Marshall W. Murphree, *Biodiversity, Rural Development and the Bottom Line: Parks in Transition*, 73.

Chapter 11

Education For Altruistic Egoism

Training a person for pure altruism can only be an idealistic task. A purely altruistic person cannot survive in a world of ordinary human beings like us. People need to work for their interests in order for them to survive. However, meeting one's interests does not necessarily require preventing other people from meeting their own interests. Thus, what is needed is to educate people on how to meet their interests without preventing others from meeting their interests or how to work for one's interests and at the same time for the interests of other people. This is what education for altruistic egoism means; it is about teaching people how to be altruistic in their egoistic endeavours. Education for altruistic egoism is to be carried out in families, schools, civil society organizations, and religious institutions.

Home education for Altruistic Egoism

Given the level of selfishness in our societies and its dangers, there is a need for the virtue of altruism to be re-emphasized in families. Parents need to teach their children about the importance and practice of altruistic egoism. This can be achieved by encouraging children to share things with children from other families, narrating stories, proverbs, and riddles that demonise solipsism and selfishness, promoting team work within the family and with neighbouring families, and assisting strangers. An example of a proverb against solipsism is the Bakonjo saying: *oyukaboha iyowene akaghunza ebisika by'omomboko*, meaning, he who ties things by himself finishes all the fibres from the banana plantation. And against selfishness, the Bakonzo use the proverb: *bayitsura mwatsura erihika liwe*, which means, a person named malice 'maliced' his own family. Parents tell such proverbs to their children to inculcate in them values such as cooperation and sharing so that the children might not become solipsists or selfish people but people who are community oriented.

The problem of egoism is especially common in urban areas and rich neighbourhoods where people live individualistic lives; children from such families can hardly become altruistic. Self-transcendence is needed on the side of the parents to allow their children interact with other children – play together, share things, and learn from one another.

Parents should never assume that their children will instinctively learn to be altruistic or that their children will acquire all of such virtues from school. It is the responsibility of the parents to lay a good foundation for an ethical and upright growth of their children. Other people can only build on what the parents have already started. Of course we are aware of existential challenges which militate against parents from carrying out their role as educators to their children. For example, in a busy city like Lagos some parents leave their homes very early for work and return very late because of the traffic jam problem. As a result, they have little or no time to educate their children. Some parents think that by paying school fees for their children the teachers should impart all the necessary knowledge and virtues to the children. But the teachers cannot replace parents; the role of the parents is irreplaceable at least as far as virtue education is concerned. Aware of this fact, some parents try as much as possible to be with their children during weekends. During such moments they try to impart some wisdom to their children. Unfortunately, some parents spend such opportune times with their friends in bars instead of being with their children.

It is of course important that parents should try as much as they can to lead exemplary lives. In ethical matters, actions speaker louder than words. Surely, it would be a waste of time for parents to instruct their children about altruistic egoism while they themselves are living selfish lives.

School Education for Altruistic Egoism

Many teachers emphasize academic excellence without showing the students how to excel in their studies. Students are left with no alternative than to become selfish; they begin to selfishly compete with one another for marks and they graduate from school with that attitude. Teachers need to show their students how it is actually easier to learn and to pass examinations through cooperation than through competition. In fact schools which put emphasis on cooperation among students, for example, the formation of discussion groups, perform better than those in which competition prevails. Moreover, as they graduate from school, students who have been assisting one another will continue to do so as they struggle to get jobs and as they establish themselves in the world. Cooperation reduces the level of corruption and consumerism in society while competition simply aggravates

196

such vices. Everybody gains with altruistic egoism while with pure egoism only a few win as majority lose.

Teachers can inculcate the spirit of altruistic egoism in their students by encouraging team work in the schools, organizing outreach programs for students to do charitable works and community service within the villages that surround their school, and asking students to donate from their little pocket monies funds that can be used to assist the poor and strangers. University students need to be encouraged to do voluntary work especially in poor communities and to design development projects that can be used to develop those communities. In order for such programs to reflect the spirit of altruistic egoism, students should be encouraged to serve in communities which are in greatest need irrespective of whether they belong to those communities or not.

A way of reducing competition among students is to identify their talents so that everybody is trained accordingly. It makes no sense for a student who is talented in music or art or sports to waste all his energy and time competing with another who is talented in sciences. However, students who have the same talent need to be encouraged to cooperate with one another in order for them to develop their talent. An education system that is based on talent identification and development empowers students for job creation and it reduces hopeless competition among society's labour force. Also, awards need not only be given to students who score high marks but more so to those who put into practice what they learn in class, thus, those who excel in extracurricular activities such as sports, leadership, community service and gardening.

Unfortunately, because of poor remunerations, some teachers have to think of other sources of income in order for them to sustain their families; some are business men/women and they are more concerned about their businesses than their profession as teachers. They do not have enough time for their students; their goal is to teach the students for purposes of passing examinations but there is no room for integral education. The focus is on passing examinations. Even the little moral education that is carried out in schools is geared towards scoring high marks but not forming students into responsible citizens. A student can score an 'A' in moral education but that does not translate into living a moral life. Also, some teachers do not provide good examples to their students. They are involved in immoral activities with some of the students, for example, sexual intercourse, abortion, assisting students to cheat in examinations, and accepting bribes from parents. Such

197

bad examples make it hard for teachers to efficiently conduct altruistic egoism in their schools. Surely, teachers who are more interested in their businesses than in their profession or those who are involved in some immoral/selfish activities with their students have no moral authority to talk about the education for altruistic egoism.

Civil Society Education for Altruistic egoism

People who are no longer in school, especially those who graduated without having been taught about altruistic egoism, and all those who did not get the chance of going to school also need to be educated about altruistic egoism. This process of sensitization will necessitate creating small groups for civic education. The first thing is to create critical thinking among the members. Members need to be critical about whatever is happening in the society. Since they are all adults, they should come for the sessions with concrete examples of selfishness and corruption that are happening in their society. Those case studies should be discussed by the group in order to compare how the evil of selfishness was dealt with in their traditional society and it is being dealt with today in the same society. The discussions should be conducted using Paulo Frere's pedagogical method whereby everybody learns from everybody; the teacher does not know it all, he learns from the students as the students learn from one another and from their teacher.

Second, there is a need for basic economic and financial management skills. The students need to know how to manage and use their resources efficiently in order to avoid being wasteful. Also, basic economic and financial management studies will enable the people to have a glimpse of how public resources are being managed by the leaders. Corruption prevails more in societies where people are economically illiterate than in societies where people are economically literate. Thus, civic education for altruistic egoism must fight against economic illiteracy so that leaders can stop perpetuating corruption by confusing people with economic jargon.

Third, people need help concerning their bargaining power. People hardly know how much bargaining power they possess. Strangers who come to a place to establish projects easily do so because the local people take it for granted that they have everything to gain while the strangers are seen as purely altruistic people. The truth however is that those strangers come with hidden motives; they themselves are going to benefit from the project, sometimes even more than the local people. They take advantage of the local

198

people's ignorance. The local people cannot ask for anything more than what the investors have decided to give them because they believe that whatever they are given is actually a privilege but not their right. People need to go through a kind of education system that will make them critical thinkers so that nobody can take them for a ride. If people know how much they are going to contribute to a project in terms of local material resources and how much the investors are going to benefit from the project, then they will be able to bargain for what is their due. Once the local people are awakened from their slumber, investors will no longer pay peanuts as wages or pollute the environment any way they want.

Fourth, there is a need to create a sense of shame for being selfish. It is not enough for the members to be critical of others; they need to be critical of themselves as well. They should be guided into an examination of consciousness so that each of them can find out how he has been acting selfishly in the past. There is need for reconciliation and repentance. The members should then be encouraged to scorn all those in their society who are selfish and to praise and emulate those who have been honest. For example, they should be able to stop adoring rich people who have achieved their wealth through corruption and instead begin to look at them as sinners in need of repentance or as patients in need of healing while people who have been faithful to altruistic egoism should be looked at as models for the group.

Fifth, the members need to know the law of their country. There are several laws about selfishness but many people are ignorant about them and so selfishness simply goes unpunished because of that ignorance. Once the members know the law and their rights, they will be able to demand accountability from whomever they suspect might have swindled public resources or acted selfishly in any other way. The members need to learn how they can stage demonstrations against leaders and fellow citizens who are selfish and which channels to follow in demanding a more equitable distribution of national resources. People have a right to *vote by their backs*, that is to say, shunning all business entities which are owned by selfish entrepreneurs. It is almost impossible to have a corruption-free nation without vigilant citizens; defeating corruption requires the collective rage of citizens. Indeed, citizens need to be liberated from the conspiracy of silence about evils such as corruption in order for their society to achieve development. They need to know that the silence of many good citizens does actually kill more people than does the selfishness of their leaders.

199

Sixth, create solidarity among the members so that they are able to work for the interests of one another and those of non-members. As they begin their journey of altruistic egoism, members need to be guided on how to work for the common good and how they can extend that good spirit beyond the group, for instance, by mobilizing resources for victims of calamities and for assisting strangers such as refugees.

Religious Education for Altruistic Egoism

Although some religious institutions have succumbed to the evil of egoism that exists in the world, religion is potentially in a better position than any other institution to make people more altruistic. Religion invites people to always aspire for the ideal. However, in order for a religion to effectively preach any gospel, including that of altruistic egoism, it must first of all renew itself from corruption, greed, and luxurious lifestyles. Unfortunately, many religious institutions have been infected with the virus of selfishness. Some of the selfishness that exists in religious institutions today has a long history. For instance, some churches in Africa own huge pieces of idle land which they did not buy but which they acquired during colonialism by playing tricks on the then ignorant owners. Unless such churches swim against the current of selfishness by giving that land back to its owners or by compensating the owners in some way, they have no moral authority to prophetically preach about altruistic egoism to a people who have been rendered landless. The best way for religion to preach is by being exemplary. Good homilies are no longer enough to convince people; there is a need for concrete prophetic actions. Also, religions must stop demonizing others as a way of luring more members. There is a need for more unity and cooperation among religions; it does not make sense to preach altruistic egoism and at the same time maintain divisions and competition among religions.

Second, after renewing itself from the vice of egoism, religion can then preach the gospel of altruistic egoism to its followers. All true religions are based on principles that can be used to promote altruism in the world. Christianity, for instance, insists on love of neighbour, self-transcendence, works of charity, and moderation. Actually almost all the Ten Commandments are against human selfishness – they fall under the category of altruistic egoism. If Christian principles are concretely (but not ideally) explained such that Christians are able to put them into practice, then the Church will have played one of its most fundamental roles. Christians will

200

not become altruistic by simply listening to good homilies about altruistic egoism; they need to put into practice what they believe. Part of this orthopraxis is for individual Christians who have been acting selfishly to repent before they can embark on the journey of altruistic egoism.

The Role of Media in the Education for Altruistic Egoism

The media can be used to propagate good or bad ideologies. Today, many radio stations, television stations, newspapers, magazines websites, and social networks are used to perpetuate selfishness by running misleading adverts. This is an invitation for civil societies and religious institutions to establish media channels for counteracting such ideologies. The media for altruistic egoism must be selfishness/solipsism-free. The first function of any medium for altruistic egoism is to enlighten people about misleading adverts. This requires accessing all the adverts, analysing them, and explaining to the people how those adverts are very misleading. Any other information in the media which contains notions of selfishness or solipsism should be analysed by the media for altruistic egoism so that the people can be enlightened accordingly. The second function is to run programs which propagate altruistic egoism. This can be done through radio talk shows and television programs to educate people about altruistic egoism. Also, success stories of people who have managed to live according to the principles of altruistic egoism can be published in newspapers, magazines, and on websites and social networks so that their way of life can be emulated by other people. The media for altruistic egoism needs to advertise for producers and business entrepreneurs who sell goods and services at genuine prices and have no intention of cheating their customers in any way.

Education for Sustainable Development in Africa

Considering that the industrialized nations have themselves begun rethinking their development-environment relationship, it is illogical for Africa to tenaciously insist on the economic growth model. Africa needs to learn from the mistakes of the western/mistaken world.[300] Education for sustainable development promotes human progress and environmental

---

[300] If Africa succeeds in shunning the economic growth model and instead develop economic models for sustainable development, then, in the future, the West will have something new to learn from Africa.

sustainability and at the same time puts into consideration important non-quantifiable qualities such as distribution, justice, equity, and happiness. African nations need to know what sustainable development really means. Sustainable development contains within it two key concepts: the concept of needs, in particular the essential needs of the poor such as food, shelter, housing, clothing, basic education and health, justice, happiness, freedom, and equity. The second concept is that of limitations imposed by the state of technology and social organization in the environment's ability to meet present and future needs. Conceptually, sustainable development can be analyzed according to four aspects: environmental sustainability, economic sustainability, social sustainability, and political sustainability. Thus, the interdependent and mutually reinforcing pillars of sustainable development are economic development, social development, and environmental protection.

Figure 1 below depicts sustainable development at the confluence of economic, social, and environmental preoccupation.[301]

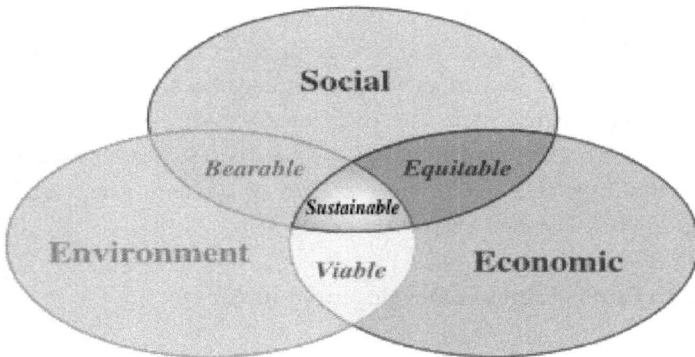

When there is a *viable* relationship between economic development and the environment, a *bearable* relationship between social development and the environment, and an *equitable* relationship between social development and economic development, then there is a confluence and this confluence

---

[301] http://en.wikipedia.org/wiki/Portal:Sustainable_development (Accessed: 19th July 2010).

indicates that sustainable development has occurred. If resources are equitably distributed, people can meet their basic needs.

For a nation to achieve sustainable development, there is a need for a form of education concerning the difference between *being* and *having*. We need an education system that propagates an economic theory of being but not of having. Gabriel Marcel says that *being* is a value that is confirmed through its relation with other beings or creatures.[302] Being as a value implies that we are inseparable from others; we are all immersed in the being and we participate together in it. This attests that we are social beings, and also intricately linked to the environment in which we participate with others – the present and future human generations, and nonhuman creatures. It is this reality that the sustainable development model seeks to unearth and sustain. In sum, sustainable development acknowledges that human beings depend upon one another and on the natural environment, that the local and global environments are fragile to human activities, the natural environment can limit human economic activity, the present and future generations need a healthy environment, and that we should not talk about optimal development by focusing on only quantifiable realities, but should include non-quantifiable realities. Thus, people need to be reminded that development does not simply mean having but being in a bearable, equitable, and viable relationship with other human beings and non-human entities. When we define life as *having*, we become possessed by our possessions and so, as William James points out, the line between what is me and what is mine becomes very difficult to draw[303] and fetishism becomes the new name for development. Life as *having* robs us of our freedom – a quality that is supposed to distinguish us from other creatures. What ought to be reduced are not necessarily possessions but the desire for more possessions. This is what the education for altruistic egoism should aim at – not the equalization or reduction of possessions but training people not to desire more unnecessary possessions.[304]

Sadly, as the saying used to go, every market has its own mad person. The situation has even worsened because of modernism. In the market of moderns, almost all lose their sanity; people hardly make rational choices.

---

[302]Gabriel Marcel, *The Mystery of Being 2: Faith and Reality*, trans. Rene Hague (Chicago: Regnery, 1960), 49.

[303] Walzer, *Spheres of Justice*, 8.

[304] Aristotle, *The Politics*, 1263a 30 and 1257b 1-5.

Thus, every market has its own mad people not just person. Sometimes people buy things just because of peer pressure – they lose their mind every time they see something new being advertised on television. As Michael Walzer wittingly puts it, if not satirically, before goods come into people's hands, they come into their minds. The mind is so obsessed that the hands must grab those goods.[305] Unfortunately, the kind of education which we have today has not helped matters in this area. Even highly educated people, including economists, make a lot of irrational economic choices. There is need for a special type of education that will enable people to make rational choices. People need to know how to draw scales of preferences that are proportional to their incomes. By sticking to those scales, they will be able to buy the most pressing needs first before they can waste money on less pressing ones. A need is said to be pressing if it is both important and urgent. Surely, it does not make sense for a poor woman to spend all her money doing her hair in a salon while there is no food at home for her children to eat. Such is a typical irrational choice; doing hair to look beautiful might be an important need but it is certainly not that urgent. The opportunity cost of making a wrong economic choice is high and people should know how to calculate the opportunity costs of their choices in order for them to become more sensitive as they decide on what to buy and when to buy it. In the nature of things, subsistence must always be prior to convenience and luxury.[306]

We believe that proper education at the level of home, school, civil society, and religion is necessary for sustainable development because "the evolution of people, we are told, is essentially an evolution of the thinking process – the mindset. Whatever the mind can conceive as possible can be done. All change begins with a change in outlook which leads to a change in attitude which leads to a change in action, and this is what brings about transformation."[307] There is no other single most valuable tool that can help bring transformation, sustainable development or sustainable human progress than proper education.

---

[305] Walzer, *Spheres of Justice*, 7.

[306] Smith, *An Inquiry into the Nature and Causes of The Wealth of Nations*, 138.

[307] Mo Ibrahim, Chairman of the Mo Ibrahim Foundation and Prize in an interview dubbed, "Inside the mind: What makes a successful business person?" with Anver Versi. See The Traveller, *Msafiri*, edition 78 (November-December 2011), 130.

From the description of a sustainable development model, it is clear that when it is applied, it benefits humanity in many ways. The following are some examples:

i.   It promotes an optimal relationship between human progress and environmental sustainability. It promotes harmonious relationship between human beings because it requires that we do to the environment what we want the environment to do to us.

ii.   It considers both the quantifiable and non-quantifiable aspects of human life, which are important for a holistic and sustainable human well-being.

iii.   It ensures the welfare of both the present and the future generations.

Notwithstanding these benefits, implementation will be difficult; there are a number of hurdles that should be cleared. These hurdles constitute possible challenges to sustainable development and a sound education system for development should create awareness about these challenges.

We have shown that causes of environmental problems are complex, both global and local in nature. The causes have economic, social, political and moral roots. The first challenge to sustainable development is on the dilemmas of cost and benefit distribution; that is local benefit versus global cost. America and China emit large amounts of carbon dioxide, which cause global warming whose effects affect Africa. How will Africa deal with such a problem in order to achieve its vision of sustainable development? Africa is weak a continent to stop the global economic and political giants such as USA from doing what they want. But, it is important that Africans know of that challenge.

Many governments, organizations, and individuals are pooling efforts to address the problem of global warming. For instance, following the Intergovernmental Panel for Climate Change's report on global warming and the plea for change in human lifestyle, the EU has resolved to cut its carbon dioxide emissions through promotion of fuel efficiency methods. The United Kingdom is the most resolute in this regard. In its efforts towards curbing carbon dioxide emissions, EU has imposed carbon taxes on airlines effective from January 2012 in order to combat climate change.[308] Although this decision has met with resistance especially from top Chinese airlines, the bottom line is that EU's effort is a positive step toward curbing global

---

[308]   http://radio86.com/focus/economy/world-viewpoints/airline-carbon-tax-row-leaves-eu-isolated-and-climate-change (Accessed: 26th February 2012).

warming. Other locally induced environmental problems result from irresponsible disposal of wastes especially in the cities, and bush burning in the rural areas. What is required in this case is responsible behaviour. Responsibility, though a hard value to achieve, is not impossible to achieve with proper education and enforcement of law. Kigali, the capital city of Rwanda, is widely known as one of the neatest cities in Africa. Like any other city, it is prone to human and industrial waste pollution. However, because of the strict application of law and the education of the citizenry, the goal of cleanliness has been achieved. The same can be done in other cities if there is willingness and proper education.

Another challenge to sustainable development is on the use of the concept "future". For some people "future" is an elusive concept, thus there is nothing like future generations. In other words, future people do not exist, so there are no specific, flesh-and-blood individuals to whom we have duties. Others acknowledge the possibility of the reality of future generations. But some wonder whether the present human generation has any moral obligations to the future generations. Would it be an evil if they never came to exist? How do we know what they will be like and what their needs and values will be? If we believe that we have an idea of their needs and values, how can their needs and values compare with those of present living beings?[309] For Martin Golding, we have obligations to the present generation and not the future generations because we are ignorant of their needs and desires.[310] These reservations about future generations, logical as they may sound, are rooted in human selfishness which does not care about the needs of the significant other.

The most obvious difference between present and future people is that the latter do not yet exist in physical form as the present people do. Does this difference in temporal location in itself constitute a sufficient reason for favouring the interests of present over future persons? It does not seem so. Location in space is not a morally relevant feature for determining the worthiness of considering someone as a person. Education for sustainable

---

[309] Robert Heilbroner, "What Has Posterity Ever Done for Me?" *Environmental Ethics: Readings in Theory and Application*, ed. Louis P. Pojman (London: Jones and Bartlett Publishers, 1994), 217-18.

[310] Martin, Golding "Obligations to Future Generations" in *Environmental Ethics: Readings in Theory and Application*, ed. Louis P. Pojman (London: Jones and Bartlett Publishers, 1994), 225.

development should enlighten people about the interconnectedness between the present and future generations. The present and the future form a continuum; they are not unrelated realities. When we take the present human generation, some people are very old and about to die; others are just born, while others are just beginning to form in the womb. This confirms that the present and future form a continuum; they are interconnected. On the basis of this, it is fallacious to claim that the future generation is not in temporal location and therefore constitutes an illusion. Moreover, we know with a high degree of certainty the basic biological and economic needs of future generations – enough food to eat, and air to breathe. The satisfaction of these needs will be a prerequisite for the satisfaction of most of the other desires and interests of future people. Besides, we inherited the environment in a particular state, and are therefore under moral obligation to leave it as it was if not better. The culture of instant gratification is against the notion of 'future' – for how long will Africans keep inheriting poverty from previous selfish generations? If the present generation does not save for future generations, poverty will remain a chronic disease.

Conclusion

Today, more than ever before, human economic behaviour deserves a renaissance. World population has skyrocketed and, as a result, the level of competition for resources has gone up. Egoism has increasingly become an inevitable trait in the pursuit of interests for human survival. Yet, it is also becoming increasingly evident that extreme egoism is dangerous especially for a planet that is overcrowded like ours. Most of our contemporary problems are a consequence of pathological egoism. The solution, therefore, lies in reducing the level of egoism and increasing the level of altruism in today's world. Human beings need to rethink the two levels of their relationships, first, the relationship among themselves as a species, and second, the relationship between the human species and non-human entities. These two levels of relationship need to be transformed from pathological egoism to an ethic that blends egoism and altruism, namely, altruistic egoism. For a better world, every human being needs to mind not only about his interests but also about the interests of his fellow human beings and the human species as a whole needs to respect not only its interests but also the interests of all the non-human entities.

Contemporary human to human relationships are in a crisis because of pathological/extreme egoism. Survival is for the fittest, public resources are used by a few individuals while majority perish in abject poverty; employment opportunities are reserved for a certain group of people while others remain unemployed despite their level of education; business enterprises exploit their workers in order to make huge profits at low costs; a few individuals hoard resources to create and benefit from artificial scarcities; people join politics for their own interests but not for the common good; democracies have become monarchies or at best oligarchies; some religious leaders squander church property; criminals walk freely on the streets after bribing the judiciary; the media is used by advertisers to confuse and manipulate consumers; one nation impoverishes another by grabbing its resources through senseless wars; multinational corporations form unholy alliances with leaders of poor countries to exploit their resources; technologically advanced countries capitalise on the ignorance of less sophisticated ones to exploit their resources; world politics is monopolised by a few individuals at the peril of billions of people in poor countries, and so on. Poverty, which is today's biggest scandal, is both a cause and an effect of extreme egoism. The same can be said about the current scandal of terrorism and interreligious conflicts and the financial crisis that is troubling the whole of humanity.

Today's crisis is not only at the human to human level of relationship. The crisis is even more acute at the level of relationship between the human species and non-human entities. Human beings behave as if the interests of other entities do not matter at all. We are guided by the ethic of anthropocentrism; both rich and poor countries pursue development with an instrumentalist mentality as far as the environment is concerned. This, however, has resulted into a serious environmental crisis. Global warming, drastic climate changes, and physical hazards such as floods, tsunamis, and droughts are some of the prices humanity is paying for all the years non-human entities have been bleeding because of our pathological egoism. The crisis has already caused a lot of untold suffering but again because of human selfishness, not much is being done to address it.

Contemporary challenges, be they local or global, will only get worse if humanity continues to become more egoistic. There is an urgent need for a change in economic behaviour. Humanity needs a new ethic, namely, altruistic egoism which, at the human to human level of relationship, requires that I should be able to meet my interests without preventing other people from meeting their own interests or that I should work for my interests and at the same time, if possible, work for the interests of other people. At the level of relationship between humans and non-human entities, altruistic egoism requires human beings to take care of their interests by taking care of the interests of the non-human members of the environment. There is need for an increase in altruism and a reduction in egoism at all levels of relationship. Instances of altruistic egoism such as differed gratification, symbiotic reciprocation, consanguineous benevolence, deontological altruism, philanthropic altruism, and others need to be more oriented to altruism than to egoism.

Education for altruistic egoism needs to be conducted at the different levels of society and by all stakeholders. Families, institutions of learning, civil society organizations, churches, the media, and government have a role to play in transforming humanity into a more altruistic species for a better world.

1. Families: since socialization begins at home, parents or guardians need to lay the foundation for their children's moral behaviour. Parents need to educate their children about altruistic egoism by emphasizing values such

as sharing, moderation, generosity, communal life, the common good, and care for the environment. Above all, since children learn more by what they see than by what they hear, parents/guardians should endeavour to live exemplary lives by shunning selfishness, corruption, greed, environmental degradation, and consumerism.

2. Schools: institutions of learning have the obligation to continue emphasizing the ethical values which children have already been introduced to by their parents. Ethics need to be introduced and or emphasized in all institutions of learning. A course in ethics should be more practical than theoretical. Teachers need to encourage cooperation and team work as opposed to competition and together with their students be involved in outreach programs for community service, caring for the less privileged students, caring for the environment of their schools and neighbourhoods. At school, students need to learn how to use their talents for the common good.

3. Civil society organizations: the formation of small groups in villages and towns for ethical sensitization is inevitable for the implementation of altruistic egoism education. The aim is for the members to become aware and critical of social, economic, political, and environmental issues in their society and indeed in the whole world. At their regular meetings, the members need to come up with ways of how to become a community in which all care for all, for example, starting small scale income generating projects purposely for common welfare. Additionally, the members deserve knowledge about economic and financial management, human rights and duties, and the law of their country. It is important for the members to demand probity and accountability from their leaders, be they political, religious, or cultural. Corrupt and selfish leaders must be impeached by the vigilant civil society organizations.

4. Religion: the only way religious leaders can teach people about altruistic egoism is to lead exemplary lives by being more accountable for church resources, caring for the needy, living moderately, and, if necessary, preach about generosity, selflessness, accountability, stewardship, charity, and all such virtues.

5. Media: education for altruistic egoism requires alternative media whose role is to counteract media that promote selfishness and luxurious lifestyles. The alternative media should instead propagate the values of altruistic egoism, advertise quality goods and services offered at lower prices,

and sensitize people about social, economic, environmental, and political issues affecting their society.

Bibliography

Andersen, L. Margaret, and Howard F. Taylor, *Sociology: Understanding a Diverse Society*. Belmont: Thomson Learning/Wadsworth, 2000.

Aristotle. *Nicomachean Ethics*. Translated by Terence Irwan. Indianapolis: Hacket PublishingCompany, 1985.

_____. *The Politics*. Edited by Steven Everson. Cambridge: Cambridge University Press, 1988.

Armstrong, Susan J. and Richard G. Botzler, eds. *Environmental Ethics: Divergence and Convergence*. New York: McGraw-Hill, 1993.

Bacon, Francis. *The New Organon and Related Writings*. Edited by Fulton H. Anderson. New York: The Liberal Arts Press, 1960.

Baffour, Ankoma. ed. "100 Greatest Africans of all Time," in *New African* (August/September 2004), 21.

Bailey, Ronald. *Eco-Scam: The False Prophets of Ecological Apocalypse*. New York: St.Martins Press, 1993.

Baker, Raymond. *Global Financial Integrity Project*. www.gfip.org (Accessed: 14th February 2011).

Barnet, Richard J. and Ronald E. Müller. *Global Reach: The Power of Multinational Corporations: Multinational Corporations or Planetary Enterprises*. New York: Simon and Schuster, 1974.

Barry, John. *Environment and Social Theory*. London: Routledge, 1999.

Beck, Ulrich. *Risk Society: Towards a New Modernity*. London: Sage, 1992.

Bell, Daniel. *The Cultural Contradictions of Capitalism*. New York: Basic Books, 1978.

Biko, Steve. "Some African Cultural Concepts." In *Philosophy from Africa: A Text with Readings*, edited by Coetze and A. P. J. Roux, 26-30. Johannesburg: International Thomson, 1998.

Boateng, Osei. "A Guest is a Stranger After all" (*New African* June 2004), 48.

Boff, Leonardo. *Holy Trinity, perfect community*. Translated by Phillip Berryman. New York: Orbis Books, 1988.

Brundtland Commission. *Our Common Future: The World Commission on Environment and Development*. Oxford: Oxford University Press, 1987.

Cannan, Edwin, ed. *Adam Smith: The Wealth of Nations*. New York: Pelican Books, 1937.

Christie, Ian and Diane Warburton, eds. *From Here to Sustainability*. London: Earthscan Publications Limited, 2001.

Collins English Dictionary Online: http://www.collinsdictionary.com/dictionary/english/egoism (Accessed: Nov.30th 2011).

Cooper, D., ed. *The Environment in Question: Ethics and Global Issues*. London: Routledge,1992.

Daly, Herman E. "Economics in a Full World." *The Scientific American* (September 2005), 78-79.
_____. *Toward A Steady-State Economy*. San Francisco: W. H. Freeman and Company, 1973.

David, Booth, ed. *Fighting Poverty in Africa: Are PRSPs making a difference?* London: Overseas development institute, 2003.

Ehrlich, Paul R. and Anne H. Ehrlich, *The Population Explosion*. New York: Simon & SchusterInc., 1990.

Ethan Lee Vita, "On Selfishness and Self-Interest": (Friday Dec 21, 2007), http://ethanleevita.blogspot.com/2007/12/on-selfishness-and-self-interest.html (Accessed May 15th 2011)

Food and Agricultural organization. *Global Forest Resources Assessment 2005*. Rome: FAO, 2006.

_____. *World Review of Fisheries and Aquaculture*. Rome: FAO, 2006.

Ghana News Agency http://www2.ohchr.org/english/law/resources.htm (Accessed: 17th June, 2010).

_____.http://www.ghanaweb.com/GhanaHomePage/NewsArchive/artikel.php?ID=199475(Access date: 14th December 2010)

Golding, Martin. "Obligations to Future Generations." In *Environmental Ethics: Readings in Theory and Application*, edited by Louis P. Pojman, 22-44. London: Jones and Bartlett Publishers, 1994.

Guest, Robert. *The Shackled Continent: Africa's Past, Present and Future*. London: Macmillan Press, 2000.

Gula, Richard M. *Reason Informed by Reason: Foundations of Catholic Morality*. New Jersey, Paulist Press, 1989.

Gustavo, Gustavo, E. "Development." In *The Development Dictionary: A Guide to Knowledge As Power*, edited by Wolfang Sach, 6-25. London: Zed Books, 1992.

Guthrie, Dale R. "The Ethical Relationship between Humans and Other Organisms." In *Environmental Ethics: Divergence and Convergence*, edited by Susan J. Armstrong, Richard G. Botzler, 292-298. New York: McGraw-Hill, 1993.

Hackman, Nana A. *Ghana's Oil Policy Debate: Stabilization Clauses and the Freedom of Parliament to impose new Taxes or Royalty*, http://opinion.myjoyonline.com/pages/feature/200912/39405.php (Accessed: 13th October 2011).

215

Hardwick, Philip, John Langmead and Bahadur Khan. *An Introduction to Modern Economics*, 5thed. London: Pearson Education Limited, 1999.

Hausman, Daniel M. "Liberalism, welfare Economics, and Politics." In *Liberalism and the Economic Order*, edited by Ellen Frankel Paul, Fred D. Miller, Jr., and Jeffrey Paul, 172-197. Cambridge: Cambridge University Press, 1993.

Hawken, Paul. *The Ecology of Commerce*. New York: Harper Business, 1993.

Heilbroner, Robert. "What Has Posterity Ever Done for Me?" In *Environmental Ethics: Readings in Theory and Application*, edited by Louis P. Pojman, 217-219. London: Jones and Bartlett Publishers, 1994.

Howard, Marilyn et al. *Poverty: The Facts*. 4th ed. London: CPAG, 2001.

http://cstl-cla.semo.edu/hill/ui429/eeglossary.htm (accessed: May 30th 2012).

http://dictionary.reference.com/browse/solipsism (Accessed: July 24th 2011).

http://finance.groups.yahoo.com/group/jfcnigeria/message/624 (Accessed: December 25th 2011).

http://en.wikipedia.org/wiki/Enlightened_self-interest (Accessed: 25th February 2012).

http://en.wikipedia.org/wiki/Portal:Sustainable_development (Accessed: 19th July 2010).

http://ezinearticles.com/?What-Causes-Sibling-Jealousy---What-Can-You-Do-About-It?&id=321373 (Accessed June 10th 2012).

http://radio86.com/focus/economy/world-viewpoints/airline-carbon-tax-row-leaves-eu-isolated-   and-climate-change (Accessed: 26th February 2012).

http://sh.diva-portal.org/smash/get/diva2:273605/FULLTEXT01
(accessed: May 30th 2012).

http://www.churchof reality.org/wisdom (Accessed: April, 5th 2011).

http://www.mgr.org/TruthAboutSomePopes.html (Accessed:

http://thinkexist.com/quotation/a-man-thinks-he-amounts-to-a-great-deal-
but-to-a/348891.html (Accessed: June 30th 2012).

Idike, Emmanuel E. "Leadership for the New Era." In *Africa: Philosophy and
Public Affairs*, Edited by Obi J. Oguajiofor, 138-146. Enugu: Delta
Publications Limited, 1998.

Iliffe, John. *The African Poor: A History*. Cambridge: Cambridge University
Press, 1987.

Jones, T. B. and Marshall W. Murphree. "Community-Based Natural
Resources Management as a Conservation Mechanism: Lessons and
Directions." In *Biodiversity, Rural Development and the Bottom Line: Parks in
Transition*, edited by Brian Child, 63-104. London: Earthscan, 2004.

Karliner, Joshua. *The Corporate Planet: Ecology and Politics in the Age of
Globalization. San Francisco, Sierra Club Books,* 1997.

Kelly, David. "Generosity and Self-Interest," *The Atlas Society* (January 2005)
http://www.atlassociety.org/generosity_self-interest (Accessed: 25th
February 2012)

Kumuyi, William F. *Leadership: The Perfect Picture*. 1st ed. Lagos, Yaba: Life
Press Ltd, 2009.

Leo XIII, Encyclical letter *Rerum Novarum, On the Conditions of Workers*, 15
May 1891(Nairobi: Paulines Publications Africa, 1990), 66.

Locke, John. *Two Treatises of Government*, ed. Thomas I. Cook. New York:
Hafner Press, 1947.

Lubasz, Heinz. "Adam Smith and the Free Market." In *Adam Smith's Wealth of Nations: New Interdisciplinary Essays*, edited by Stephen Copley and Kathryn Sutherland, 45-69. Manchester: Manchester University Press, 1995.

MacIntyre, Alasdair. *After Virtue: A Study in Moral Theory*. 2nd ed. Notre Dame: University of Notre Dame Press, 1984.

Mammo, Tirfe. *The Paradox of Africa's Poverty: The Role of Indigenous Knowledge, Traditional Practices, and Local Institutions— The Case of Ethiopia*. Asmara, Eritrea: The Red Sea Press, 1999.

Marcel, Gabriel. *The Mystery of Being 2: Faith and Reality*, trans. Rene Hague. Chicago: Regnery, 1960.

Mchome, Erick. "Suicide: Why Students are Killing Themselves." (The Citizen: 5th June, 2012).

Millennium Ecosystem Assessment. *Ecosystems and Human Well-Being: Synthesis*. Washington, D.C.: Island Press, 2005.

Muller, Jerry Z. *Adam Smith in His Time and Ours: Designing the Decent Society*. Princeton: Princeton University Press, 1993.

Myers, David D. *Psychology*. 5th ed. Michigan: Worth Publishers, Inc., 1998.

Natalia Mirovitskaya, and William Ascher, eds., *Guide To Sustainable Development and Environmental Policy*. Durham, North Carolina: Duke University Press, 2001.

Norton, Bryan G. "Environmental Ethics and Weak Anthropocentrism." In *Environmental Ethics: Divergence and Convergence*, edited by Susan J. Armstrong and Richard G. Botzler, 326-338. New York: McGraw-Hill, 1993.

O'Connor, Anthony. *Poverty in Africa: A Geographical Approach*. London: Belhaven Press, 1991.

218

Orobator, Agbonkhianmeghe E. *From Crisis to Kairos: The Mission of the Church in the Time of HIV/AIDS, Refugees, and Poverty.* Nairobi: Pauline Publications, 2005.

Pachauri, Rajendra. *State of the World 2009: Into a Warming World* at http://www.worldwatch.org (Accessed: 20th July 2010).

Palmer, Joy A., ed. *Fifty Key Environmental Thinkers on the Environment.* London: Routledge, 2001.

Pannenberg, Wolfhart. *Human Nature, Election, and History.* Philadelphia: The Westminster Press, 1977.

Peschke, Karl-Hienz, ed. *Ordo Socialis: Social Economy in the Light of Christian Faith.*Cologne: Paulinus-Verlag, 1991.

Pius XI, Encyclical Letter *Quadragesimo Anno*, 15 May 1931, *AAS* 23 (1931), 528.

Pojman, Louis P., ed. *Environmental Ethics: Readings in Theory and Application.* Boston: Jones and Bartlet Publishers, 1994.

Porter, Roy. "The Enlightenment." *The Hutchinson Dictionary of Ideas.* Oxford: Helicon, 1994.

Rahnema, Majid. "Poverty." In *The Development Dictionary: A Guide to Knowledge As Power*, edited by Wolfang Sachs, 158-176. London: Zed Books, 1992.

Rand, Ayn, and Nathaniel Branden. *The Virtue of Selfishness: A New Concept of Egoism.*New York: Signet, 1964.

Reisman, G. "The Toxicity of Environmentalism." In *Rational Readings on Environmental Concerns*, edited by Jay H. Lehr, 819-845. New York: Van Nostrand Reinhold, 1992.

Remenyi, Joe. "What is Development?" In *Key Issues in Development*, 22-44. New York: Palgrave, 2004.

Rist, Gilbert. *The History of Development: From Western Origins to Global Faith*. London: Zed Books, 1997.

Rodney, Walter. *How Europe Underdeveloped Africa*. Harare: Zimbabwe Publishing House, 1972.

Ruffin, Roy J. and Paul R. Gregory. *Principles of Economics*. Glenview, Illinois: Scott, Foresman and Company, 1983.

Saccomandi, V., and J. D. van der Ploeg. "On impact of Endogenous Development in Agriculture." In *Beyond Modernisation: The Impact of Endogenous Rural Development*, 10-28. Amsterdam: Van Gorcum, 1995.

Sachs, Jeffrey. *Common Wealth: Economics for a Crowded Planet*. London Penguin Books, 2008.

_____. *The End of Poverty*. New York: Penguin books, 2005.

_____. "Can Extreme Poverty be Eliminated?" *Scientific American* (August 22, 2005).

Sanks, Howland T. "Reading the Signs of the Times: Purpose and Method." In *Resources for Social and Cultural Analysis: reading the Signs of the Times*, edited by Howland T. Sanks and John A. Coleman, 3- 10. New York: Paulist Press, 1993.

Schumacher, E. F. *Small is Beautiful: Economics as if People Mattered*. New York: Harper and Row Publishers, 1973.

Smith, Adam. *An Inquiry into the Nature and Causes of the Wealth of Nations*. Edited by Bruce Mazlish. Indianapolis: Bobbs-Merrill Educational Publishing, 1961.

Speth, James G. *The Bridge at the Edge of the World: Capitalism, The Environment, and Crossing from Crisis to Sustainability*. New Haven: Yale University Press, 2008.

The Challenge to the South. *The Report of the South Commission*. Oxford: Oxford University Press, 1990.

The Justice Development and Peace Commission of the Catholic Bishops Conference of Nigeria. *Nigeria: The Travesty of Oil and Gas Wealth*. Lagos: Catholic Secretariat of Nigeria, 2006.

The Millennium Development Goals Report 2010. New York: United Nations, 2010.

The Proceedings of the United States National Academy of Arts and Sciences, 2007.United Nations Environmental Programme, "At a Glance: The World's Water Crisis," http://www.ourplanet.com/imgversn/141/glance.html (Accessed: 20th March 2011).

The Traveller, *Msafiri*, 78th ed. (November-December 2011).

Thevenot, Xavier. *Sin: A Christian view for today*. Missouri: Liguori Publications, 1984.

Tirop, Benedict and Jackline Moraa. "Two Girls commit suicide over KCPE results." (Saturday Nation, 31st December 2011).

Tribe, Keith, "Natural Liberty and laissez-faire: How Adam Smith became a free market ideologue." In *Adam Smith's Wealth of Nations: New Interdisciplinary Essays*, edited by Stephen Copley and Kathryn Sutherland, 23-44. Manchester: Manchester University Press, 1995).

State of the World 2009: *Into a Warming World*, http://www.worldwatch.org (Accessed: 15th June 2010).

UNDP, *Human Development Report 1991*. Oxford: Oxford University Press, 1991.

Van der Ploeg, *et al.* "Rural Development: From Practices and Policies Towards Theory." In *Sociologia Ruralis*. 40:4 (2000), 391-408.

Vasagar, Jeevan. "Storms lie ahead over future of Nile," http://www.ntz.info/gen/n01799.html (Accessed: August, 31st 2011).

Vatican II, *Gaudium et Spes*, 7 December 1965, *AAS* 58 (1966), 104.

Walting, J. L. "Descartes." In *A Critical History of Western Philosophy*, edited by D. J. O'Connor, 170-186. New York: The Free Press, 1965.

Walzer, Michael. *Spheres of Justice: A Defense of Pluralism and Equality*. Oxford: Basil Blackwell, 1983.

Weir, David. *The Bhopal Syndrome: Pesticides, Environment, And Health*. San Francesco: Sierra Club Books, 1987.

White Jr., Lynn. "The Historical Roots of our Ecological Crisis." In *Environmental Ethics: Readings in Theory and Application*, edited by Louis P. Pojman. London: Jones and Bartlett Publishers, 1994.